Fragments of a Forgotten War

Fragments of a Forgotten War

Judith Matloff

PENGUIN BOOKS

PENGUIN BOOKS
Published by the Penguin Group
27 Wrights Lane, London W8 5TZ, England
Viking Penguin, a division of Penguin Books USA Inc, 375 Hudson
Street, New York, New York 10014, USA
Penguin Books Australia Ltd, Ringwood, Victoria, Australia
Penguin Books (NZ) Ltd, 182-190 Wairau Road, Auckland 10,
New Zealand
Penguin Books (South Africa) (Pty) Ltd, Pallinghurst Road, Parktown,
South Africa 2193

Penguin Books (South Africa) (Pty) Ltd, Registered Offices:
20 Woodlands Drive, Woodmead, Sandton, South Africa 2128

First published by Penguin Books (South Africa) (Pty) Ltd 1997

ISBN 0 140 26619 4

Typeset in 10.5 on 12.5 point Bembo
Cover photograph by Joao Silva
Author photograph by Paul Gordon
Printed and bound by Interpak, Natal

In memory of my father
and
to ajh

He who drinks from the River Bengo
will never forget Angola

– Traditional Kimbundu saying

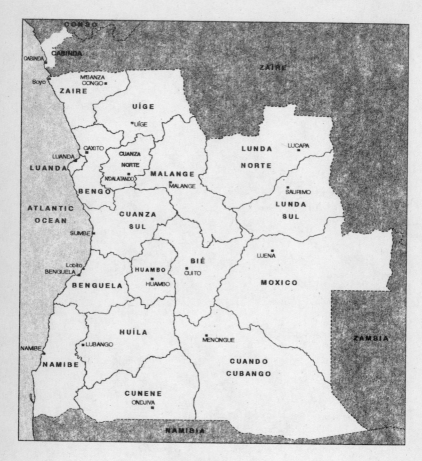

Map of Angola

Contents

Acknowledgements

Many different people steered what started as a vague notion into a book. It is impossible to mention them all, but I would like to name a few special participants.

I begin by thanking Andy Hill for introducing me to Africa. Waldemar Bastos, Manuela Teixeira and João Martins were valuable guides who led me into that world which is Angola. Tony Smith, Tom Cohen, Prexy Nesbitt and John Carlin kick-started me from talk into action.

The John D. and Catherine T. MacArthur Foundation generously provided the funding which made writing the book possible. My employers, *The Christian Science Monitor*, kindly allowed me leave to complete the project. I thank in particular Editor John Cook and Foreign Editor Clayton Jones.

Pam Thornley and Alison Lowry at Penguin Books had valuable ideas for improving the manuscript and I am grateful for their efforts.

Hamilton Wende and Lex Faure read and re-read ungainly drafts, injecting healthy doses of lateral thinking. Because of their tireless efforts, the end product is far more imaginative than initially envisaged. Lex's dedication was such that he broke a leg in the rush to dispatch some comments. Fred Bridgland shared his crucial insights. Edward Burke and John Fleming contributed Angolan verification on research gaps. Patrick Collings lent technical assistance at a critical juncture.

Fred Bridgland and Jorge Ntyamba kindly granted me permission to quote from their published works.

Last, but surely not least, I owe a measureless debt to my mother, my sister and John van Schaik. They endured many trying moments with unconditional love and support.

Prologue

Luanda is a city of few monuments; just some rusty tanks mounted on concrete slabs to remember the civil war. But at Camama cemetery at the edge of town, a pauper's grave which no one ever visits serves as a macabre reminder of an inglorious past.

Poor people in Angola adorn their relatives' graves with something simple — a twig, a shoe, a soda bottle or a small stone — because they can't afford anything else. But this burial plot in a desolate corner of Camama will remain unmarked for ever.

I do not know the men's names or how old they were. All I know is that they were believed to be members of the UNITA rebel movement, among 10 000 similar suspects who were rounded up door to door and massacred on Halloween weekend in 1992. According to the grave-digger, the men were lined up at the cemetery's perimeter white wall and shot before being thrown into a hole in the red earth. Judging from the number of bullet holes on the wall they must have shot at least half a dozen men.

The executioners were so eager to get rid of the bodies that they shovelled too quickly and didn't properly cover them with earth. A couple of the corpses were partly exposed in Luanda's debilitating heat. A long index finger pointed rigidly from the mound at the very spot of the execution.

I went there a week after the massacres. People living behind the cemetery said they heard the shots but didn't see them being fired. The grave-digger, reeking of beer brewed from corn, wasn't very coherent and gave few clues.

1

I returned several times hoping, I suppose, that the accusing finger would be covered by now or the mound dignified by a marking, even a little pebble. It seemed no one ever paid a visit. Even the drunken grave-digger refused to go near the spot as though it had been cursed. Mourners at other grave sites averted their gaze.

The skin of the finger grew leathery in the sub-equatorial sun, and then withered away slowly. But the white bone continued to point towards the bullet-pocked wall.

1

The Wave

For months after I left Angola in 1994 I had a disturbing dream which I couldn't recall. I would wake everyone in the house with my screams but could never explain to them why.

Finally the dream made its way to the surface some time in 1995 and I awoke each morning with a bitter after-taste. In the dream I am sitting on a cliff with green shrubs overlooking a village on the beach and the immense ocean beyond. I am alone; it is a clear sparkling autumn day. Suddenly I see a distant big wave, like a Japanese print of a tidal wave I once saw, rolling in from afar. It is a huge wave, the height of a New York skyscraper, and its edges are curled with deadly white foam. The people in the village below cannot see the wave coming and they are going about their daily routines, the sounds of voices and clanging and animals rising to my vantage point. I am too far away to shout a warning to the people below. I cannot call others to alert them. So I sit powerless and aghast as the wave slowly engulfs the village, drowning its inhabitants.

✛

This book is about being in the wrong place at the wrong time in history. It's about getting so inexorably drawn into a situation that when it was time to leave I kept going back.

In 1992 I accidentally went to Angola and fell into a war that was not supposed to happen.

I travelled to Angola expecting to write about the reconstruction of one of Africa's potentially richest countries, the end of the Cold War and a new world order of peace. Instead, I found myself following a UN peace mission of absurd incompetence and the resumption of a war which for nearly a year was the world's most ferocious.

I never intended to cover a war, anyway. The little bit of violence I had seen in Latin America and South Africa had made me even more determined to avoid conflict. I was convinced that I was not among the ilk that thrives on the adrenalin of danger.

I was born in Queens in New York City and perfected my Spanish while studying Latin American matters at Harvard. I pretended to speak Portuguese fluently because I needed a second foreign language to get a job with Reuters. I also pretended to know something about economics. My bluff must have been convincing because Reuters hired me as a financial writer and sent me forth into the world to write about oil, coffee and fish in Lusophone countries. I covered Angola from afar in Portugal for more than two years and charted the peace talks as the Berlin Wall fell.

When peace seemed to arrive they assigned me to cover the reconstruction of Angola. I went to Angola to write about the rebuilding of a vast country blessed with oil, which was once one of the world's biggest coffee and diamond producers and now hoped to prosper with peace after 16 years of war. Instead, I found myself in the middle of a conflagration whose dimensions no one knew.

I stayed there during the six months of fighting when more people died every day in Angola than in any other conflict in the world, including Bosnia. I went back time and again in the years following that. It was a tough order for a relative novice to Africa. My employers had given me a satellite telephone for filing urgent election results, not to report on numbers of the dead.

4

Angola was to be one of the first post-Cold War test cases of a foreign-mediated conflict resolution. Instead it became a cautionary tale for peacekeepers. Lessons have been learned, one hopes, from the experiences in Sarajevo, Somalia, Mozambique, Rwanda and Liberia. But mistakes are still being repeated today in Angola. It was a colossal tragedy that the international community did not want to assume responsibility for.

I don't claim this to be a definitive treatise on Angola. It begins roughly with the UN-supervised peace accords in 1991 and ends with the UN still struggling to contain the conflict today, in 1997. I was there at a time when there were few witnesses and I felt compelled to chronicle what I saw. I have tried to make sense of why things fell apart.

The book is a series of fragments from a fragmented time. There are only parts of memories. There were and are a lot of ellipses. If one looks at the map of Angola during the war it was split into isolated parts, between government and rebel territory, like the broken pieces of mortar and brick in the cities. So, too, was the disjointed international response and my own feelings of impotence and moral indignation.

✝

Angola is an operatic sort of country where everything is on a Wagnerian scale and can be described in superlatives. Except for Sudan, the fighting has been going on the longest of any conflict in Africa since 1961.

The UNITA rebel leader Jonas Savimbi is often described as 'the most resilient' or 'the most charismatic' guerrilla chief in Africa. When the superpowers got involved, the Soviets behind the MPLA government and the US with South Africa behind UNITA, they unleashed some of their most expensive weaponry in Angola. Angola is blessed with every conceivable natural resource – rich agricultural land, rivers, seas, diamonds, oil, minerals, beaches. That is part of its tragedy; everyone wanted a piece of Angola's wealth and yet, because of the war, few harvested it.

Angola is a country of paradoxes. I was in despair much of the time I was in Angola, but moments of absurd comedy punctuated the gloom. It is a country of illusions, where things are never quite what they seem. For a journalist, it was a frustrating yet fascinating struggle to excavate the truth.

There is the official story: Portugal colonised Angola for nearly 500 years and hastily withdrew in 1975 after its own coup. Conflict developed between three Angolan liberation groups, the FNLA, UNITA and the MPLA. The MPLA got the support of Cuba and the Soviet Union and reigned from the capital, Luanda. UNITA became the main rebel force, fighting with the help of Washington and Pretoria. Then the Cold War ended and the superpowers decided to withdraw. A peace accord was signed between the MPLA and UNITA in 1991, but fighting resumed after Savimbi rejected his election defeat in 1992. Another peace accord was signed in November 1994. Fighting continues today.

Then there is another more murky story.

The rebel leader is a Maoist who got support from rabid anti-communists. Hundreds of millions of dollars worth of diamonds are dug out of Angola's soil each year but the profits do not appear on any public balance sheets. For several years, Cuban troops guarded American oil installations in Angola whose profits were shared with the very same Luanda government that Washington was trying to topple. Angola has banks which no one uses; tellers report to work behind empty counters while the real money trading takes place on the streets. Companies have offices with no signs; officially they do not exist. South African mercenaries deny they are in Angola, yet you meet bearded white men in shorts, boasting of battle. Officially there is peace, but everyone is still fighting. Both sides churn out propaganda and lies. Usually the truth lies somewhere between the rumours and the denials.

You can't write anything about Angola without writing about the fighting which has been going on there for 35 years. There is a land-mine buried in Angolan soil for every man, woman and child in the country. More than half of Angola's ten million people are below the age of 25. That means they have never known anything but loss, refugee camps and weapons. Even if you wrote something about the music, you would find that most of the lyrics are about exile and tears. The closest thing the country has to a national emblem is a sad-looking wooden statuette called *O Pensador*, The Thinker. He seems to embody the national melancholy, brooding over the fractured nation's destiny.

Despite my abhorrence of conflict, I feel oddly privileged to have had an opportunity to peep out of my own narrow world and enter another for a short time. War is a fact of life for several million people on earth; I felt I should understand it, although I feared it. My grandparents fled to America to escape the pogroms in Russia and I was weaned on their tales of dislocation. When I was young my parents showed me news clips of the liberation of Nazi concentration camps with the piles of skeletal remains in mass graves and said: 'Remember. Do not forget.' A quarter of a century later I visited a refugee centre outside Luanda called *Boa Esperança*, Good Hope. Looking at 30 000 frightened women and children who had nowhere to go, I could honestly say I would not forget.

One is taught in journalism that the cardinal rule is to be objective and never use the word 'I'. Any semblance of objectivity that I had quickly evaporated in Angola. The Polish film-maker Krzysztof Kieślowski once said in an interview that the only grudge he bore against film school was that no one told him that the only thing he could really call his own was his life and his point of view. This all made sense after Angola, and I've struggled ever since to maintain my distance from my subject when writing.

If there was one important lesson to be learned, it was from the Angolans themselves. In a country where no one remembers when there wasn't war, people try to maintain a tenuous semblance of normality even in the most trying of conditions. People go about their lives in an almost matter-of-fact way, improvising order and routine out of destruction. Artillery fire could slam into the house next door but they still pulled out cards and played poker, and saved their spare batteries so that they could play music on the radio and dance at birthday parties.

A few months after the end of what was one of the most brutal 22-month sieges in the history of modern war I revisited a town called Cuito, a town like dozens of others. It was a fresh spring day in Angola and people living on the main street which had once been the front line were going about their normal routines. Mortars were sticking out of buildings like giant nails; someone had hung a towel on a shell to dry in the sun.

The apartments all had their facades blown off, exposing the rooms inside like a big doll-house. You could see clearly into one family's living room; they were sitting drinking coffee on a lounge suite like a family anywhere, the only difference being that the front wall was gone. Someone had put up lace curtains as a homage to domesticity. They had eaten all the canaries and puppies during the siege, but someone had found a monkey by the river and it crawled around the parlour on a lead.

In spite of the war, or maybe because of it, Angolans have an indomitable zest for life. Residents proudly took me to see Cuito's new discothèque, which was one of the first places to rise up from the ashes. It was a modest open-air affair, really nothing more than plastic sheeting donated by foreign charities and held up on poles. Generators provided the only power. People had few outfits because of the war but they dressed in their cleanest clothes when they went to the disco and polished their shoes with spit. The disco was positioned next to a park, which was bumpy with mounds where the victims of the fighting had been buried. And so the survivors danced, just metres away from the graves.

The ruling MPLA party has a slogan, *A Luta Continua*: The Struggle Continues. Ordinary Angolans just shrug and say: Life goes on.

2

Saudades

The first time I went to Angola I was actually in Lisbon. Or let me phrase it differently. The first time I discovered Angola I was 9 000 kilometres away in Lisbon.

It was June 1989 at the Ritz, a night-club which had evolved over the years variously from house of ill repute, hangout for leftists, and working-class dance hall. Now it was the favoured night spot for Africans in exile who had come to Lisbon and didn't have much money.

The Ritz had a perpetual layer of smoke and grime, which people tried to escape by seeking refuge on the wooden staircase or on wrought-iron balconies overlooking the dance floor. There were a few fought-over tables with chairs on the edge of the dance floor. But as that filled up the tables were pushed back to the walls and it was uncomfortable to sit there with the dancers hovering above you. Conversation was out of the question because of the noise. Things never got started until well after midnight on Friday or Saturday nights, but then suddenly the floor was so full you couldn't move beyond a confined, tiny space. Within 20 minutes your clothes were stuck to your skin with sweat. The band usually played until dawn and would then abruptly announce that the night was over and pack up and leave.

For years the same band played at the Ritz; I believe it still performs there today. As the years went on its repertoire grew worn and tired and the numbers shorter. But the band continued to draw the crowds.

Many of the African clientele were in Lisbon for political reasons. Some of the others came to make money or to escape the draft, poverty or wars back home. But most of the ones I met at the Ritz were in Lisbon to raise funds, to mobilise support and even to get guns. There were Guineans operating a clandestine movement via fax-line. I met Mozambicans who wanted to stop the massacres back home. There were Cape Verdeans and São Tomenses whose governments weren't at war.

And then there were the Angolans.

At the Ritz you could spot the Angolans' political divisions by the line-up at the dance floor. The MPLA government sympathisers tended to be lighter-skinned and dressed fashionably in soft leather jackets and crisply ironed jeans. They stood at the back or on the balconies, whiskies in hand, and only danced as the night got older. You could smell them as they danced; the men wore cologne. They commanded rather than asked me to dance and held my arm up tightly in the air, like an AK-47 rifle. The UNITA men stood by the bar on the edge of the dance floor; they were dressed in worn, ill-fitting clothes like labourers and were not selective about whom they danced with. They sweated earthily without the cloak of perfume. They stayed all evening, until the club closed, and then would move on to another spot. And they would get angry with me if I danced with someone from the other side.

✛

There is a word in Portuguese which exiles use – *saudades*. The closest translation is homesickness or nostalgia. *Saudades* echoed around the Ritz. My dance partners had *saudades* for palm oil stew, for grilled prawns with red hot piri-piri chillies on the beach. The piri-piri was weak in Lisbon, they said, it needed the bitter bite of home. They had *saudades* for home towns they hadn't visited in 20 years and for childhood sweethearts who

11

had died. They especially missed the music, the mamba beats and slow mournful songs.

It was at the Ritz that I first learned about the tragedy of Angola. At first there were snippets of conversation between dance sets, as everyone tried to cool down with beers at the bar and the tape played reggae. The geography of Angola, its cities of Luena, Cuito and Huambo, worked their way into my vocabulary and my curiosity. I bought a map so that I could locate the latest battles and the birthplaces of my new acquaintances.

One of the Angolans I met at the Ritz was the singer Waldemar Bastos. He and his family quickly became close friends of mine. Each Angolan side had its muse and tall, proud Waldemar was the MPLA's chosen minstrel. UNITA's musician was Bonga, whose voice sounded like gravel and whose lyrics made Angolans emotional. Bonga had originally been with the MPLA, but had later switched sides. For two men who were bitter rivals professionally, their music and life circumstances were remarkably similar. Both sang songs of liberation and both lived in exile – Bonga in Paris and Waldemar in Lisbon.

The songs of both men were about *saudades* and war. Waldemar's fans knew all the words to his *Pitanga Madura* (Mature Fruit) and *Um Futuro Melhor* (A Better Future). But Bonga's followers insisted that there was more raw poetry in his hits *Olhos Molhados* (Tearful Eyes) and *Acacias Feridas* (Wounded Acacias).

Estamos Juntos was the title of Waldemar's most popular album. It was what the MPLA men would say as a farewell: 'We're together.'

To keep the crowd happy, the band at the Ritz – made up of neutral Mozambicans, Cape Verdeans and São Tomenses – played the music of both sides. Both men wrote catchy dance tunes and sometimes an MPLA supporter would find himself dancing to Bonga.

Waldemar had charisma and looked like a bronzed model.

He had the sort of Romanesque profile women wanted to run their hands over. The word usually summoned up to describe him was 'classy'. He had a more highbrow, if smaller, following than Bonga and was disdainful of his rival's gold lamé jackets and his performances at UNITA rallies. He sniffed dismissively when I described a party held by Bonga. The venue was an aeroplane on the edge of Lisbon that had been converted into a bar, where the waitresses were dressed like stewardesses. Waldemar preferred classic cafés and smoky clubs. He insisted that he was independent and that the MPLA had adopted him rather than the other way around.

'At least the people who come to hear me buy their tickets, rather than attend because they are ordered to,' Waldemar said about his rival.

Bonga was more conciliatory towards Waldemar. 'I like his music,' he confided to me. 'He's good.'

Whatever their differences, both men agreed that they couldn't make music back in Angola.

'There's no safety and no studios,' said Waldemar one time. 'How are you supposed to record if the electricity is always going out? And who has money to buy tapes when they can't even afford food?'

Bonga said simply: 'I need to get away from the war to create.'

✢

After my first meetings at the Ritz, the pamphlets and news releases, communiqués and statements were not long in arriving. Streams of propaganda came in via mail, fax and messengers from the various liberation groups. The man from the Guinea-Bissau opposition movement Bafata was convinced the secret police had tracked him to Lisbon and would never identify himself when we spoke by telephone. The representative of the Mozambican rebel group RENAMO was a

13

melancholy thin man with stomach problems and sore feet who periodically dropped by the office with crumpled communiqués and requests for lunch. He seemed too gentle for a movement reputed to mutilate its victims. Once he confessed that his deepest desire was to be a humanitarian aid worker.

I often met my new contacts at the old cafés in Lisbon's downtown section called the Baixa. We'd sit amid the art nouveau décor and sip bitter strong coffee cut with a dash of milk. The cafés were messier than in Paris or even Madrid. The chairs were older and rusted. If they dated, as they often did, back 90 years or so it was because the owner could not afford to replace them. At the turn of the century, Lisbon's intellectuals and poets sat in these cafés whose tables spilled on to the cobbled sidewalks on warm days. Now African exiles occupied these seats, passionately talking about faraway wars.

The Angolan ambassador, Rui Mingas, was a former soccer player and musician who was affable but, like the other diplomats at the embassy, he was fairly inaccessible. They obviously felt they didn't need to court the press and were suspicious of Western journalists like myself. But the UNITA men embraced me, like an American sister. This was useful, although it made me uncomfortable that they assumed that I automatically supported their cause because my government did.

I spent a lot of time at the UNITA office in Lisbon, riding up to the third floor in the caged metalwork elevator to pick up communiqués or to attend press conferences. It was a simple office, near a big park and an easy walk from our office. Any interview was monitored by a sinister-looking man in dark glasses, Adriano Dachala, whose raison d'être seemed to be to ensure that no one from the delegation revealed too much information or acted out of line. He would hover at the back of the room during an interview, silently observing. I never heard him even cough.

There were two people I cultivated at the time, who seemed so different it was hard to imagine they were from the same movement. The more senior was General Adolosi Mango Aliçerces. His name provoked many jokes in the press corps about banana republics and fruit salads. I felt sorry for the way this thin, solitary figure struggled with the city. Mango seemed too vulnerable to command a battle. He had just come from Jamba, UNITA's bush headquarters in southern Angola, and frequently lost his way in Lisbon. Once I made the mistake of inviting him to a business lunch at one of the finest restaurants, an English-style establishment where people whispered over their roasts and puddings. Mango seemed intimidated by the array of cutlery and held up a fish fork with a bewildered plea for explanation. After that we met at a little café around the corner from his office. Mango seemed homesick for Angola and brightened every time he was recalled to Jamba for consultations. I never saw him in the night-clubs.

The press man, Norberto de Castro, on the other hand, was a high-living *mestiço* (mixed-race) Angolan who had no desire to leave Lisbon's gorgeous women and plentiful bars. He appeared apprehensive when summoned from Lisbon's liberating decadence to the discipline of Jamba. He often invited me to his preferred hangout, Bana's Cape Verdean club, offering me entire bottles of whisky which I declined. They thought I was their friend; I saw them as mere work contacts. I tried to avoid talking politics with them after hours.

✛

I often associate the datelines I reported from with colours. Madrid was a bold, fire-engine red. London was grey and Geneva a pale blue. Lisbon was a yellow-green, like new leaves in spring.

It might seem odd that I linked Lisbon with green when in fact the city is replete with pinks and blues like Venice. It is true that Lisbon is filled with plants; geraniums bloom on windowsills and gardens abound. But my associating Lisbon with green is more a matter of the freshness of the atmosphere. Lisbon is a light and relaxed place.

Lisbon was a gentle city then, with a Moorish castle at its heart overlooking the River Tejo. Growing up in New York, I connected castles with fairy tales: now I could pass one on the way to work! Lisbon's castle was run down, but it was a castle all the same. The entire city had a decayed charm about it, a sense of being frozen in another era; it was filled with old cars and turn of the century furniture and chandeliers. The pastel-coloured paint was peeling off the buildings and the blue and white tiles, or *azulejos*, that covered the walls were chipped. It all seemed very attractive, as did the fact that the residents never paved over the cobblestones in the streets and travelled by little trams up and down the hills.

It has changed now, but Lisbon in those days was an enchanted place. The beach was a quick drive across a magnificent bridge like San Francisco's and I could walk in the dunes alone, or stroll unbothered at the docks at night. Even the rain seemed softer and fresher than London from where I had just moved. The summers were longer. Lisbon had a beach, not a grey dirty river. The weather was so mild I once swam on New Year's day. At night Lisbon took on another look, cloaked by a yellow light which made the buildings look like they were carved out of ivory. I slept with my veranda windows wide open without fear. The cobblestones seem clean in my memory, although when I go back I remember they weren't.

The Portuguese on the whole are industrious people, and gentle like their beloved capital. The national folk music, *fado*, is mournful and often about *saudades*. The films are ponderous. The grammar is simple and straightforward, devoid of the bewildering exceptions of French and Spanish. Even Portugal's former dictator, António de Oliveira Salazar, was stern but not malevolent like Mussolini or Hitler. Under his isolationist 36-

year reign the twentieth century passed the country by. The revolution staged on 25 April 1974 by leftist military officials occurred with minimal violence. I remember it well and was struck by its passivity after the brutality of Chile's coup and the war in Vietnam. Other movements have adopted symbols of guns or machetes. The Portuguese revolution took as its trademark a flower, the red carnation.

I had come to Lisbon to recover from two big losses – my father's sudden death from a heart attack and the breakdown of a long-term love who was killing himself with drink. I wanted to get away from the bad memories of London to somewhere where I had no connections. Lisbon was a healing refuge. I experienced my serenest moments there.

I landed in Lisbon by a circuitous route of linguistic exaggeration and aversion to archive dust. It began by wandering into journalism, just like Angola later on, by pure accident. Having grown up in bilingual New York, I developed the strong conviction that I needed Spanish to survive in the world. So when I went to Harvard I decided to study Latin American literature and politics. Upon graduating I went to Mexico on a Fulbright fellowship to research an obscure religious crusade of the 1920s. Needing some extra cash, I adopted the freelance cast-offs of some reporter friends, writing for a couple of alternative newspapers back in the States and later for the United Press International wire agency. It seemed more exciting than interviewing octogenarians who were living in the past, or facing eight more years of cloistered study towards the next degree. I said goodbye to academia with no regrets.

A year later, in pursuit of a coveted job at Reuters in London, I made it through the required trilingual interview by adapting my Spanish to sound like Portuguese. For two weeks before the interview I had practised polished replies to what I thought would be 15 potential questions. Sure enough, some of them were asked: Why do you want to be a journalist? What do you think of the Latin American debt question? Will El Salvador's rebels win the war? My doctored accent was convincing enough. I passed the test.

Portuguese is easy to pick up for anyone who speaks Spanish and has some patience to make the change. But to the untrained ear, the slurs and shushes of Portugal are closer to the Slavic steppes than Iberia. Reuters thought it was an exotic language and few journalists claimed to speak it. This meant that my linguistic fib haunted me during my first five years at Reuters, propelling me to a country where I couldn't properly communicate at first. Twice I was summoned with dread to assess the language speaking skills of people who had been raised in Brazil.

I dodged the first interview by professing to have a sore throat. I used diplomacy to get out of the second one.

'But Jim is much, much more senior,' I told the woman from personnel, pointing to a colleague sitting across the room who had lived in Brazil. 'I'm sure he would be terribly offended if he found out I was chosen to conduct the interview rather than him.'

'You're absolutely right,' she said, looking very relieved at avoiding a hierarchy faux pas. She beamed at me. 'I owe you one. Thanks for saving me.'

'My pleasure,' I said, settling back happily behind my computer.

✛

The first time I was sent to work in Portugal was at the start of 1985, ten years after Portugal had liberated its colonies. The Lisbon bureau chief had fallen ill and I was summoned from Madrid, where I was then based, to 'help out'. The beleaguered office was struggling to cover more than it could handle: a constitutional crisis, a port strike, membership negotiations with the European Community and attacks on NATO installations by FP-25 guerrillas. Upon this brimming news plate was placed

Angola: the superpower battlefield in that distant strange continent, Africa, which was covered from Portugal because Western journalists so rarely got in. I couldn't communicate very well, but I loved Lisbon and vowed to get back there.

Then in 1989 I was assigned to Portugal full time. It took a good six months of hazy missed sentences before I was able to understand the news on television or conduct interviews. But, finally, I awoke one morning and realised that I had dreamt in Portuguese, past, present and future tense, subjunctive mood and all. I had arrived linguistically.

My news editor had been surprised when I had volunteered for the job, which was far from a promotion. Portugal was on the margins of world events and most writers wanted to go for the Big Story. In those days it was the disintegrating Soviet bloc, Israel and Thatcher's London.

'Nothing is happening in Portugal,' he said, puzzled.

'Great,' I thought. It was just what I needed. I wanted some peace and Lisbon seemed like a quiet place where I could be ignored.

The editor conceded, however, that maybe it was the right choice because my writing was deemed to be so dry.

'I don't think you have the flair it takes to write about things like war,' he concluded.

I got the job.

⊹

Portugal is probably the only former imperial power whose erstwhile colony Brazil makes jokes about it and is a bigger economic force. Portugal was such a peripheral country that Africa was the centre point of the assignment. Most of the stories I wrote about were on Angola, because so little was happening in Portugal. And as time went on, Africa also became the centre of my life.

It wasn't just because of the people I met at the Ritz, where

I became such a regular that they let me in for free. It was that Portugal couldn't let go of Africa. Portugal was the first European empire to colonise Africa, 500 years ago. It was the last out in 1975, more than a decade after everyone else. The Portuguese had intermarried more with the locals than other colonials. Africa was in their blood, and their blood was left behind in Africa in the progeny they had sired.

There were hints of Africa everywhere in Portugal. I went to the Alentejo and the acacia bushes, the harsh dry sun and the cracked earth felt like the Horn of Africa. Trás-Os-Montes in the north was like a cold version of Africa; its villagers travelled on dirt roads, shitted in outhouses and cultivated their fields with hand-held ploughs. All that differed from Africa was that the man everyone respected was the village priest instead of the tribal elder.

Africa was not something I had seriously considered before and now it was creeping into my life. I had fancied myself an expert on Latin America, particularly Mexico. Africa seemed distant, especially from my American perspective. I was raised in a city of millions of immigrants who spoke Spanish, not Swahili or Xhosa. Africa was dangerous and chaotic.

When I was little I wanted to be a taxidermist or a zoologist and I dragged my parents every possible weekend to New York's Museum of Natural History. I spent entire days staring at the display cases of stuffed creatures. You could almost feel the heat from the painted backgrounds of distant deserts and mountains. The African animals were the strangest, most wonderful beasts, as fantastic to me as unicorns or griffins. They had evocative names: Okapi, Gnu, Dongo. I saw the film *Born Free* three times and begged my father to move us to Kenya so that we could raise lions. I wanted a pet antelope, not a caged hamster.

But that was when I was small. Later in life, Africa faded out of my emotional realm and imagination, except for raising money for the anti-apartheid movement in South Africa and taking a course in African politics at Harvard for one semester. I glided through the reading superficially, skimming it with my mind on other continents.

But suddenly this had changed. I now felt a whole world was opening up and I experienced a revival of my childhood wonderment. I seemed to see Africa everywhere I looked.

For some reason nearly all my Portuguese friends were *retornados*. Maybe it was because they felt foreign too, although they were Portuguese citizens. The *retornados* were the half-million colonials who hurriedly abandoned the five African colonies during independence in 1974–75, some packing up with only a day's notice. This human wave descended upon Lisbon's shores within a mere few months. They left behind their plantations, large villas and beautiful gardens. They abandoned their clothes, furniture and possessions to settle in a country which couldn't properly absorb them. They came back to no jobs and often no homes. They camped out in churches in Lisbon or in the living rooms of relatives or in sheds on the family farms. Some had been born and raised in Africa. Others had left Portugal when they were young and had only the faintest memories of it. The *retornados* felt different from those who had never left Portugal and their traumatic return was not welcomed.

Now, ten years later, they, like the African exiles, had *saudades* for that distant continent. *Saudades* gave them a fraternity with the very Africans whom they had never treated as equals. The *retornados* clung to memories of dancing at the *Costa do Sol* nightclub on Saturday nights in Maputo. They still called Maputo by its old name, Lourenço Marques. They remembered tranquil beach holidays on Benguela's white sands. They had photographs of tame pet monkeys who scrambled in the bougainvillaea. Life would never be the same again.

✦

Like the *retornados* looking back towards Africa across the sea, Lisbon has its nostalgic reminders of its lost maritime glory located on the bank of the River Tejo: the Belem Tower and the Monument of the Discoveries. Both are temples to the past, paying homage to the oceans and Portugal's long-lost glory when it explored the world. The monuments both jut out to sea. The first was built at the height of the Discoveries in the fifteenth and sixteenth centuries, a delicate structure that looks about to sink. The latter is solid, carved in a fascist style. Its muscular figures are triumphantly moving towards the ocean.

The sea is omnipresent in Lisbon. There is even a special architectural style developed during the Age of Discoveries, called the *Manueline*, which specialises in maritime motifs such as seashells. The *azulejos*, the blue and white tiles which cover the walls of buildings, depict scenes of ships and the empire. In Lisbon you eat food from the sea, you smell the sea, you complain about paint peeling because of the humidity. People catch coughs from the damp. It is not just a beach city. It is a sea city. The ocean provides food and pleasure and swimming. But it's more than that. It also provides identity and soul.

✦

There was a big public garden on the corner of my street, filled with lush plants and red flowers whose names I didn't know at the time. When I later went to Angola I saw the same vegetation there, but more exuberant and untamed. My flat in Lisbon was in an old house whose huge terrace became a Mecca for my African friends.

After a late night at the clubs we'd tramp back to my flat arguing about politics and why I couldn't dance properly. I'd leave them debating in my living room and go to the sanctuary of my bedroom just before dawn. Then I'd awake the next afternoon to dark roasted coffee and a stew on the boil for Sunday lunch. People would sprawl all over the sofas or in the spare room. Talk would have moved on over the hours from why Cape Verde and Guinea-Bissau could never unite to whether there was anything ideologically different between UNITA and the MPLA. And why so many Portuguese African revolutionaries were poets.

Then sisters and cousins and other people would pour in for lunch and the living room would be crowded with more talk and laughter and warmth. One Mozambican came for a weekend and stayed for six months; something containing coconut was always simmering in the kitchen. Waldemar dropped by occasionally for parties or meals. He never sang, disdainfully rejecting requests. But what he held back musically he made up in conversation.

I loved those weekends and my friends said it reminded them of other times.

'*Muamba* is a Sunday dish, it is as sacred as church,' said Luzia, pounding palm nuts for a chicken stew. 'Done properly, you must have lots of whisky, family and more family,' she added. Her eyes misted.

Food was one of my entrées into people's lives. I had a notion in those days to write a Portuguese-African cookbook, which is now a heap of recipes in my kitchen. I periodically excavate them when creativity and nostalgia strike. My culinary curiosity gained me access to people's homes; everyone's mother or wife made the best dish and wanted to let me in on the secret.

'What! A *Matapa*? She doesn't know how to do it; try mine,' someone would say about the manioc leaf and crab stew from Mozambique.

'Come to our house and we'll show you the best white beans in town,' someone else said.

How could I say no?

I spent many hours at a tiny cramped Mozambican restaurant in Lisbon's maze-like old quarter. Known simply as 'Aziz', the restaurant took its name from its owner, a refugee from northern Mozambique. He later died, from a mysterious wasting disease which no one wanted to admit was Aids. Like the Ritz, Aziz's place was frequented by many of the exiles and one could pick up news tips there. It was at the restaurant that I heard about Mozambique's fledgeling peace talks. It was over a grilled chicken prepared by his wife that I was shown the manifesto of the Bissaun opposition.

Nearly every weekend someone in Aziz's huge extended family had a birthday or wedding anniversary. Aziz and his wife would close the doors and lay out a feast for their many cousins and most intimate friends. To refuse an invitation would be to risk banishment. We'd gorge ourselves on prawns and coconut rice and sticky sweet cashew until our stomachs were swollen. Then they would pull out the whisky and dance to Afro-Latin rhythms crackling from an old record-player.

Since my job entailed reporting on Portugal's former colonies I made a convincing case to my bosses to cover the political changes in Cape Verde and Guinea-Bissau in mid-1991. The two countries were slowly opening up to multiparty rule and I argued that I should go there to write about it. I also ended up writing about a Bissaun film-maker who shot movies in a leaking, roofless building with barely literate actors who had trouble reading their scripts. I made a pilgrimage to the house which was the birthplace of Amilcar Cabral, the great revolutionary hero of Guinea-Bissau. It was boarded up and in shambles, rather like his dream of a glorious liberation.

When I went to Cape Verde and Guinea-Bissau it was with a long list of instructions from friends to collect sacks of dried fish and den den, palm nuts which are crushed into a bright orange, acidic oil. When I visited Mozambique several months later, Aziz gave me names of relatives to contact. I took his sister canned goods and clothes and in return was laden like a donkey with bags of cashew nuts, limes and manioc leaves. The white customs officials at Lisbon airport waved me through with a wink, even though I was probably breaking every agricultural rule in the book. They probably missed the stuff as well.

✛

Despite all the *saudades* that the Portuguese have for Africa, when I look at photographs from the colonies I am struck by an enduring impression of the colonials' inability to blend in with their adopted environment.

Take, for instance, an old book I have of Luanda, Angola's main city for 400 years. The photographs are from around the time of the 1884-85 Berlin Conference, when European imperial powers carved up Africa's borders. Portugal was so worried about losing its five-country African empire that it immediately launched into three decades of expansion into Angola's unexplored interior.

The book is about life in 'Old Luanda'. It is about the carnivals, the festivities, parades and picnics. It is about the charmed existence of people who transcended the obscurity of poverty back home to preside over big villas with crystal chandeliers and servants.

Angola was Portugal's richest and most beloved colony in Africa. It was their home away from home. My old map book of Angola is filled with the names of saints and famous Portuguese men: Porto Alexandre, Novo Redondo, Duque de Bragança, São Salvador, Silva Porto, Sá da Bandeira, Salazar, Dom Pedro V, São António and Teixeira da Silva. Some, such as Nova Lisboa (New Lisbon), were named after towns back home. They are pretty names from another world. Since independence towns have regained the indigenous names that rumble with ancient authority: Cuito, Huambo, Bailundo. But when the Portuguese ruled they tried to impose their shadows of Lisbon on Africa.

The Portuguese had an ambivalent attitude towards their black subjects. Depending on whom you spoke to, the relative poverty of the Portuguese settlers compared to the Belgians and French was a negative or positive factor. The British explorer David Livingstone noticed this dichotomy when he travelled to Angola in 1854. He wrote that he was pleased to see that the Portuguese colonials treated their half-caste children as well as they did their white children. But he also found that hostility from local people increased as he approached each Portuguese settlement.

Many of the people sent to settle in Angola were of distinctly low calibre. The colony became a repository for exiled convicts or illiterate peasants. The right of many of these new Portuguese colonials to impose their 'civilisation' was dubious.

It is undoubtedly true that the middle- and upper-class British and French who colonised their parts of Africa left far superior systems of education and civil service than the Portuguese. But while the French were convinced that their colonies were privileged to be Francophised, the Portuguese coexisted with the Africans in a more modest fashion. They begat children with local women, and in the more remote areas they drank coffee with their black neighbours because there was no one else around. Some had been barefoot farmers before they came to Angola.

Superficially, therefore, there was a greater psychological affinity between the Portuguese and the blacks. But this made the masters enjoy playing landlord all the more. The intrinsic social fact was that they would never see themselves as equals to the *pretos* – the word for blacks that Angolans still find derogatory today.

The belief in the motherland of its multiracialism became a myth which was summoned up to justify continued colonialism. The late dictator Salazar put a name to this supposed multiracialism, calling it *Lusotropicalismo*. Salazar liked to describe the Portuguese possessions in Africa as provinces rather than colonies, as though this were a less severe form of subjugation. But the racial tolerance seemed mainly to take the form of sexual activity. Beyond that, Angolans tell a story of exclusion from power, exploitation, and virtual social apartheid.

Looking at the photographs of this alleged African paradise,

I feel that something is wrong. These Portuguese settlers did not conquer or blend in with their environment. There is a gulf between them and the Africans, who are hovering bare-chested in the background. The Portuguese have tried to duplicate a Lisbon tea party but their gentility is illusionary. The heat is too great and the vegetation thick with malaria lurks untamed behind them. Girls sit in starched white dresses, tendrils of hair escaping from their prim plaits in the humid heat. Men languish in hammocks, carried by porters. But even in the fading grey and white photographs you see the disorder spilling out from behind the banana trees and the high grass. Just beyond the terrace and the picnic there is something that corsets and top hats cannot contain.

The next series of pictures I have are more sinister. They are from the 13-year colonial war when 500 years of the charmed life ended. Women are still well-coiffed, their hair sprayed into bouffants, their heels high and their flowered shifts fashionably above the knee. They stand awkwardly as soldiers give them shooting lessons so that they can defend themselves while alone on the farms. By that time hundreds of women and children on isolated plantations had been slaughtered with machetes and guns. They weren't executed quickly; the photographs of their corpses show multiple hacks on the legs and arms. These are the slashes of slow-burning rage.

The most poignant pictures of failure are of the teenage soldiers in fatigues on patrol. They look defensive – no, downright scared. Many of the photographs are of ambushes: aircraft shot down, mangled helicopters and planes crumpled like tin foil. An armoured vehicle is lifted out of water where one hundred people had drowned; cars are turned on their sides and crushed. The grass is taller than the uniformed youths, who huddle around stricken vehicles holding their guns close to their bodies. And from the bush appears a huge serpent, lying lethargically on the ground with its belly grotesquely swollen. The curious soldiers cut it open – and find the decomposing but intact body of an African youth.

✝

We know little about Angola's original inhabitants, other than the names of mythical kings which some elders still remember. The name Angola derives from a Kimbundu word, *Jingola*, which means a small piece of metal. It became a symbol of political authority. Later the word *Ngola* became the title of the monarch of the Ndongo kingdom situated in western and central Angola south of the Congo.

Anthropologists believe the first inhabitants of what is modern-day Angola migrated around AD 500 from Nigeria and the Cameroon to the Congo basin. Then from the twelfth to the fifteenth centuries there was mass migration to what is today Zaire and Angola. Around 1400 two major kingdoms were formed: that of the Ndongo, and the Congo dynasty in the north-western corner.

Portuguese colonial occupation began with the discovery of the mouth of the Congo river in 1482 by explorer Diogo Cão, who struck up a friendship with the Congo King. The King in turn began corresponding with the King of Portugal. The Congo monarch converted to Christianity, changed his name to Afonso and adopted Portuguese aristocratic titles. M'banza Congo, his headquarters, became the first Catholic settlement in Africa. Portugal's contact with the Congo royal family was fairly egalitarian – until the start of the slave trade.

The Portuguese began to conquer the country in earnest in 1560. Luanda was settled 16 years later. It was a strategic port because of its access to the Atlantic, and became Angola's main city for 400 years. Luanda also became a major base for the slave trade and military expeditions were launched from its garrisons in pursuit of more slaves. Some three million Angolan slaves were shipped over three centuries to Brazil, the Caribbean and South America's River Plate area. A further seven million died in transit. Angolan slaves were deemed especially attractive; they were tall and handsome and strong. The Portuguese encouraged tribal rivalries to bolster their slave trade, buying prisoners to send across the ocean. Their biggest ally was the King of the Congo, who sold them prisoners captured during his battles with the other kingdoms.

But this was not taken passively by the local populations who staged rebellions and uprisings against the Portuguese. The Ndongo in particular put up stiff resistance, although the Portuguese eventually succeeded in destroying the kingdom by 1670. Around the same time a similar fate befell the Congo kingdom. Finally turning against the Portuguese, the Congo was in disarray in 1665 after a fierce conflict.

✦

Angola is a big country. It is the size of Germany, France and Spain combined. There was a lot to colonise, but the Portuguese tended to stick to the coast where their biggest settlements were around Luanda and Benguela, further south. It was only after the Berlin Conference, in the early part of the twentieth century, that major expansion into the interior occurred.

Angola's white population was never more than 10 000 until the start of the twentieth century. The colonials set up an apartheid-style separation of the races, with *mestiços* given a higher status than most blacks. In Luanda itself, it was mainly the whites and *mestiços* who lived in the houses and flats. The blacks were relegated to the *musseques*, the sand slums on the periphery of the town.

There was a tendency by the Portuguese to lump the various ethnic groups into one category: African. There was little appreciation or distinction made of the vast differences between the clans and linguistic groups: the cattle-raisers on the border with Namibia, the Herero desert people, Ganguela fishermen and nomadic bushmen.

The Chokwe people of the centre-east Lundas region at the end of the nineteenth century were considered by the colonials to be among the most aggressive and independent groups. Their economic power was reinforced by the fact that ivory, rubber and beeswax, the main commercial items at the time, came from the areas under their control. They had firearms and female slaves. But by the twentieth century their influence had waned compared to that of the biggest groups – the Ovimbundu, the Kimbundu, and the Bakongo.

The Kimbundu were descendants of the Ndongo kingdom. Today they comprise 16 per cent of Angola's population. In Luanda, the Kimbundu tended to mix more easily with the Portuguese whites than other ethnic groups. Indeed, some were proud of their association with the Portuguese and the role they played in helping to subjugate Angola to the colonial power. The word *Mundele* was applied to some of them: it meant a black with shoes. The Kimbundu began a literary tradition in Luanda at the end of the nineteenth century and formed part of a new elite involved in commerce, civil service and intellectual life.

The Bakongo people came from the area of the old Congo kingdom. They make up about 13 per cent of the population today. Based in Cabinda, Zaire and Uíge provinces, the Bakongo are closely linked ethnically with people in the former Zaire and Congo.

The Ovimbundu are Angola's biggest ethnic group, making up an estimated 35 per cent of the population. At the end of the nineteenth century the Ovimbundu were organised politically into 12 kingdoms of which the biggest were the Bailundo, Huambo, Bie, Chiyaka, Galangue and Andulo. The Bailundo king was for a time the most powerful of them all. Largely peasants who worked the land, the Ovimbundu were the most homogeneous group linguistically; other ethnic groups tended to be split into dialects. They were dispersed over the most populous parts of Angola, excluding the capital, from south of the River Cuanza throughout the central highlands known as the Planalto Central which spans the provinces of Huambo, Bie and Benguela. They generally lived in big villages of one hundred to a thousand people, inhabited by kin of blood ties.

The colonial rulers used forced labour to cultivate plantations, displacing the Ovimbundu in particular to work on the coffee farms in the north. This, as well as the seizure of traditional lands, prompted various rebellions by the local populations. There were uprisings by the Dembo tribe northeast of Luanda, and the southern Cuanhama people challenged the Portuguese from 1904 to 1915.

Arguably, the revolt with the most lasting consequences was the four-month Bailundo rebellion of 1902. The revolt was brutally put down, a humiliating fact which had a bearing on the success 60 years later by UNITA rebel leader Jonas Savimbi in garnering support among the Ovimbundu.

Once the slave trade ended, Angola became something of an economic burden for Portugal. This continued into the mid-twentieth century, despite lucrative prospecting for diamonds and the country's status as one of the world's largest coffee producers. But Lisbon continued to pour in resources nevertheless.

In the 1950s, Dictator Salazar began to pursue a policy of greater economic investment in Angola. The capital was a hub of construction. From 1955 to 1959 the colonials built 1 400 new buildings in Luanda alone. Aside from apartment blocks and offices, they also constructed dams, railways, factories, harbours, bridges, airports and roads. Earnings were coming in from the Benguela Railroad, a feat of engineering that stretched 1 301 kilometres from the Atlantic port of Lobito and then forked out to Zaire and Zambia. Built between 1903 and 1929, it was the main artery to the sea for those two countries. Precious freight was moved to the Atlantic on the railroad. European travellers arriving in Lobito would travel in high style on trains offering showers, silverware and Portuguese wines.

In the 1960s the economy took off, thanks to oil. Angola quickly became sub-Saharan Africa's largest producer after Nigeria. By independence Angola was producing 150 000 barrels per day. Meanwhile, total revenue on the Benguela Railroad peaked at $43 million in 1974, moving a total freight of around 3 million tonnes. That same year, diamond production hit a peak of 2,3 million carats. Coffee production was around 210 000 tonnes.

Few of these riches were enjoyed by the Angolans themselves. The public works were largely cosmetic for most Angolans and, in the view of many, came far too late. An urban, intellectual elite of *mestiços* had emerged – a result of the scarcity of white women, which encouraged colonial men to take local lovers. During the time of the slave trade *mestiços* had played a role as intermediaries. But few black Africans enjoyed privileges. The Portuguese, generously so they thought, devised a special class – the *assimilados*, or assimilated ones – who had a special status. But the qualifications to join this special club were ridiculously tough. An applicant had to speak fluent Portuguese, be at least 18 years old, earn a decent income, produce a birth certificate, a health certificate, two references and a statement of loyalty. By 1960 only one per cent of Angolans were *assimilados*.

It was little wonder, therefore, that the liberation fever in British and French Africa spread to the Portuguese colonies. But the Portuguese weren't prepared for the hatred which ensued. Three movements sprang up – the MPLA, the FNLA, and UNITA – all of which had external links.

Practically from the moment the liberation struggle took root the three groups were in competition, trying to wipe each other out. They were neatly divided on ethnic lines, although all three have denied that they were tribalist and non-representative.

The MPLA (Popular Movement for the Liberation of Angola) was formed in 1956 under the leadership of Agostinho Neto. The movement's roots and support base were mainly in Luanda and Bengo, Cuanza Norte, Cuanza Sul and Malange, as well as the intellectuals of Benguela. Its support basis was largely among the *mestiços* and Kimbundu. Many of its leaders were intellectuals who had studied or spent time in Portugal.

The FNLA (National Front for the Liberation of Angola) was founded by Holden Roberto. It was strong among the Bakongo in the northern provinces of Zaire and Uíge. Roberto's ancestors were part of the Bakongo royal family and he was related by marriage to the president of Zaire, Mobutu Sese Seko. The FNLA was based in Zaire for a while and enjoyed the support of the CIA in the 1960s, before the Americans switched their support to UNITA.

Jonas Savimbi's UNITA (National Union for the Total Independence of Angola) was based in the central highlands of the Ovimbundu people. It broke away from the FNLA in 1964, initially with Chinese support. After 1975 UNITA formed a close alliance with South Africa.

The enmity between the three movements led to a dispersal of what could have been a joint force against the Portuguese. But it also created a three-pronged rebellion with distinct methods.

The French, British and Belgians tended to abandon their colonies when the pressure became untenable. But Portugal held on, with a tenacity unparalleled elsewhere. The colonies served an emotional and nationalistic purpose; they were a source of pride in a now faded imperial power stretching back to the glorious Age of Discoveries. It was hard to let them go without a struggle.

The Portuguese fight to retain their African possessions was unrivalled in modern history. Brazil became independent in 1822 in relative calm. Goa's incorporation into India occurred with relatively limited conflict. East Timor's brutal invasion by Indonesia came after Portugal had withdrawn peacefully. Macau today is being handed over to China with minimal problems.

The African war of attrition took its toll economically but the Portuguese stuck it out, sending out thousands of young men to fight a war they couldn't win. They employed counter-insurgency strategies pioneered in Algeria and Vietnam. What made their job so tough was that they were dealing not with one but with three liberation movements. The Portuguese would pacify, or try to pacify, one area. Then they would be hit in another. And besides Angola, colonial wars were also being fought in Guinea-Bissau and Mozambique.

The uprisings were a huge drain on Portugal, both financially and psychologically. More than one million Portuguese emigrated, including about 100 000 draft dodgers who left the country. Casualties from the colonial wars were high: 11 000 dead and 30 000 wounded or disabled. In the final years of the fighting one half of Portugal's annual budget went on military spending.

For the Portuguese in the colonies, there was a sense that everything was disintegrating around them. Neighbours and servants whom they had trusted suddenly turned against them. Women had to learn to use guns and families had to travel in convoys. They were no longer safe at night in their own homes.

For the Angolans, it was a chance to claim what they felt was rightfully theirs.

'It wasn't that we were against whites per se,' explained one man, Casimiro Dembo, who had fought with the MPLA in the early 1970s. 'There were individuals that I liked; I encountered some good people. But the fact of the matter was that we were like slaves in the farms and factories. We were not allowed to attend secondary school; I wanted to study but the system didn't allow it. I was brought up with the anger of my parents about the injustices of the system. So when a guy I knew in the neighbourhood started talking about the MPLA it all made sense. I joined up and fought.'

What finally ended the war was not a military victory on either side. It was the fact that Portuguese leftist military men, tired of 40 years of dictatorship and the costly colonial wars which they couldn't win, decided to take matters into their own hands. They staged a coup and on 25 April 1974 a new era began. Portugal's new leaders moved quickly to divest the country of its colonies. Angola was the last of the five colonies to gain independence, which was declared on 11 November 1975.

During the year and a half between and coup and independence, about 800 000 Portuguese colonials packed up and left the colonies, about 335 000 from Angola alone. They went back to the motherland, leaving a trail of turbulence behind. Many left the week Angola declared independence, taking flight at the absolute last minute. By that time the capital Luanda was a war zone. The MPLA had declared itself the new rulers and UNITA and the FNLA were trying to close in from outside.

With civil war breaking out, the panicked colonials took everything they had and escaped from Luanda by air or boat. They left as little as possible behind intact. Light bulbs were smashed, electrical wires were cut. There were apocryphal accounts of fleeing Portuguese pouring cement down drains so that those inheriting their property would not enjoy it. From being the masters of estates, they were suddenly reduced to little more than refugees.

'Our world vanished in a week. We lost our status and were torn from our friends, our dogs and our furniture,' was how one *retornado* described the trauma. 'Maybe you took your clothes with you. But you lost your context.'

But their fate was not as bad as that of the Angolans. The *retornados* left behind a country where practically no one knew how to read, let alone run a government.

Before its quick exit, Portugal tried to set up what it believed was a power-sharing mechanism between the three rival guerrilla groups. In the so-called Alvor agreement, signed on 15 January 1975, all four parties mapped out a transitional arrangement until a new constitution could be drawn up and elections held for a new constitutional assembly.

This was asking too much. A lot of weight was put on the good faith and political will of groups that had little reason to trust one another. The constitutional assembly was never elected. What didn't help was the vague wording of the November independence statement which bestowed power on 'the Angolan people'. This was open to interpretation, especially by the MPLA which immediately declared its own Democratic Republic of Angola in Luanda. UNITA and the FNLA were left out.

When Portugal withdrew, foreign meddlers jumped into the vacuum. South Africa wanted a base from which to strike at SWAPO (South West African Peoples' Organisation) guerrillas in what later became Namibia. Pretoria also wanted to destabilise any leftist threat in nearby black states. Zaire wanted to prop up its ally next door, Holden Roberto's FNLA. The US and the Soviet Union, which respectively supported UNITA and the MPLA, wanted to pursue ideological expansions and a military balance. Cuba backed the MPLA, likewise, to increase its sphere of influence.

At the peak of the war, US officials estimated that Soviet aid amounted to $800 million in a year. The Soviet Union gave an estimated $6 billion in total military support to the MPLA. In turn, US support to UNITA was estimated at about $60 million annually in the final years. This US aid was covert for the first ten years, but became open after 1985 when Congress lifted a law preventing official American aid to the rebels.

South Africa occupied large parts of the Cunene and Cuando Cubango provinces in southern Angola from 1981-88, creating a buffer zone between Namibia and the rest of Angola. But this led to a stalemate. By the late 1980s UNITA claimed to have 70 000 men but, even with the help of Pretoria's regular raids and sabotage operations, could not defeat the MPLA's FAPLA army.

The 1986–87 battle for Cuito Cuanavale, in the south near Namibia, marked a turning point in the civil war. The South African Defence Force could not break through the MPLA army's defence and lost control of the air war, suffering hundreds of wounded and dozens of dead. This drove home to Pretoria's apartheid leaders that South Africa could not win militarily in either Namibia or Angola.

Following this realisation, contacts intensified to try to find a peaceful solution. US Assistant Secretary of State for African Affairs Chester Crocker and other negotiators shuttled between Lusaka, Luanda, London, Brazzaville, Havana and Cape Verde. They concentrated on linkage: withdrawing Cuban soldiers once South Africa left and accepted the independence of Namibia. On 22 December 1988 the Tripartite Accords were signed in New York between South Africa, Cuba and Angola. UNITA, however, did not take part in the negotiations or the accord, on the insistence of the Angolan government.

On 11 November 1989 the Berlin Wall fell. For Angola, a whole world of opportunities opened up.

✛

Opportunities opened up for Portugal, too. Only a changing world order could mean that peace talks for Angola could be hosted by its former colonial master.

The time was ripe for peace for ordinary Angolans. The war had maimed or killed an estimated 600 000 Angolans and inflicted material damage worth $30 billion. By 1990, there were more than 300 000 refugees and 800 000 displaced people. Oil, which accounted for 90 per cent of export revenue, was pumping at a comfortable rate of more than 500 000 barrels per day. But much of that revenue went to the war effort. Other sectors of the economy were ruined; diamond and coffee production was severely down. The mighty Benguela Railroad was virtually paralysed except for a 40-kilometre stretch. Adult literacy was a pitiful 30 per cent, only one third of the population had access to basic health services, and only one in ten to adequate sanitation.

There already had been strong signals that something was coming. In Gbadolite on 22 June 1989, the first agreement was reached since Alvor in 1975 for a cease-fire in Angola. At a meeting of several African heads of state in Zairian President Mobutu's residence, Savimbi and Angolan President José Eduardo dos Santos shook hands. Two days later they both disagreed about what they had agreed on and the truce fell apart. Mobutu continued to offer his mediation services, but these were declined by Dos Santos.

There was momentum behind the scenes, however. Between 27–30 January 1990 Savimbi made his first visit to Portugal in 30 years. His trip was delayed by a week because of fighting in Cuando Cubango. Then he left early, due to an offensive near his Mavinga stronghold. But the fact that he came at all seemed to indicate that negotiations were picking up pace.

Meanwhile, the political situation in South Africa was changing. Apartheid was withering away after the release of African National Congress leader Nelson Mandela and the legalisation of black political groups in February 1990.

In Lisbon, Reuters closed the office for the day and we watched the live television transmission from Cape Town as Mandela left prison a free man, hand held high, with his wife Winnie. The moment the image appeared on the screen the phones began ringing insistently.

'It's just a matter of time now,' an Angolan friend said, just one of several people calling to share the moment. 'Our liberation from war comes next.'

The following month Namibia declared its independence. In Rome, tentative peace talks had begun between RENAMO rebels and the government in Mozambique. The superpowers expressed their desire to disengage from Angola. They were winding down the Cold War and Angola was among the most expensive proxies for both sides. They were working together to end conflicts in southern Africa and the Horn.

Meanwhile, Portugal was trying to recapture its past diplomatic weight now that it had joined the European Community. Businessmen wanted access to African markets and to reclaim their nationalised land. Perhaps just as importantly, the Portuguese wanted to come to terms with their collective guilt over abandoning their colonies in such an abrupt fashion. Promoting peace talks seemed to be a way to redress their error.

When UNITA and the MPLA finally met on 24 April 1990, I wasn't surprised. The only thing which was surprising was the venue – Évora. Évora is a pretty little tourist town with Roman ruins in Portugal's Alentejo region. It seemed an unlikely choice, with its souvenir shops and hotels frequented by German tourists. But the security was deemed good, a major factor in the months to come.

The following 13 months of peace talks were like a revolving tour of the military installations surrounding Lisbon. The talks took place roughly every month and were surprisingly businesslike considering the rancour and distrust of the two adversaries. Despite the periodic deadlocks and stalemates there was an overall sense of progress.

Part of that no-nonsense atmosphere was attributable to the competence of the main mediator, Portugal's then Secretary of State for Foreign Affairs and Co-operation, José Manuel Durão Barroso. A young man in his thirties, Durão Barroso had been a Maoist activist as a student and was now a rising star in the Social Democrat government. He was very bright, very ambitious, and both Angolan sides seemed to trust him.

The pace of negotiations was given an added push by the involvement of the superpowers, who until then had been watching from the sidelines. After several sessions in 1990, they decided that the Angolans and the Portuguese meant business. From the fourth round of talks, in September 1990, the US and the Soviets stepped in and began to play a bigger role as mediators. Their presence encouraged the process further.

Despite my professed enjoyment of the slow pace of Portuguese news, it was a relief finally to have a proper story to get involved in. I savoured the negotiations, realising that actually I had missed proper reporting. I tracked every little nuance, every subtle change in position, every breakthrough, every hitch. The more the talks became technical, the deeper I followed them.

All the participants, whether from Luanda or Jamba, seemed to have noms de guerre. The MPLA men took dramatic, although essentially nonsensical names such as Nando, N'dalu, Loy. The UNITA men had childish sounding nicknames: Gato (Cat), Mango, Ben Ben. But their negotiators were no fools and won many concessions with wily bargaining.

The US was the weightiest of the three mediators involved. Portugal should have had a big say, being host to the talks. But it was a small country. Besides, its clout over UNITA was limited because the latter accused it of harbouring sympathies for the MPLA. The Soviet Union was falling apart. This gave UNITA an advantage because its benefactor was intact, unlike its rival's.

There were huge gaps in confidence and fighting was continuing despite the gains in negotiations. Both sides were keen to keep up the military pressure, hoping that the battles would intensify their bargaining leverage. And while the superpowers were edging closer to a common position on Angola, from late 1988 to mid-1991 they poured increased military aid into their proxies. In the final years of the war, the growing momentum for peace was accompanied by escalated military activity. Nowhere was that more evident than in the last big battle of the war, UNITA's siege of Luena, the capital of eastern Moxíco province. The city was pounded with artillery and traumatised for 45 days.

There was a fair amount of horse-trading and posturing by both sides, which included stalling on mutual demands for explicit recognition of each other. December 1990 proved to be the critical turning point. US Secretary of State James Baker and his Soviet counterpart Eduard Shevardnadze decided they needed to play a more active role in the negotiations. Meeting with their top aides, they drew up an outline linking a UN-supervised cease-fire with a date for internationally monitored elections and ending military support to their proxies after the truce.

On 13 December 1990, in Washington, officials of the two adversaries and the Troika agreed on a blueprint for a peace accord. It included the above items as well as the creation of a multiparty democracy and of a single national army after the cease-fire and before the elections.

It appeared that a breakthrough had finally been reached. However, it took further rounds of intense negotiating before the deal was finalised. The election date emerged as the biggest sticking point. UNITA, with the backing of the US, wanted elections within nine months. The MPLA wanted the poll to be held within three years. A compromise, proposed by Durão Barroso, was eventually reached: elections within 16 months.

On the surface the accord had similar components to the Alvor agreement: there was to be a cease-fire and a transition period before multiparty elections took place. A new joint military was to be created. But there were also major differences to the Alvor agreement. This time one of the two adversaries was actually in power. Now Portugal was a mediator, not a disengaging colonial master. What also differed was that these mediators set up conflict resolution mechanisms – a joint political and military commission observed by the Troika – to oversee the truce and the creation of the new armed forces.

On 1 May 1991, UNITA vice-president Jeremias Chitunda

and Angolan government representative Lopo do Nascimento initialled the Estoril Accords, which took their name from the town where the final negotiations took place. They stipulated that a cease-fire would come into effect within two weeks and that the final signing between Savimbi and Dos Santos would take place on 31 May. On 6 May, the MPLA government approved constitutional revisions for the introduction of a multiparty system. The siege of Luena lasted until the moment the cease-fire began on 15 May, and on 25 May the last Cuban soldiers left Angola.

At the initialling ceremony in Estoril, a colleague from Paris stood behind me and did a jocular rendition of a horse race report as though the signatories were competing to reach the finish line. The rotund Chitunda was lagging far behind his svelte MPLA counterpart.

'And there's Chitunda, straggling behind. The MPLA is miles ahead. There! He signs another page. And another. And yet another. Chitunda is still on his third page. Can he catch up? No! And there's the MPLA, stretching their lead even more . . .'

I giggled a little too loudly and someone in the diplomatic corps looked at me sharply. It seemed cruel to mock Chitunda, his face crunched in concentration and his thick fingers awkwardly gripping the pen. He looked anxiously at his counterpart, but he couldn't catch up.

My colleague continued. 'And there's the MPLA . . . they're close, ladies and gentlemen, very close. And they're there! They have crossed the finale! Ladies and gentlemen, the victor of the Biçesse Accords is . . . the MPLA!'

Just how apt this was became clear only months later.

✢

The final signing of the peace agreement, called the Biçesse Accords, on 31 May 1991 created an explosion of euphoria in

Lisbon. This was Portugal's moment. It was a diplomatic victory. Biçesse served not only to put Portugal on the map but also to assuage the collective guilt about the way Lisbon had so appallingly abandoned its colonies. For two days Portugal was no backwater; Lisbon was at the top of the news items. World leaders converged upon Lisbon; bodyguards and motorcades surrounded the top hotels. The joint signing by President José Eduardo dos Santos and Jonas Savimbi took place under the watchful eyes of international figures: UN Secretary General Javier Pérez de Cuéllar, Organisation of African Unity President Joweri Museveni, US Secretary of State James Baker and his Soviet counterpart Aleksandr Bessmertnykh.

The latter two men declared that the agreement signalled the end of the Cold War in Africa.

Chester Crocker, who had worked for so many years for this moment, summed up the hope that so many people felt that day.

'As I listened to the speeches that evening and watched MPLA and UNITA leaders mingling, I knew that we were celebrating the end of an era,' he wrote in his book *High Noon in Southern Africa: Making Peace in a Rough Neighborhood*.

'Angolans could now begin to shape their own destiny after centuries of foreign domination, living with foreign legacies and foreign conflicts. It was also the time for a fresh start for Portugal in Africa; peace would open up a vast, constructive potential between these peoples tied by language, blood and culture.'

That night Lisbon held the party of all parties. Bells rang out in every church in the city exactly at midnight. The clanging was so loud and I was so emotional that I had difficulty concentrating on finishing my final story of the night. I kept writing the word singing instead of signing.

An Angolan friend had rung home and reported that the mood in Luanda was more cautious. The prevailing sound was not of church bells but of the guns that revellers shot in the air in lieu of firecrackers. Many people stayed inside their homes and pondered the implications of peace.

'They say they are almost too scared to hope,' my friend said. 'It seems too good to be true.'

That night I went to the Ritz where the festivities were as frenzied as on New Year's Eve. People gathered in the streets in front of the entrance and stood on top of cars because there was no more room inside the club. Mozambicans were embracing Guinea-Bissauns who were hugging the São Tomenses, who had never had a war of liberation. No one could afford champagne so they were drinking beer. The band played the liveliest music it knew. But they steered away from songs of Angola. The music from Angola was about exile and tears. They wanted a new start.

The iron balconies at the Ritz looked as though they might collapse from the weight of all the bodies. I waded through hundreds of people on the stairs to reach the dance floor. It was so full no one could move sideways.

One person wasn't dancing: a UNITA journalist who was standing glumly by the bar on the side. He had a mug of beer in his hand and he seemed uneasy. I asked him to dance but he just shook his head.

'*Vamos vêr*,' he said. 'Let's see.'

3

Respite

My Lisbon idyll was too good to last. Every month, week and day after I hit the two-year mark I tensed when the telephone rang, fearing it was my news editors calling to offer me transfers. I had turned down Brazil postings twice already. I likewise shunned an offer of Spain. Everyone said I was crazy to stay on in a place of so little news. But I didn't want to leave Lisbon's cocoon.

The lure of the big story didn't attract me much, so I said. But now that the negotiations were over I had grown lazy. The job became something to fill in time between meals rather than a raison d'être. I began eyeing property to open a bar and talked about buying a house, an old house in the medieval section within sight of the castle.

'Who needs the aggravation of a busy story?' I said to a friend one evening as we ambled along the docks. It was a mild spring evening and, as always, I could smell the sea and squid fried in olive oil.

'It's stressful. A beeper strapped to your waist, telephone calls summoning you to write stories in the night. You can't be master of your own life.'

He nodded, gazing at Lisbon, luminescent across the river. 'The pressure. The egos. The power games.'

But I thought twice when the Johannesburg posting came up and my news editor in London telephoned to offer it to me in November 1991.

'It won't just be South Africa,' he said as a sweetener. 'And with your Portuguese, you'll have Mozambique and Angola too.'

I debated for days, running all the arguments pro and con through my head like a piece of film. I sought the advice of all the people who had served as mentors to me. They told me what my heart didn't believe: that I should go.

It was Waldemar who finally convinced me. We were dining at Aziz's restaurant, eating hot piri-piri chicken basted with coconut milk. He had to shout, something he didn't ordinarily do, because the music was so loud.

'You've become complacent. Momentous things are happening there. It's the last liberation. History is being made – don't you want to witness it?' He saw another musician and got up to greet him, turning as he rose. 'Angola's just around the corner, you know. Even if you leave, *estamos juntos*'.

✣

Once I had made up my mind, I called the news editor who was growing tired of my wavering.

'Good girl,' he said. 'I was afraid we'd never get you out of Lisbon.'

My farewell parties were held at the Ritz and at Aziz's restaurant. Someone asked me to bring back a jar of sand from Luanda beach next time I passed through Lisbon. I received an array of farewell gifts that were typically Portuguese: a crystal decanter, local perfume, *azulejos* and books. And a leather belt.

I tried it on. It was way too large and wasn't quite my style. I contemplated how many holes would have to be cut into it for it to fit me properly.

'It's to whip those bad guys into line,' someone said, explaining that it was a joke.

'I thought there weren't any left,' I answered.

'There's always some. I'm sure you'll have no trouble finding them.'

✣

Johannesburg was unlike any African city I had seen and I disliked its oppressive air of control. The sterile, grid-like streets were more like Middle America than the other places I had visited on the continent. Apartheid had ensured that even the townships were orderly, compared to elsewhere in Africa, with their neat rows of box houses.

Even the red car that Reuters allotted me seemed to be rotten, like apartheid. The Citi Golf emitted a strange odour, like the smell of meat that had gone off. I regarded this as a bad omen. Repeated washing of the car's seats and floor failed to exorcise the stench. It haunted the vehicle like a bad-tempered ghost. One day while changing the battery I finally discovered the source: the decomposing skeleton of a bird was lodged in the engine.

Driving was just a small part of a big adjustment to a very different way of life. After Lisbon's villagey feel, Johannesburg was relentlessly demanding. There were thousands of people to meet. The foreign press corps numbered in the hundreds instead of half a dozen. I had been accustomed to running my own office; suddenly I was part of a ten-person team. The work never seemed to stop. You could stay in the office overnight and there would be plenty to write about: massacres, shootings, statements, negotiations, fighting. Sometimes we worked through the night because there was so much happening.

Where Lisbon was all softness, Jo'burg was dry and hard. So many people I met were veterans of the war in Angola. In Lisbon there was a sadness about the loss of an empire, even a sense of relief to be rid of the evil responsibility of colonialism. In South Africa, there was an ambivalence about not having got it right. Portugal's domination of Angola had happened so long ago it could be ignored. Let bygones be bygones, many people felt. But Angola was South Africa's Vietnam, a shameful, wasteful war of attrition with all the accompanying regrets. There was little to be proud of in a war fought for naught.

There were no two ways about it. I hated Johannesburg,

47

hated it as much as I loved Lisbon. It was a dichotomy that had nothing to do with the job. It was something that professionalism could not transcend. South Africa was historical and important. But Lisbon had soul.

I had constant flashes of *saudades*. I confessed this to the brother of a friend from Portugal, who lived in Johannesburg. He took me to the four square blocks of Portuguese cafés in the city centre which had names like Belem and prepared prego steak sandwiches and egg yolk desserts just like in Lisbon. But the sterile formica counters, burglar bars and women in shapeless dresses were not in the least reminiscent of Lisbon. I yearned for Portugal even more.

My friend's brother must have seen the disappointment on my face and was anxious to please.

'I think a lot of Angolans come here,' he said, looking at the door as though they were just about to enter.

They didn't.

✢

My first view of Angola from afar was in Lisbon. The second view, from South Africa, was from a completely different angle. Despite the proximity of the two countries and their political entanglements over the years, few Angolans settled in South Africa. The South Africans I met had had a completely different experience with Angola and another way of relating to it compared to the Portuguese. Some of the African National Congress members had trained in Angola, or worse, been detained and tortured in camps there by their own party.

Many of the South Africans I knew who had spent time in *Angolsh*, as they called it, were cameramen or photographers. They had been young white soldiers who had fought in the Caprivi or at Cuito Cuanavale. The South Africans were reputedly among the world's best when it came to filming conflict and many of them thrived on the adrenalin rush one gets covering violence. Angola had taught them not to flinch under fire.

So many people were asking me about Angola that I felt I really ought to get there quickly in order to give informed replies. However, it was hard to find a quiet moment when I could leave the demands of South Africa and stage a reconnaissance. Finally, after three months, Johannesburg came the closest it ever did to a news lull and my news editor suggested that I go before something else ensnared my attention in South Africa.

✦

It was the boxes. I had seen this before on flights from Lisbon to Cape Verde, Guinea-Bissau and Mozambique. Luso-Africans without money didn't travel with normal luggage like suitcases. Instead they travelled with cardboard cartons wrapped several times over in masking tape so that they looked shiny, the destination written in heavy black marker. They were always heavier than the permitted luggage allowance. This had to be the check-in counter for Angola.

It was April 1992 and there were still no direct flights from South Africa to Angola. There was no Angolan embassy in South Africa either, so I stopped over in Namibia to obtain my visa and flight. I stayed with a friend who introduced me to the Angolan ambassador, a former liberation fighter now decked in a crisp lightweight suit. He granted me a visa immediately.

Taking the Luanda flight via the Angolan airlines TAAG was a more confusing prospect. You could spot the Angolans a mile away, sprawled on the airport's immaculately polished floors. The unruly crowd shouted and swore in Portuguese. Their bodies were pungent with sweat. Even their clothes were visually loud – prints of every colour. The heated discussions seemed to centre on one particularly high pile of cardboard cartons, enough to fill a trailer. A stout woman dressed in a purple gown had placed a baby with a leaking diaper on top of the pile as though to press her point: 'This plane is not going anywhere without all of us.'

It was a scene that was repeated many times on my subsequent trips to Angola. It was particularly bad flying out of Johannesburg. Angolans would come to South Africa to buy as many sanitary napkins, earrings, powdered milk, lingerie, onions and potatoes as they could stuff into their cardboard boxes. The goods would be resold at exorbitant prices back in Luanda. Often Angolans would buy two tickets under false names, and check in the baggage without boarding.

It happened on every flight I took for four years and the crew never grew any wiser. Each time, after all the baggage had been loaded, we would sit in the plane on the tarmac for up to five hours while the boxes were unloaded and the passengers filed out to identify their loads. The unclaimed boxes would remain on the tarmac and the delayed flight would finally take off. It was the flight the stewardesses dreaded the most. They had to be especially vigilant to ensure the passengers didn't steal the seat cushions.

But I discovered this much later. Now, surrounded by a swarm of gesticulating Angolans, I wasn't sure whether I would ever even get to board the plane. Suddenly I saw the Angolan ambassador in the crowd. He seemed harassed and his suit was creased and limp. He was trying to assist some passengers to check in their bags, and finally reached the counter with the satisfied smile of a victorious marathon runner. The passengers safely at the front, the ambassador turned around and approached me. He explained what all the commotion was about.

Apparently the plane was delayed for anywhere from six hours to three days, the ambassador said. The fact that all the passengers and their cargo were ready was irrelevant. These things were capricious matters of fate.

'You haven't even arrived in Angola and already you're

impatient,' he said in mild reproach.

Windhoek airport was one of the most modern and polished in Africa, and reflected the country's Teutonic emphasis on tidiness. Its conversion into a purgatory for raucous Angolans awaiting their uncertain flight was a weekly event the cleaning staff resigned themselves to. A woman with a broom followed by another with a mop persevered with determination in their mission to pick up every last piece of paper trash on the floor and wipe away the muddy footprints.

I had it easier than most, I had to admit. At least my own luggage was a single satchel carried by hand. The friend in Windhoek had advised me not to check in any bags and to take only what I could run with to make life easier upon arrival in Luanda.

'Sometimes they cut the suitcases with knives. Other times they just wrench the locks out with scissors, even on the tarmac itself. And sometimes porters offer to carry your bags and then run off with them,' she warned helpfully.

Much of what was packed inside my small bag was food. I had been bombarded with stories about the 1980s, when shortages left even the hotels and shops bereft of food. I dutifully packed provisions of nuts, dried fruit, crackers, biscuits and canned fish. These proved to be unnecessary, however. When I got to Angola, I found that times had changed.

✢

Eight hours later we boarded the plane. The two and a half hour trip was bumpy and the meal consisted of a stale roll with a tired slice of cheese the colour of glue.

The man sitting next to me was a Portuguese businessman whose family had fled Angola to South Africa after Angola became independent. He was now going back to see whether he could reclaim the family property which had been seized. He was also looking into new business opportunities.

'What sort of business?' I asked conversationally.

'Dried fish. Tyres. Soft drinks. Paper. They need everything. The country is like a mouth missing teeth.'

+

Most of the flight was through a cloudless sky, revealing just how few settlements there were in the immensity of the land below. In many parts of Africa fast population growth is overwhelming the environment and trees are sacrificed in the name of human survival. Angola was sparsely populated, the official figure being ten million people. However, no one knew for sure how many people there really were because a proper census hadn't been done for years. And no one had counted the unmarked graves from the war.

The landscape below changed from desert to rolling highlands to lush fields. Then the ocean came into view and as we descended I saw a stretch of brown next to the sea with some box-like patterns which on closer inspection appeared to be homes. A peninsula stretched protectively around the city, like a gently curved arm. It was then that I registered the colour that I would thereafter associate with the Luanda dateline: rich brick brown.

The pilot landed with a jarring thump. The man sitting next to me applauded with obvious relief. I was one of the first out of the plane and ran across the tarmac to the immigration building with my small canvas bag under my arm. Passengers must have been backlogged from an earlier flight because there were hundreds in the building.

The air was muggy with a musty smell of sea and garbage. Some fluid dripped on my forehead and I wiped it away with the back of my hand. It smelt awful.

'It's piss,' the woman standing in front of me said, looking at my disgusted face. 'It appears they still haven't fixed the plumbing upstairs.'

She reflectively checked her head.

Once I reached the immigration desk, I waited for an hour in what approximated to a queue. Already my cotton shirt was stuck to my body from the humidity. The woman inspecting passports was surly in the heat. She studied the Ecuadorian visas in my passport upside down for a long time and then stamped it brusquely and handed it back.

I had asked the state-run press centre to send someone to meet me but the flight had been delayed for so long they had obviously left. There were no telephones I could use to find out if they could send someone else. There were also no taxis or buses, so I hitched a ride with the Portuguese businessman who had sat next to me on the plane. He had arranged for a car beforehand and his chauffeur had waited.

'It sure has changed,' he remarked, as we passed rotting plants in what was once a flower-bed on a traffic island.

Some boys were kicking a soccer ball improvised out of rags. The streets were littered with soggy refuse. A mass of humanity was walking by the side of the road. They were limping and hopping too: legions of amputees, their stumps wrapped in dirty cloth. Angola has the highest per capita land-mine victim rate in the world, higher than Cambodia. Many *mutilados*, as the amputees were called, had converged on the capital looking for food and work. Some were lucky enough to have proper crutches but many were making do with sticks, planks of wood or branches.

On the way to town the businessman pointed out some of Luanda's sights. The entire shabby city was a monument to decay. In its heyday in the 1960s Luanda had been called the Rio of Africa for its mosaic promenades and graceful bay. It was more cosmopolitan than Maputo, more Latin than South Africa, and the shellfish was renowned. Luanda had largely been insulated from the war; and very little fighting had actually taken place there. But when you looked at the advanced state of neglect you'd never believe that.

On a hill overlooking the city was the old fort from which

53

the Portuguese had defended their African prize for centuries. The harbour was filled with the rusted hulks of ships that had sunk. The mausoleum where the remains of Agostinho Neto, founding father of the MPLA and independent Angola's first president, were laid to rest was an unfinished bare concrete structure the shape of a spaceship. Its pointed top reached upwards like an angry finger emphatically jabbing the sky.

I saw hints of Lisbon in the remnants of Portuguese tiles and fountains. The streets resembled Lisbon's cobbled mosaic sidewalks with the wave patterns. The military buildings were painted a soft shade of pink, just like in Portugal. The 1950s apartment blocks resembled those in Benfica, a working-class area of Lisbon.

For a militarised country which had been at war continually for 30 years, I thought it odd that military installations were painted such a feminine colour as pink. This delicacy seemed ironic considering that museums in Luanda are generally dedicated to the most brutal episodes in Angola's history: slavery and war. I never managed to enter the war museum, which was housed in the Dutch fort on the hill overlooking the city. It was always closed. As for the slavery museum, I only went there years later when Angola thought it might be able to attract genuine tourists who weren't South African mercenaries or European aid workers. The walls were whitewashed, but the manacles were still stained with ancient blood.

Unlike Lisbon, which was quaintly dilapidated, Luanda was downright rotting. The buildings had lost many layers of paint and were exposed down to their corroded cores. In Lisbon, the paint had merely flaked off. Here it had peeled like skin off a bone, taking with it the top layers of plaster and some of the cement underneath.

Turn a corner, and a hint of a colonial building appeared. The tiles were worn and chipped, chunks of masonry were missing, and wiring sprouted out of the walls. It was a city that made no sense of its present. The streets carried the signs of the old names but had been given new names that had no signs. There was a Baixa downtown, like in Lisbon. But the shop windows were bare. The cafés served only imported Nescafe, although Angola grew its own coffee.

But, like Lisbon, the sea was omnipresent. The Portuguese chose to build their colonial cities by exquisite beaches. Bissau had a port, like Lisbon. Maputo had one too, and so did Luanda. In Lisbon, there is a treacherous winding highway called the Marginal on the road to the suburban beach resort of Cascais. It follows the seaside, curving suddenly at the narrow points. There are terrible crashes on the Marginal late at night when drivers return from parties and the mist comes off the ocean. Maputo has a Marginal, too. So does Luanda. Luanda's Marginal is a wide, palm-lined boulevard by the side of the water. You could squint your eyes and imagine you were in Lisbon.

Later, I realised that there were strong echoes of Lisbon in Angola's other 17 provinces too. Benguela had gardens and squares reminiscent of northern Portugal. In Lobito there was a big cross with a statue of Jesus Christ, like the one on the other side of the bridge from Lisbon over the Tejo river and the one overlooking Rio de Janeiro. Lobito's cross was smaller than the other two, however, and maintained a vigil not over a bay but over a sad panorama of empty scrub-land.

✣

After months of South Africa's sterility and race consciousness, Luanda's vitality shouted joyously at me. The city was a mess and the air heavy with the smell of diesel and shit. But it was alive. All my senses were assaulted. Even inside the car I was hit by the constant din of conversation, haggling, gossip, car horns and construction.

I checked in to the Hotel Trópico, up the rubbish-strewn hill from the government press centre. A churlish woman at reception showed me to a lift which didn't work and a room where the bath had run dry. The slimy bar of pink Lux soap was flecked with the previous guest's dirt. The hotel was as central as could be but there were no taxis to hail in the street. As much as I disliked driving, I now wished I had a car.

The first port of call for any foreign reporter in Luanda is the state-run press centre. The centre was a left-over from the days of socialism when the government wanted to maintain control over what was written about the country. There was still a great deal of censorship in the local press and access to government ministers was limited. Getting an interview required constant nagging of the press centre staff, whose main job seemed to be to obstruct the search for knowledge. The infrastructure available at the centre also did not aid the dissemination of information, once you'd gathered enough information to write a story. The row of ancient telexes with the Portuguese keyboards was rarely functional as the power always cut out. Phone calls were subsidised and cheap – a half hour call to New York was just a couple of dollars. But getting a working line was a challenge.

My transport problem was resolved partly by Vita, one of the first people I met in Luanda. Vita worked at the press centre as a sort of Mr Fix It. Like the other staff at the press centre he had a reserved air, the demeanour of a man trained to listen and ever poised for a hard currency tip. Vita and the others spent hours on end in apparent idleness, poring day after day over virtually empty folders. He was an easygoing, round-faced fellow from the Cabinda oil enclave who, like many Angolans from the north, had moved to the capital in search of work. He had found it as a minder at the press centre, but with Marxism-Leninism officially disbanded these days that job description had grown obsolete. So he did odd jobs setting up interviews, translating and – most importantly for me – driving visitors around.

As Vita's car seemed to break down every other day, I often

had to find alternative means of transport. The opposition parties, desperate for good foreign press, offered their jeeps and sedans to show me around the town. The UNITA press man from Lisbon, Norberto de Castro, had relocated to Luanda with other UNITA returnees from abroad and from Jamba. He gave me rides in the group's blue 4x4 vehicles, which had been donated by the US government.

'At least my taxpayer's money is going to good use,' I half-joked, as I stepped awkwardly into one of the vehicles, with a certain prick of conscience at accepting a ride from a political party.

Norberto looked at me sharply. It apparently wasn't funny.

✝

One of the first places Vita took me was to the *musseques*, the sand slums. I realised that these mud and wattle structures were the boxes I had seen from the plane. The *musseques* were built with bricks fashioned from the grey clay, giving them the appearance of being carved out of the earth. From the sky the *musseques* looked like a waffle-grid of uniform brown. But on the ground there were splashes of colour in between the cinder block buildings: flashes of baobab trees, bright blue plastic water buckets and the palm-fringed beach. The landscape looked as dry as North Africa but Vita said that when it rained in Luanda the mud rose ankle-deep. The rains strip Luanda of its last remnants of beauty. The city looks dingier when the skies are overcast with impending rain. The oppressive grey clouds obscure the faded pastel pinks and ochres of the buildings. One sees only the grime.

In many parts of Angola rain signifies good luck. But in the *musseques* rain meant illness: cholera and deadly, malaria-carrying mosquitoes. Luanda residents have an aversion to breezes. In every hotel and home I have stayed in there, people shutter up the windows and endure stuffy stifling heat to keep the air out.

They know as doctors do that dysentery doesn't just travel from handling soiled *kwanza*, shaking an unwashed hand or drinking dirty water. Disease also travels with the wind, which swirls through the open sewers and carries infected dust into the house. They know that a virus can be inhaled as easily as it can be imbibed.

Vita took me to his in-laws' home in the *musseque* named Samba. The dwelling was on a plot that used to be a Portuguese vacation home. Now the land had been divided into many sections.

'We're very lucky,' he said, opening a door and then hitting the hinge with his hand to reattach it to the frame. 'Some people live in tents on the beach or in containers.'

Vita's younger sister gave me a welcoming gift, a necklace of dry beans. Then she fetched a lukewarm Fanta from a dark room inside. No one else was drinking and I had the distinct impression that this was their last soda. The house was cramped but was luxurious compared to others I had seen nearby. The chintz curtains and china dogs reminded me of my grandmother's décor in Queens, New York. The women of the house took great pride in the home and they swept the red dust which blew in several times a day. What they could not sweep away, however, was the smell of blocked drains.

Vita said that much of what happened in the *musseques* went unreported, especially what happened after dark. The *musseques* were hotbeds of resistance during the liberation struggle; the miserable conditions were a prime breeding ground for discontent and the maze-like lanes were ideal for evading the police. Most of Luanda's estimated two million residents lived in the *musseques* – Rocha Pinto, Sambizanga, Prenda, Samba, Praia do Obispo, Bairro Azul, Golf, Rangel, Cassenda. The *musseques* were also called the *bairros*. *Bairro* means neighbourhood, but it is the name in any Portuguese African country for a poor neighbourhood. The inference is that affluent people are insulated from the poor, living behind big walls and guarded by armed watchmen.

My other guide in Luanda was my musician friend Waldemar, who had gone back to Luanda from Lisbon for an extended stay to investigate the possibilities of relocating.

'It's a recce visit,' he explained, when he picked me up at the hotel to take me for a drive.

He had many things to sort out first, namely finding somewhere to live and work.

'If I can get a regular electricity supply maybe I could set up a studio here. But first I need a house.'

Houses were a big problem and Waldemar's brother was living in a hotel like many of the returnees to Luanda. Waldemar's one relative who did have a house was his cousin Zeca, who had remained in Angola during the war. Zeca was a man about town who ran a detergent factory. He was not rich but was a long-term MPLA activist, and his party card and reputation gained him access to private clubs where he could dance and drink with the political elite as a respected citizen. Zeca was a man of enormous girth and rotten teeth, but he acquired elegance while dancing.

Zeca and his wife treated me as one of the family, inviting me to eat dinner at their large house whenever I could. Zeca was comfortable, and meals were a sign that life was good. His favourite pastime was eating. Zeca liked to spend Sunday afternoons at a Portuguese restaurant downtown with his family, eating crayfish and rich stews of creamy codfish. That, and drinks on the terrace of the Meridien Hotel overlooking the sea, were proof that he had made it.

Zeca and Waldemar introduced me to the Ilha, the peninsula jutting out from the city where most of the open-air bars were. They said that since the peace accords had been signed new eateries had proliferated. Many still did not have electricity and as we drove past the fishermen's huts, paraffin lights and candles flickered, illuminating the boys holding up wriggling crayfish or garoupa for sale. From the darkness glowed the coals of charcoal grills with savoury chicken cooking on top.

Sitting by the beach at little plastic tables with umbrellas, we devoured prawns and warm Sagres beer from Portugal. Waldemar was popular among the local womenfolk. Girls stared at us and flirtatiously approached the table to greet him.

Waldemar hummed a couple of bars from his song *Angola Minha Namorada* (Angola My Love). The words were about how he shouldn't be asked when he would return, because he would never leave Angola.

Zeca sighed. 'It's going to be good here from now on.'

Zeca and Waldemar grew more excited as they moved from beer to whisky and began to argue. Zeca took offence at Waldemar's assertion that UNITA wasn't really all that bad.

'I'm tired of the MPLA and its hypocrisy,' Waldemar said.

'Sure, that's easy for you to say. You haven't lived here, with UNITA blowing up electricity pylons,' Zeca retorted. 'You've been living in Lisbon drinking coffee the whole time.'

'Well, I left because things got so bad,' Waldemar said. He gestured at the waiter to bring the bill and pulled some crumpled currency notes out of his pocket.

We rose from the table. I changed the subject, asking Waldemar whether he was inspired by being back.

'Enough of this politicking. I'm going to write songs about love from now on,' he said as we walked to his cousin's car.

Some girls overheard and called out from the darkness coquettishly.

'Waldemar! Here we are! *Alô!*'

✛

Angola in 1992 was like a Rip Van Winkle yawning and stretching awake after the moribund days of socialist deprivation. The days of spies and using eggs as a bartering currency were over.

'You can get dollars! You can get shaving cream!' exclaimed Vita. That is, if you had the money.

One night at dinner, Zeca and his wife described the long queues of the socialist days. They called them *bichas*, which also means worms, because of the way they wound around the block. By their accounts, life in Luanda in the 1980s was overwhelmed by shortages and people waiting miserably on long lines. The only ones who didn't have to wait in interminable queues were the MPLA elite; they had their own private clinics and supermarkets stocked with Italian chocolates and fatty red meat.

There were *bichas* for the old and sick, and different ones for men and women. There were *bichas* for rice, meat and potatoes. Sometimes people had to wait on line for three whole days, missing work to remain in the queue. Those with money paid less fortunates to keep their places.

'Babies were born on those *bichas*!' Zeca recalled.

As with all shortages, there'd be a rush when a certain item became available, Zeca said. He called those the 'moments'.

'There were the moments of the red wine. Suddenly red wine was everywhere. A friend of mine got sick because he drank an entire litre in five minutes because he had missed red wine so much. Then there was the whisky phase, suddenly there was whisky,' Zeca said. He was smiling faintly at the absurdity of it all.

'But beer, well, those in the know could always get beer. In the 1980s it was better than *kwanza*. Two crates of beer could buy you a round-trip ticket to Lisbon!'

What Zeca and his wife didn't like to talk about were the purges. They lowered their voices the first time I asked about them. It was a difficult thing to reconcile, if you were a member of the MPLA and believed in it.

The politics of fear under the MPLA was a legacy of the Portuguese secret police. Or maybe the MPLA had learned too well from its Soviet allies. The MPLA surveillance system meant that no one felt safe. The secret police would denounce you, or your neighbours would if they didn't. Neighbourhood cells in the *bairros* served as an excellent network for spying.

The purges were reminiscent of Stalin, Zeca said. People were dragged out of their homes at night to torture cells. Some were shot and their corpses left on the streets. Others simply disappeared.

The so-called *Golpe Nitista*, or Nitist coup attempt, began officially on 27 May 1977. Luanda residents awoke before dawn to the sound of shooting and grenades exploding near the radio station. The radio station and a prison were taken over for several hours by supporters of Nito Alves, the former interior minister. Bernardo Baptisto Nito Alves had set up his own power base to challenge Agostinho Neto's leadership of the party. To critics, he was an opportunist who evoked racist passions and tribalism to further his own position. But to his supporters, he rightly criticised the inadequacies of the MPLA bourgeois leadership to deliver on their promises for a better life for all Angolans.

Nine hours after it began, the mutiny was quashed. Shortly thereafter the ringleaders of the abortive putsch were executed. But, according to Luanda residents, so too were innocent people. They said the persecution of those suspected of taking part lasted for days afterwards.

People were more relaxed by the time I visited Luanda. But I never was able to get a full picture of the MPLA's brutal side. Very little has been written about the Nitist coup and its bloody put-down. Residents of Luanda, like Zeca, spoke about thousands being killed. But history books written in the 1970s and 1980s were penned mainly by apologists who exhorted the workers' party of the MPLA. I never found out the full story.

Much later on, I went on a mission to try to decipher that fractured period. The national archive seemed to be the most logical place to start. But visiting it gave me a revelation of a different type.

The entire country had been looted, sacked and ruined. Hospital supplies had been stolen. Museums had been robbed of their sculptures. But in a country where few people read, no one thought of robbing the archives. Here lay a veritable treasure of brittle, yellowing papers documenting the minutiae of 500 years of life – yet no one thought to venture in except for some bugs.

The sporadic electricity cuts turned off air conditioning which would have protected the papers from the ravages of the sea air. The archive's director complained that there was no place, not even a desk, to receive visitors. She had the fervour of a zealot as she flipped through titles and subjects on her flimsy laptop computer. The computer was stuffed with information which she was furiously trying to catalogue before the termites ate away the paper.

The vast reading room was empty. I asked the director about the purges.

'Pardon?' was the response. I realised I wasn't going to get very far.

The only other visitor was a bald elderly man who shuffled in seeking to identify faces in a newspaper competition. The newspaper had published pictures of famous people under the title *Rostos da História* (Faces of History). Eager to have something to do, the sole librarian obliged the old man, enthusiastically bringing out old MPLA posters and books. The icons of the MPLA were identified. But not, of course, Nito Alves.

☩

Another great myth is the MPLA's professed national unity. 'From Cabinda to Cunene – One People, One Nation' was its slogan. But nothing could be further from the truth.

The tribalism which the MPLA purported to eradicate, and which Nito Alves evoked, was deep, very deep.

The divisions of the various groups were as disparate as the landscapes from which they sprang. They all had their landmarks and their pride. They varied from the white desert sands of Namibe to the bushy scrub-land of Cuando Cubango to the gentle hills of the Planalto plateau and the lush jungles of Zaire province. Benguela was the graceful 'red' city of white leftist intellectuals whose residents thought themselves superior. Lobito was proud of its huge statue of Christ. It had cattle and vineyards. Its climate was dry and healthy and didn't breed illness like elsewhere in Angola.

Then there was the Cabinda enclave. Sandwiched between Zaire and the Congo, Cabinda was cut off from the rest of Angola. And within the enclave was another enclave – the American oil company base. If it weren't for the monkeys and the dense jungle, one would have thought Chevron's Malongo oil complex was part of the United States. The mess hall served regulation hamburgers. The bungalows were built on trimmed green lawns. The men played golf on a nearby course. The accents hailed from Texas.

Chevron thoughtfully arranged flights home for its men – one month on, one month off – via Europe. This way they could avoid passing through Luanda. They also avoided going to the town. The town was filled with rundown wooden houses with flaking paint and overgrown gardens of mango trees. The Cabindans earned barely enough to eat meat for Sunday lunch, while two-thirds of the country's oil exports were drained away into the pockets of the Luanda government and foreign oil companies.

Isolated from town, Malongo's American residents avoided the locals. Many of the locals were believed to be members of the various factions of FLEC, the separatists who had been fighting since the 1960s.

Cabinda was the forgotten war within the forgotten war. The hope in the rest of Angola was that elections and peace would lead to greater democracy, opportunities, prosperity and normalisation. But the peace accords had not been signed in Cabinda and FLEC had not agreed to lay down its arms. The expatriates travelled to town in helicopters after a series of ambushes had occurred. The local staff braved the roads.

✛

This new peace in 1992 was the first Angolans had known for 30 years. Suddenly, small shops were opening and people were plastering over the bullet holes and painting their houses. Foreigners were coming in, looking for good business deals. Suddenly, too, there was a proliferation of cars – and traffic jams.

Bars were opening everywhere. The favoured one at the time was the *Bar Aberto*, or Open Bar, which was on a rooftop and played the latest techno-rap music from New York. I never ceased to marvel at where all these trendy people in tight black outfits appeared from; you never saw such hip well-dressed characters on the streets during the day.

There was so little space that sometimes private houses were converted into clubs or restaurants. The most eccentric one on the Ilha was called Number 8. It was a Vietnamese restaurant run by a Scandinavian in the garage of the military attaché of the British embassy who was known as Colonel Bob. Bob was a mischievous man with a sense of the absurd who liked to walk about in full uniform, complete with braided epaulettes. I once saw him smoke a cigarette underwater through a tube in the British ambassador's swimming pool. Bob bought a little parrot which perched on his shoulder. He tried to teach it to say: 'Pieces of Eight! Pieces of Eight!'

The optimism that followed the Biçesse accords led to talk of physical reconstruction. Consultants and experts flew in to calculate how much it would cost to repair the shattered country. The World Bank estimated it would take a decade to fully rebuild the roads, bridges and other infrastructure. One of the more ambitious projects was reviving the Benguela Railroad (estimate: $340 million). Portuguese citizens visited factories and farms that had been nationalised with a view to buying them back.

The end of the war was also accompanied by greater mobility across the country. People could now revisit their villages which had been cut off for 16 years. There was a negative side to this freedom of movement, however: Aids. Angola was one of the last African countries to suffer an Aids epidemic. The war had acted like a giant condom by insulating much of the population from the disease. Foreigners had had trouble getting into the country. Soldiers spent long years on the front in remote areas, so the illness didn't spread very much.

But now borders were becoming more porous and infected Zairians were sneaking into Angola. Prostitutes were brazenly soliciting in Luanda, a new phenomenon after the long years of socialist puritanism which had kept them off the streets. There were just a couple of hundred registered Aids cases, according to the World Health Organisation. But its experts said that the situation was changing fast.

Another negative side of peace, for the MPLA at any rate, was that it could no longer blame the ills of urban life on the enemy. Earlier it was UNITA which had thrown the city into a waterless dark by sabotaging electricity pylons and water tanks. But now that the rebels were in Luanda the MPLA had to assume responsibility for the deficiencies of city life.

These deficiencies were myriad. The MPLA as administrators embodied the worst of Portuguese bureaucracy, African lack of training and Marxist-Leninist inefficiency. Luanda had become a monster of a city.

For most of the population – and one-fifth lived in Luanda – there was no proper health care or education. Public services had all but broken down. I saw this most clearly at the city morgue, which I visited by accident. I was suffering from symptoms of malaria and a friend took me to the military hospital to be tested. I was advised to take my own clean needle to avoid the possibility of contracting Aids from the used ones they had at the hospital. When one entered the clinic one became keenly aware of one's mortality: it was right next to the morgue. The building emitted a terrible stench. As the Cuban doctor pricked my finger for blood I heard what sounded like a small explosion.

'What's that?' I asked. Another noise followed.

'Oh, it's probably a body at the morgue,' the doctor said nonchalantly. 'When the electricity goes off the refrigerators go warm. Then the bodies swell up and pop.'

✧

For citizens of a country which had been so interfered with by foreigners, Angolans were quite open to yet another alien like myself. Even the fact that I was from the United States, UNITA's big backer, did not seem to put off the MPLA stalwarts who were willing to give me the benefit of the doubt.

Angola attracted legions of foreign do-gooders and sinners, a motley crew of expatriates whose common characteristic was toughness and an appreciation of adventure. This international interest in so rundown an African country gave Luanda a cosmopolitan air. The city was cloaked in a veneer of self-importance. During the many subsequent months that I worked in Angola I lived under the illusion that I was at the centre of the world – even when my dispatches went ignored and unpublished. The energy was such that every news event and nuance, no matter how small, seemed like a matter of life or death.

The first foreigners I came across were present in wall murals and street signs: Che Guevara's picture was painted on every government army barrack I visited. Major avenues and boulevards bore the names of Vladimir Lenin and Karl Marx.

With the icons of socialism came their proponents: legions

of advisers and pilots and technicians from Cuba, Vietnam and the Soviet bloc. One also found the occasional well-meaning Scandinavian. By the time I got to Luanda, Cuba had withdrawn its 91 000 troops. A small group of Cuban doctors and construction workers remained, living in a compound and socialising mainly among themselves. Despite a similar language and Latin lifestyle, the Cubans were often resented by the Angolans, particularly by the men who feared the lighter-skinned Caribbeans would steal their women. But for these Cubans, whose own country was falling apart, there was little to go back to.

The *cooperantes*, as foreign helpers were called, who came to Angola during the socialist era rarely stayed on through the 1990s. Life in Angola was tougher than in Mozambique, they said. 'You can get a tan with your revolution,' was how one Scandinavian described the Mozambican scene, where foreigners were rewarded with luxurious housing and status. But Angola's physical deprivations, rampant malaria and its being a virtual police state took a toll on the more delicate European socialists. They had come to the chaotic African country seeking ideological inspiration and found instead corruption and spies.

There were still human remnants of the socialist past: correspondents from Mozambique, Cuba, Yugoslavia and the Soviet Union were all posted to Luanda and produced reams of dispatches for editors in faraway lands who no longer had a strategic interest in Angola. The Finnish woman who ran the press centre, Katia, had married and divorced in Angola yet had decided to stay on. It wasn't that she was happy with the life, which she bore with stoicism. There was nowhere else to go. The ice of Finland no longer seemed like home.

Katia lived on the bottom floor of what was probably once a sought-after apartment building across the street from the main cemetery. She earned enough to buy a generator and rented out her spare bedrooms to visiting correspondents. The house was filled with *mestiço* grandchildren and mosquitoes. Katia was a well-read woman who treasured her books. The best gifts to bring her, like offerings, were mosquito coils and additions to her private library which bulged from the living room wall.

✛

As I got to know Luanda better over the coming weeks I realised that it was a city of illusions and phantoms.

First of all, there was the pretty little *Palácio de Ferro*, the Iron Palace, which was speckled with rust after years of neglect. Everyone said Eiffel had built it. A visit to the building was an obligatory stop on any tour given by Luanda residents, who proudly pointed it out as proof that their city was once a more cosmopolitan place. The Palace was not really a palace per se; it was a small two-storey house with delicate metal pillars and ornamental trimming. But had Eiffel really built it? And why on earth in Angola? No one could confirm the story or offer any evidence.

These days the Iron Palace had lost any Parisian charm, if it had ever had any. It was invaded by squatters, who hung torn laundry from the windows and the palm trees outside. To get to the entrance one had to step gingerly through the mud past reeking rubbish containers. Most of the windows were boarded up with planks of splintered wood. I peeked inside and saw coils of excrement on the empty floors.

I went to the National Institute of Cultural Heritage to glean some insight into the origins of the Iron Palace. I climbed the steps of the Institute's pink nineteenth-century building, taking care not to trip on the chunks of masonry which had broken off the balcony. It must have been a grand and elegant building a century ago. In the reception room a bored woman flicked through a magazine, sitting by a telephone which didn't work. The light fixture hanging above her lacked a bulb.

'I'm looking for some information about the Iron Palace. Is

there anyone who can tell me whether Eiffel built it?' I enquired. The woman looked irked that I had disturbed her.

'Check and see if there's a plaque on the building,' she replied, without looking up from the magazine.

'I did. There's nothing,' I said. She remained silent. Her apathy irritated me. I insisted: 'Don't you have records?'

She looked at me as though I was mentally defective and didn't say anything else.

I wrote to an archivist at the Eiffel Tower in Paris, hoping for clarification. I asked whether Eiffel had indeed designed the building in Luanda, as well as another one in Maputo which was alleged to be his work. Did Eiffel have some special connection with Portuguese Africa? I asked.

The reply saddened me: 'I am sorry but to my knowledge Gustave Eiffel has no works in Angola neither in Mozambique,' Marie-Claude de Maneville wrote to me. 'At the end of the last century there were a lot of companies which specialised in metallic construction. But only Eiffel is still famous . . .!'

The other great monument in Luanda was one that was closed to the public. It was the mausoleum of Agostinho Neto. The mausoleum remained unfinished during the five years that I visited Angola, a red construction crane poised half-way up the entire time. Few people had been inside this sacred resting place of the great man. Those who had ventured within told of Russian embalming experts who had tended to his corpse in the great socialist tradition. I asked some Soviet diplomats for permission for an introduction to the embalmers but they politely evaded my request. After the peace accords, Neto's remains were discreetly moved to another government building and properly entombed. Popular wisdom had it that the MPLA was afraid that UNITA might seize the body and desecrate it.

The biggest illusion of all was that of the economy. The one building in Luanda which was impeccably restored was the one that had limited purpose: the central bank. The Banco Nacional de Angola was the city's best maintained building. It was a graceful pink colonial masterpiece on the Marginal, with rounded windows and an exquisite wall of *azulejos* in the foyer. I felt there was a certain irony in keeping up the appearances of a formal economy which basically didn't exist. The real economy was the so-called parallel one on the streets.

It was hard to arrive at reliable economic statistics in Angola. In most countries there is a shadow economy. In Angola, the shadow takes on a mythical proportion that no one can measure. For all the MPLA's talk about adopting a market economy and privatisation, little had been done to stop the mismanagement of the country's wealth. Accumulated inflation in 1992 was more than 1800 per cent and about a third of petroleum production was mortgaged ahead as a guarantee for medium- and short-term credit lines. Agricultural production fell rather than rose. The *kwanza* was devalued regularly.

Diamonds were no longer a source of major revenue, despite the fact that Angola was potentially the world's fourth largest producer. Peace had ironically ushered in the government's loss of control over diamond prospecting. Until the 1991 peace accords, only the government diamond company Endiama could dig, own and sell rough diamonds. Then it passed a law allowing anyone to possess them as long as the stones were sold to the state. The result was a proliferation of wildcat mining in the Lunda provinces. By mid-1992 smugglers were openly offering diamonds to visitors in the streets and bars of Luanda. Endiama had lost its grip.

Angolans were keenly aware that government officials pocketed whatever they could in case they were sacked. Jokes abounded about the Planning Ministry. Angolans called it the Lack of Planning Ministry.

The MPLA elite benefited from subsidies for imported cars, telephone calls and aeroplane tickets which were among the cheapest in Africa. Abundance was the word that best described the spreads and drinks at ministers' cocktail parties that I attended. But *gimnastica económica* – economic gymnastics or contortions – was the phrase employed by ordinary Angolans to describe how a person earning $10 a month managed to feed six children, and pay rent and other services totalling $20. With 800 000 displaced people needing to resettle and 300 000 refugees planning to return to the country, the economic pressures were only increasing.

Many people I met had two jobs so that they could feed their families. Others turned to crime. The city's port resounded with gunfire every night while robbers broke into containers. For police, who earned a mere pittance, taking bribes was the answer. They never called them bribes, preferring the more refined word 'fines'. But it was the same thing. I was continually stopped for going through fictitious stop signs or stoplights that didn't work. One policeman wanted to 'fine' me for making an illegal left turn.

'But there's no sign indicating that it's prohibited,' I said, pointing ahead of me.

He didn't care. 'There used to be a sign before independence. You should have known,' the policeman insisted, his hand resting on his AK-47 rifle to stress his authority.

People rarely put their money in banks. I went to various banks and saw bored tellers with no customers to attend to. If you made money you converted it into dollars or diamonds. But you were unwise to deposit your cash savings into an account where it would lose value, or worse, disappear. The real banks were on the streets; the women who sat by the kerb and waved wads of bills and always quoted the same rate, even on opposite sides of the city. They used the parallel rates of the *candango*, or contraband. Some used *moeda alternativa* – alternative money – which was just another phrase for bartering. Stores were only just beginning to reopen and most people bought their goods on the streets.

The biggest open-air market was named after a fictional character from a Brazilian soap opera: Roque Santeiro. Roque was one of the largest markets I have seen in Africa. On a good day as many as 10 000 people crammed into it, haggling for anything from an aspirin to a washing machine. It was a dangerous, dense place where arguments often led to shootings. Some women I knew refused to go there without male chaperons to serve as bodyguards. Roque spilled down a hill towards the sea and was as well organised as a department store. If you stood on the ridge overlooking the market, it looked like a commercial Dante's Inferno, smoke and dust and smells rising from each level.

The appliances were half-way down the hill. Then there was the barber section, with painted wooden signs depicting the various styles of hair-cut one could choose. The pharmacy area and cold drinks stands were nearby. There was even a shoelace section. You could buy a diamond or stolen sacks of grain donated by the US government. The guns were buried in the thickest part in the market's heart.

✝

The irony was that I felt very safe in Luanda, despite the lawlessness and the lack of effective policing. Perhaps I was desperately naive, but I walked the streets at any hour of night just as in Lisbon, without fear.

One night, just before returning to Johannesburg, I strolled with two friends through the streets of Luanda. The electricity wasn't working in this part of town and we couldn't see very well in the dark. We were looking for one of the private houses that had been converted into a night-club, but had lost our way. We saw a home lit by candles where music was playing loudly.

'Let's go in,' said one of my companions. 'Looks like quite a party.'

Inside a birthday celebration was under way, 60 people dancing around a huge cake displayed in the middle. No one seemed to think it odd that three strangers had walked in off the streets and joined their party at one in the morning. For a country emerging from 16 years of curfews and war these are pretty trusting people, I thought.

'Have you known the birthday boy a long time?' asked one of the guests, handing me a plastic cup of wine and a slice of cake. The cake had blue icing and I could make out the letters of the word 'happy'.

'Um, only recently,' I replied. I took a sip of the wine. It was sweet and lukewarm but tasted good. I toasted him: 'To your health.'

'To Angola,' he answered. 'The new Angola.'

We raised our glasses again.

4

The Night of the Generals

There is a word which Angolans use when things go amiss –
confusão. *Confusão* is literally translated as confusion but it is
more like disturbance, trouble or even anarchy. It can apply to
something as mundane as an argument between friends at a
market or something as serious as a war. And *confusão* is what
people said about the UN's ill-fated peace mission.

✢

When I first visited Angola in April 1992, the UN special envoy
Margaret Anstee bravely tried to make light of the impossible
task assigned to her.

'I have been given a 747 to fly with only enough fuel for a
DC3,' she said in a joking reference to the UN Security Council
Resolution 747, the mandate for the UNAVEM II peace mission
she had been appointed to supervise.

As time went on, Angolans changed the apocryphal quote
to 'only enough fuel for a car'.

The country's first multiparty elections were less than six
months away. Anstee was concerned. Her mission comprised
just a few hundred observers with a limited mandate. The two
enemy armies were to be pared down and merged by 1 August
1992, creating a new armed force of 50 000. Demobilisation
and the assembling of troops at camps had only just begun.

It was my first visit to Angola and we were sitting in her

'office' at the UN headquarters, which was not much more than a collection of trailers fitted with desks, beds and electricity. Anstee was an athletic businesslike Englishwoman, educated at Cambridge, who looked far less than her 60-odd years. Her office was neat and stacked with piles of official-looking papers.

'It is the world's cheapest peacekeeping operation,' she said, with a trace of complaint. Anstee called in her Scandinavian assistant, who carried a stack of documents to prove her point. Anstee ruffled through them, pointing to a budget of $132 million for the peace observer mission in Angola. By contrast, Namibia had been awarded $430 million and Cambodia $2 billion. Cambodia had 22 000 UN personnel to oversee its peace process.

Anstee returned repeatedly to the case of Namibia, which had a mere 1,4 million people versus Angola's population of ten million. But Namibia had been assigned 10 000 UN personnel including an 8 000-member armed military and police force to supervise its transition to peace and its elections. True, Namibia had undergone a guerrilla liberation struggle. But Namibia had suffered nowhere near the physical and psychological devastation of Angola, where perhaps one million people had died during 16 years of civil war which had also wrecked the country's infrastructure. Angola had been assigned a mere 350 UN military observers, 90 police monitors and about 400 civilian election observers. A further 400 foreign election observers came later. Angola is a country five times the size of Britain and 5 820 polling stations were set up. It was impossible to monitor them all.

From the moment it was formed, the UN Angola Verification Mission (UNAVEM) II was poorly conceived. UN peacekeeping was still embryonic in those days. UNAVEM II was an experiment in post-Cold War conflict mediation and the Angolan accords were hailed as a model for making the transition from war to peace elsewhere. The lessons of Somalia, Liberia and Rwanda had yet to come.

The Troika – Portugal, Russia and the United States – which was overseeing the 1991 peace accords was eager to wrap up the costly mission and push through the elections. The US and Russia, which had invested billions of dollars in supporting their Angolan proxies, had taxpayers to answer to and wanted to close this African chapter of the Cold War. They were under pressure to hold the polling before the rainy season began in October, which would have made it impossible to get a decent turnout or to supervise logistics for several months.

UNAVEM II had only a peripheral role as an observer; neither UNITA nor the government wanted too strong a UN presence which could actually enforce peace. Optimism about the changing world order was such that warning signs were ignored. No one thought about the implications of a peace accord reached after neither adversary had had a decisive military victory and where elections were seen as a way to win a conflict that hadn't been resolved on the battlefield. Everyone was saying it would be all right, like an anxious family practising denial at the bedside of a cancer victim.

But things weren't all right and they didn't get better as the 29 30 September elections approached. Anstee maintained her proverbial British stiff upper lip and wrote memos to New York which were never satisfactorily answered.

One of Anstee's biggest problems was logistics. She had to cope with a ruined infrastructure, a critical lack of resources and a bureaucracy that was Kafka-esque in its inefficiency. It seemed an insurmountable problem to move sufficient supplies and men across the country, where the only way to travel was by air. Hundreds of bridges had been blown up and the few asphalt highways were mined. The Benguela Railroad was paralysed. Anstee offered to get me on one of the few flights across the country, in a military transport plane leased by the UN, so that I could see for myself the challenges she was working against.

✢

'We lack decent quarters, transport, communications, systems, infrastructure and time,' said General Abilio Numa, a former UNITA fighter who was now one of the two provisional commanders of the new joint army. 'Oh yes, and don't forget money.'

Numa, a thin amiable man, was mopping his forehead with a handkerchief in the sweltering midday heat while he stood on the tarmac of Luanda's military airport. He had been stranded in the capital for the second consecutive day. He was trying to get to the coastal city of Benguela to oversee the formation of a new peacetime force. But the one pilot who knew how to fly the Soviet-made Ilyushin 76 transport plane was ill and no other aircraft was available. Numa was irritated but there was nothing even he could do. We drove back to town.

During the ride, he spoke about how rioting was breaking out at the demobilisation camps. There was nothing to do except play cards and there was not enough food and water. Some of the men hadn't been paid for months.

'Boredom and hunger are our new enemies,' he said, as we drove past a group of amputees begging at an intersection.

I gleaned a better sense of what he was talking about several days later, when I rode on a UN flight to Luachimo in the diamond district near the border with Zaire. Luachimo was a rundown place where the grass sprouted waist-high in the town centre. There didn't seem to be any working plumbing and the only electricity was provided by generators. The buildings, once painted bright pink, ochre and blue, were now grimy and faded from neglect.

The UNAVEM men in town in their isolation seemed pleased to see me and my travel companions, two colleagues from Portugal. They drove us in military vehicles to the demobilisation camp, which was a few miles outside Luachimo town. 'Don't expect much,' one of the men warned as we neared the site.

Indeed, the camp wasn't much, just a collection of tents in

the middle of the bush. There was no water nearby and it was hot. It was already ten in the morning and I wondered how the men managed to get anything done in the middle of the day when the heat was at its worst. About 50 former MPLA soldiers in a mixture of civilian and military dress – a camouflage shirt over jeans, some in sandals, some in marching boots – sat in the shade of the trees, playing cards and listening to Latin dance tapes on a ghetto-blaster. They were so excited to have visitors that they surrounded us, pulling at our shirt-sleeves and all talking at the same time.

The UNAVEM observers took us on a tour of the 'facilities'. These comprised one tent where the soldiers were supposed to hand over their weapons and uniforms. It was empty except for a small pile of boots and clothes in one corner. They were crumpled and worn out. There were some old AK-47s and cartridge belts in another corner. Anyone could have picked them up and made off with them. After all, how do you lock a tent?

'Arms have been disappearing,' said one of the UNAVEM men, who was from Brazil. 'Besides, we have no way of knowing if these men have hidden rifles somewhere else. We don't have enough people to supervise this properly.'

But that was not the worst of his problems. 'Deserters slip away at the weekends, and get into drunken fights in town,' he said. He lowered his voice. 'They've also raped women.' He expressed the fear that the men, their $80 a month salaries eight months in arrears, were getting involved in diamond smuggling which was rife in the area. 'What do you expect? Even their two helpings a day of rice isn't constant.'

As though on cue, soldiers – some of whom looked no more than 15 years old – nudged me insistently, asking for food and help. One, named Carlos, wouldn't let go of my arm.

'I've been fighting since I was 14,' Carlos said. Now he was 30. He showed me his ID card which had his date of birth. The photograph must have been taken a while back because he

79

looked softer in it, the cheeks fuller and the eyes bewildered. He said he was from a village 3 000 kilometres away and hadn't seen his family since he had gone to fight. There had been no letters or telephone calls or telegrams. He had been robbed of his youth and he hadn't had a proper girlfriend for 16 years. Now he wanted to go home. But he didn't know when that would be or even if his house was still standing. He had no skills other than using a gun and didn't remember how to farm. He didn't know what he'd do, other than 'start a family, I guess'. Did he look forward to peace? Carlos responded with an anxious look. 'I've never known it.'

It was time to go; the plane back to Luanda would be leaving soon and we didn't want to be stranded in Luachimo for what could be days. The UNAVEM observers gestured at their watches and the waiting jeep. Carlos touched my arm again. 'Please tell them I want to leave. Please tell them to let me go home.'

+

When I returned to Luanda Anstee had flown off somewhere. Her Scandinavian assistant told me that she flew all the time across the 1,25 million square kilometres to try to supervise matters. Sometimes, to save time and fuel, she had to cover five places a day, stopping at each for only an hour at a time. 'She does what she can,' explained the assistant.

Anstee clung to one promising sign. She noted the remarkably few cease-fire violations in the 16 months after the Biçesse agreements were signed, an achievement for a country which had been so heavily embroiled in war. Only a few minor incidents were discussed in great depth at the Joint Political and Military Commission, known by its Portuguese acronym CCPM. The CCPM was designed for maximum consultation; it comprised representatives of the erstwhile foes and of UNAVEM and the Troika. Its role was to probe alleged cease-fire violations and ensure compliance by both sides. The CCPM aimed to work out disputes by mediation and allowed UNITA some political power for the first time.

The peace accords also established a joint commission for the creation of a single army, which comprised the two parties as well as military experts from Portugal, Britain and France who were helping to train the new force. The military men at the top levels of both armies had a solid rapport, probably better than their counterparts on the political side. Men on both sides were sick of the fighting and found they actually had a lot in common.

One day in April I drove out to Viana, one of the poor neighbourhoods on the outskirts of Luanda. There, on a dusty patch of earth, barefoot teenagers were playing football. Viana had been in MPLA hands during the war but after the peace accords UNITA supporters had moved into the area. Sympathisers from the two sides seemed to get along these days; even disputed penalties during the soccer match were debated in a relaxed fashion. It was the first time some of these youths had met the former enemy face-to-face. I asked them after the game how they felt about it.

'They're good football players,' said a boy named Jorge from the MPLA side. 'But they're a bit weak at defence.'

Similar bonhomie was present in the upper echelons of the military. Numa and his MPLA counterpart, João de Matos, spent a lot of time together and appeared to relish each other's company. During their free time they went everywhere like conspirators – the beach, bars, parties – and behaved like two rowdy college boys on the prowl. I was staying at the Trópico Hotel which was a popular meeting spot and often saw them there hanging around the lobby drinking beer, sprawled over the sides of the armchairs.

On one occasion they were joking about the times they had nearly killed each other. They were so playful you'd have thought they were talking about an innocuous game of tennis instead of battles where thousands of men had died.

'He caused many problems for us,' De Matos said about Numa, whom he had fought several times in the south-eastern Cuando Cubango province. He prodded his former nemesis on the shoulder, making rude remarks in Portuguese.

'And what about you?' Numa retorted jocularly. 'Every where João de Matos went we had trouble.'

'Yeah, right. Well let's make some trouble now,' De Matos said.

'Now you're talking,' said Numa, springing out of his chair and heading towards the door. They glided out of the hotel into the poorly lit night, laughing.

✛

Life had a sense of impermanence in those days. Part of it was due to the fact that for many people accommodation and jobs were temporary as the country made the transition from war to peace. The telephones didn't work so the United Nations, businessmen, diplomats and, later, UNITA officials walked around with walkie-talkie radios. They became so ubiquitous that enterprising craftsmen in the market made wire and wood models of the radios and sold them to aid workers.

Because of the severe shortage of housing, anyone who was new to town stayed in hotels. Businessmen, rebels, journalists, even diplomats lived and worked out of tiny cramped rooms. Savimbi had a lovely mansion on the top of the hill overlooking the bay in a diplomatic area called *Miramar* (Sea View) right next to the American embassy. But his aides worked out of these small hotel rooms.

During my first visit I could only get a room in the Trópico Hotel in the city centre. The great advantage of the Trópico was that some of the UNITA leadership stayed there.

Half of the city's hotels were managed by a short, warm Portuguese man named Carlos Amorim, who was one of the few people in Luanda who managed to remain popular with UNITA and the MPLA alike. He was an extremely gracious individual who always had time to help me, whether it was to find a working telephone or give me tips for stories.

Political strategy and business deals were formulated in those musty hotel rooms. You could tell a person's rank by which hotel he or she stayed at. Some of the UNITA political officials stayed at the Trópico which cost about $60 a day. A few UNITA military men were at the more upmarket Turismo which cost more. Portuguese diplomats and the CCPM took over the Hotel Império which cost about $100 a night. Leaders of the FNLA – the third liberation movement of the 1960s and 1970s – chose the Meridien, which cost about $150 a night. Only the MPLA could afford to put people in the Hotel Tivoli for $165 a night. The Tivoli was where the Brazilian public relations firm which was organising the government's election campaign stayed.

The hotel guest registration read like a Who's Who of recent Angolan history. Holden Roberto, the FNLA leader who had largely drifted into obscurity in Zaire after the CIA shifted its support from him to UNITA, was back in town heading what he hoped would be a comeback in the elections. Frequenting the restaurants and bars were some prominent MPLA dissidents who were heading their own independent parties, including Daniel Chipenda.

A lot of UNITA men who had been legends in the bush were now walking around in shorts on their way to the beach, or sipping coffee like any other citizen of Luanda. Sometimes ordinary Angolans would gather at the entrance of the Turismo and gape as General Arlindo Chenda Pena 'Ben Ben', the head of the military machine and Savimbi's relative, walked in and out.

The Trópico was the temporary home of Jorge Valentim, UNITA's information secretary whom the MPLA called the Butcher of Lobito for the massacres he was allegedly responsible for in that Atlantic port in the 1970s. Also staying at the Trópico was the movement's shadow culture minister Jaka Jamba, an avuncular man known as a moderate and UNITA's most prominent intellectual.

Businessmen hoping to get rich on the reconstruction were ubiquitous. Everywhere you looked there were people trying to sell something. Most of them were South African, Portuguese or Brazilian businessmen. Fruit juice, construction services, tyres, beer, can openers to open the beer, or furniture. Everything.

For the UNITA men accustomed to living in the bush under the most trying of conditions, this new accommodation was the epitome of luxury. They set up camp in these small hotel rooms, hanging laundry above the bed, installing women and children in a single bed, stacking cardboard boxes in the corners alongside chairs and tables waiting for a real home. The government was vague about when housing would be available but the UNITA men were patient. They expected to win the elections – and with victory would come big homes.

Because such important people were staying at the Trópico, other UNITA luminaries stopped by regularly. I spent a lot of time chatting with the foreign affairs chief, Abel Chivukuvuku. He was a lanky, handsome man in his thirties who looked like a model and was tipped to be Savimbi's successor. Chivukuvuku had spent a lot of time in Washington and was comfortable with Americans. He was slick, and in his striped shirts and silk ties he bore more resemblance to a public relations man from Madison Avenue than a guerrilla fighter.

✝

There were some disturbing signs. Savimbi said repeatedly in interviews that he would lose the elections only if there were fraud, ruling out even the slimmest chance of an MPLA victory. For a man who was credited with being the most charismatic guerrilla leader in Africa, I found him rather tedious and even a bit desperate.

Before the elections, Savimbi was quite accessible for interviews. He was hungry for exposure. But his people always made it seem hard to get hold of him. Every time I went to his mansion, up on the hill in Miramar next to the American compound, I was made to wait. It didn't matter whether I arrived early or late for the appointment. Savimbi always kept people waiting.

There were a lot of ironies in his house. Savimbi hated the Portuguese, yet the mansion was the model of a red-tile roofed, white Portuguese villa with blue and white *azulejos* imported from the motherland. The house and its sturdy carved furniture could have been straight out of Porto or Lisbon. Savimbi never liked the cities very much and he looked uncomfortable in the sumptuous splendour, as though he never quite believed it was really his. The other irony was that Savimbi lived far more comfortably than his American benefactors, who were next door in what were essentially converted trailers.

Most people in Luanda were suspicious of Savimbi. At first, when he returned from the bush in early 1992, they gave him the benefit of the doubt and turned out in their tens of thousands to catch a glimpse of this legendary figure whom they had loathed and feared for 30 years. But UNITA grew defensive over the months and its rhetoric became more bellicose.

At a campaign rally in Rocha Pinto in the *musseques*, UNITA trucked in 5 000 people. No one in the crowd looked terribly festive until they brought in crates of beer. I didn't understand the message; it was in Umbundu, the language of Savimbi's Ovimbundu people. Most of those in the crowd were Ovimbundu, as were the speakers – Valentim and Chivukuvuku. I asked a woman wearing a cotton cloth with a picture of UNITA's black cockerel emblem what they were talking about. 'He's saying that Ovimbundu are different and that when UNITA comes to power we'll inherit the country,' she said, her eyes on the wooden platform. Behind the podium, Valentim was trying to liven up the crowd; he'd shout a command and they would clap.

A group of journalists based in Lisbon flew up to Uíge in the north on a UNITA aeroplane to hear Savimbi address a rally. It was an important rally at which he coined his campaign slogan, *Calças Novas* – meaning 'New Trousers'. The crowd went wild and thereafter the slogan was painted in red and black all over buildings in Angola.

I stayed behind in Luanda because I had malaria and so missed the rally. My friends came back later that day with a report that they had seen an unusually big pile of explosives on the floor of the plane. 'It was very odd,' said one of the journalists, looking disturbed. 'What would they need it for?'

I went up to the fifth floor of the Trópico and knocked on Jorge Valentim's door. He grinned his manic grin and waved me in. 'Come into my office and abode.'

There was nowhere to sit because a young woman of about 17 was occupying the only chair. Several boxes covered the bed. I stood awkwardly at the door. I mentioned the dynamite.

Valentim frowned and waved his hands in the air in a dismissive gesture. 'I don't know anything about it. But it probably was for construction purposes or something.' He looked at me intently. 'Really, it's nothing.'

✢

The UNITA general Peregrino Wambu told me in an interview three years later that something had indeed been afoot. He said that he had been summoned with other UNITA military men to Uíge in April 1992 by Savimbi and had received instructions for a contingency plan. UNITA was concerned about the MPLA mobilising a paramilitary force and decided to hedge its bets.

'After April 22 the military Chief of Staff practically left Luanda for Huambo, only coming back for meetings and the elections,' he said. 'The first time we realised that plans were afoot for war was when the MPLA moved troops to Huambo and put police uniforms on them. There was clearly no demobilisation intended. It was a violation of the peace accords and we brought it up time and again in the CCPM but no one answered our concerns. So in April we received instructions to go to Huambo. After that we called the commanders and told them things were not good.'

✛

I didn't know then that the meeting had taken place, but I left Luanda troubled by the dynamite incident. I returned to Johannesburg to cover the political changes taking place there. News about Angola was meagre and for the next two months I concentrated on South Africa's transition to democracy. The multiracial talks between Nelson Mandela's African National Congress and the white minority government were breaking down over a massacre in Boipatong township outside Johannesburg. Violence was rising.

My next trip to Angola was scheduled for June 1992, and it seemed like a distant notion. Angola was a mere entry in my diary for a future date but was not etched much on my mind. Having finally visited Angola I could put it aside for the time being. I was settling into a new job and Johannesburg was slowly starting to feel like home. I had arrived in South Africa in late January and was only now hanging pictures on my walls and unpacking my files. Angola was my secondary beat, it was a place I would visit only occasionally. In South Africa there were sources to develop, rallies to attend, townships to get to know and negotiations to follow. South Africa was compelling, more important in the grand scheme of things. If South Africa's transition didn't succeed, the region would sink.

It did, however, seem ironic at the time that after Pretoria's destabilising role in Angola, Angola presented a more hopeful case of a peaceful transformation than South Africa.

✛

When I returned to Luanda in June the mood seemed much more tense. My ostensible reason for being there was to cover the visit of Pope John Paul II, who was giving his blessing to the new era of peace. But it was a good time also to judge how things had developed.

By all accounts, they hadn't developed well. The two armies were to be merged by 1 August, with a new joint armed force of 50 000. By June only 60 000 of the MPLA's 150 000 troops had reported to the assembly points. Only 2 000 of UNITA's 50 000 men were at the cantonment areas. Diplomats estimated there were maybe 3 500 UNITA men walking around fully armed in Luanda.

Rhetoric was growing more hostile between the two parties and meetings at the CCPM were still quite polarised. The MPLA was dragging its feet on accepting UNITA into the police force. In turn, UNITA would not allow the MPLA to establish central administration in much of the territory under rebel control. Mutual distrust was not lessening. UNITA viewed the UN as pro-government because Anstee's operation was based in Luanda, the capital of its enemy. The MPLA, meanwhile, saw the appointment of Elias Salupeto Pena, Savimbi's nephew and a general, rather than a political official, as head of UNITA's CCPM negotiating delegation as a breach of good faith.

The papal visit was supposed to be the crowning moment of the peace process. First the superpowers and the United Nations had given their endorsement. Now it was the turn of the Vatican. But like many things in Angola in those days, it actually highlighted how terribly wrong everything was.

The Pontiff's open-air mass in Luanda was the centrepiece

of the trip. It was delivered on a desolate plot of land and – ironically for the anti-communist Pope – within sight of the mausoleum of Neto, the founding father of the Marxist MPLA.

We left the car far behind and walked through the crowd. There were a lot of amputees in wheelchairs and on crutches in the front of the audience, waiting to be blessed. Both UNITA and the MPLA were using the mass as a campaign event, joining the diplomatic corps and other elite assembling on the stage. The UNITA men were mostly Protestants and they looked uncomfortable.

Suddenly a sinister presence emerged: men in black leather jackets, starched blue uniforms and sun glasses so dark you couldn't see their eyes. Someone had obviously told them to keep the crowd away from the Pope and they were taking their instructions seriously. Anyone who moved too close to the Pope faced dire consequences. One of the uniformed men had a whip and he was lashing at the cripples sitting in the front. Another seized a photographer, Alexander Joe, and hauled him into a car with threats of arrest. Meanwhile the Pope was talking about peace, oblivious of the mêlée offstage.

'Who are these guys?' I asked an Angolan colleague, as one of the men dived into the crowd to push back a wheelchair. The force with which he did this was so great that the wheelchair tipped over.

'Ninjas,' my colleague said, ducking a new advance by the men in blue. 'The new elite riot squad. Apparently they've been trained by the Spanish. They're paid more than ordinary police. Many are demobilised soldiers.'

I withdrew to the safety of the sidelines.

UNITA was outraged that the MPLA had mobilised a paramilitary force of several thousand men. The government first began to transfer demobilised soldiers into this new crack unit in March 1992 and their first operation was during the Pope's visit. The force was a source of debate at the CCPM meetings but UNAVEM didn't insist that the government disband it. The government claimed there were only about 1 500 Ninjas but diplomats put it at 10 000 several months later. We didn't know it at the time, but UNITA was making its own plans to counter the Ninjas.

Another unpleasant incident occurred at the Pope's Luanda mass, indicating that all was not well. The UNITA military staff were allowed to carry guns. A UNITA journalist with the weekly newspaper *Terra Angolana* had driven to the rally to hear the Pope, so he said. Police stopped him, searched the car, and found a trunk-load of guns. The journalist said he had borrowed the car from Valentim's deputy, Norberto de Castro, who was a brigadier and therefore entitled to carry weapons. The journalist was thrown into jail, to the protests of UNITA who claimed that the police were harassing its members.

The incident blew over when the journalist was freed several days later. But I wondered uneasily what sort of peace accord allowed people to walk around fully armed with shotguns in their cars and pistols under their jackets and let others form paramilitary forces with impunity.

✛

One area which worried the international observers was the high level of hostile propaganda by both UNITA and the MPLA. The official election campaign was supposed to start on 26 August but both parties had already begun months before. The Biçesse peace accords clearly stipulated that belligerent propaganda should cease. But, if anything, it seemed to worsen as the elections approached. The MPLA had the advantage of having a monopoly on the sole television station, the *Radio Nacional* network, the news agency ANGOP and the *Jornal de Angola* daily newspaper. UNITA had only its new weekly newspaper, *Terra Angolana*, and its radio station *Vorgan* (Voice of Resistance of the Black Cockerel). You needed a short-wave radio to pick up *Vorgan* in many parts of Angola – a distinct disadvantage for UNITA. And most Angolans, being illiterate and poor, relied on the radio for their information.

Hoping to defuse the situation, American diplomats organised a seminar to teach journalists of both sides about reporting on 'free' elections. The communications officer invited me to lead the discussions.

I had taught a couple of journalism workshops in Mozambique and Swaziland the previous year and fished out of my memory simulated reporting exercises that I had used before. My favourite was a mock press conference held after a mysterious bomb goes off in a country at war. It served as a good vehicle to judge the participants' prowess in interviewing and objectivity. The exercise usually led to emotional discussions about accountability and the responsibility of the media.

This time it took a while to get started with the assignment. The UNITA reporters were outnumbered and the warming-up debate deteriorated into a slanging match between the two sides. They began murmuring their mutual dislike, and their differences reached a loud crescendo within minutes. They blamed each other for the war, calling each other liars and murderers.

The diplomat who had organised the session looked distressed at this display of anger and waved his hands, as though that would bring the debate under control. Eventually he succeeded and they quietened down like disgruntled children. Sufficient calm was restored for me to begin the exercise.

One of the MPLA journalists put up his hand.

'Excuse me,' he said politely. 'Do we cover this like a real reporting assignment or write propaganda like we normally do?'

✝

The journalists' workshop was held the day before I left Angola. I packed and went to the airport feeling uneasy. But the US diplomat who had organised the seminar was upbeat.

'That kind of tension is par for the course,' he said. 'They've been fighting for so many years that there's bound to be some lingering distrust. It can be worked out.'

✢

It was not until three months later that I had a chance to see for myself whether things could be worked out in Angola. When I got back to South Africa there wasn't even time to think, there was so much work to do.

Angola seemed remote, partially due to the fact that communications were so difficult. When it rained, you didn't even contemplate trying to get through on the telephone. At the best of times the lines were clear only at night. There was virtually no news about Angola during this time in South Africa. If I wanted to find out what was happening I called my old office in Portugal where Angola was front-page news. Reuters had a stringer in Luanda, Anita Coulson of the BBC, and when the telex was working she wrote disturbing stories about clashes between UNITA and MPLA supporters as the election campaign heated up. But generally Angola was off the news map and out of my mind, obscured by South Africa's own dramatic quagmire.

I had little idea of what had transpired during my absence from Angola and telephoned around to various embassies to get some information before flying there in September 1992. Reuters specialises in financial information and there was a great need to provide stories about the newly liberalised diamond trade, the oil industry which provided 90 per cent of Angola's export revenues and what exactly UNITA's economic programme was. I didn't expect to be away for more than two weeks as there were pressing developments in South Africa which required coverage.

'Remember, speed is of the essence,' said the news editor as he handed me a pile of instructions on how and when to file election results. 'This could move markets.'

I arrived in Luanda about a week before the 29-30 September 1992 elections, flying in from Johannesburg with Howard Burditt, a freelance photographer from Zimbabwe whom Reuters hired occasionally. From the moment we touched down at the airport there was an air of anxious expectation.

The election campaign had begun in earnest and the drive from the airport to the city was festooned with posters and banners. Most prominent were the signs of the MPLA with the words *O FUTURO SEGURO* (THE SECURE FUTURE) and a picture of an amiable-looking Dos Santos. Other posters sported a big red outline of a heart with the words *ANGOLA NO CORAÇÃO* (ANGOLA IN THE HEART). A lot of people were wearing T-shirts with blue doves of peace which had been handed out free by the independent National Electoral Commission (CNE).

We took along a satellite telephone this time, thinking that the world would be awaiting the election results and we would need to get them out quickly. Luanda's normal telephone system was too unreliable to depend on; it could take hours, if not days, to get an international line and even ringing from one side of the city to another was difficult. The satellite telephone operated like a normal telephone at ten times the cost. It could be hooked up to a laptop computer and photo transmitter to send pictures and text to our news-desk in London. We set up a makeshift office in a suite on the twenty-first floor of the Hotel Meridien, the city's highest building, which had a panoramic view of Luanda.

Our satellite telephone, known as the satphone, was a huge contraption which weighed more than my 45 kilograms and which I couldn't lift without help. Because it was so bulky, about the size of a coffee table, Howard couldn't do it alone either and he enlisted the help of two colleagues. We, or rather Howard and the others, hung the dish precariously outside the window, swivelling it around several times with compass in hand as a guide until we got a signal from somewhere above the Indian Ocean. In time I became adept at putting together and dismantling the plastic parts within minutes and knowing just how to tilt the dish to capture a perfect signal. But for someone who had trouble operating a VCR at home, this sophisticated piece of machinery seemed terrifying at first.

We got off the plane and went immediately into a press conference at the CNE. At least 200 journalists from around the world had converged on Luanda for the elections. Most were filing at the press centre. A row of new orange telexes had been set up; they were computerised and unlike the old ones where your fingers got caught between the keys.

Howard set up a darkroom in the bathroom of his hotel room. Every day he'd hang his favourite photograph of the day on the wall so that a pictorial narrative emerged of the story we were covering. We didn't expect to stay very long so he didn't leave much space.

His first pictures were happy: youths with big flags of the MPLA hoisted high as they danced on the beach; a kid with a papier mâché mask, half black, half white, plastered with a sticker of Dos Santos, grinning friends surrounding him. They looked playful and jubilant.

To cover a story for a news agency in a foreign country like Angola, you need a good stringer. A stringer is someone who is usually underpaid and overworked, who sets up interviews for visiting correspondents and does legwork on all areas of coverage. Often it is the stringers who do the real work, and this case was no exception. The BBC correspondent introduced us to a stout, fortyish woman named Manuela Teixeira whom she described as a 'rough diamond'. Manuela's husband, Bento, called her *Rusa*, or little Russian, because of her MPLA affiliations. Manuela was always impeccably coiffed even when the water was off (which was much of the time). She generally had a cigarette in her hand and managed to run remarkably quickly on high heels through Luanda's cobbled streets.

Manuela had suffered terribly at the hands of the FNLA in Uíge in 1975, an attack that was so horrendous and humiliating that she didn't like to talk about it. All the same, she had remained in Angola and saw these elections as a sort of deliverance. She had made sacrifices for the MPLA but never had doubts. She wasn't what you'd call an objective reporter; we'd drive by posters of the Heart and she'd cry out: 'Good! Another sign up! That's the way to go!' Thanks to Manuela's MPLA connections we could barge into ministers' living rooms any time we needed an interview, even late at night.

Neither Howard nor I wanted the hassle of driving ourselves through Luanda's chaotic streets. The only maps available at that time still had the old Portuguese colonial names which had been changed 17 years before. Besides, most landmarks like the *musseques* were off the map and many streets weren't marked even with the new names. Howard didn't speak Portuguese and he didn't want to try negotiating with the police, who regularly stopped drivers to demand bribes. So Manuela's husband, who ran the bar at the state-run press centre, introduced us to his friend Mena.

Mena was an Angolan of Portuguese descent who drove a battered white van which resembled an ice-cream truck. He was a big, gentle, plump man with a droopy black moustache and unkempt hair that hung down to his collar. Mena did odd jobs here and there, and although he seemed to be permanently unemployed, he had enough money to maintain a nice flat in the Avalade area where many whites lived. He drove as though he was in a chase scene in the movies. Even if we were going out for a leisurely snack he'd race through intersections, shouting at pedestrians that they'd die if they didn't get out of the way. They probably would have.

Mena thought our job was great fun and joked constantly

about becoming a journalist. But his plans changed from day to day. 'Judite, I want to be a photographer like Howard,' was Monday's idea. On Tuesday: 'Actually Judite, I think I prefer television. More impact.' By Thursday he had changed his mind again. 'Newspapers, definitely. That's where it's at. Writing is more intellectual.'

Unlike Manuela, Mena was apolitical and hadn't quite made up his mind whom he would vote for. 'Probably the MPLA because they've been there always,' he said. But then other days he thought maybe he wouldn't vote at all. 'I don't get involved in that stuff; that's for the politicians. I just want a quiet life.'

✦

Margaret Anstee probably yearned for a quiet life as well. Her concerns were growing. One major worry was that she didn't have enough staff to properly supervise the 5 820 polling stations across the country. The independent National Electoral Commission (CNE) had no aircraft at its disposal and relied on those of UNAVEM. At least two helicopters had crashed, depleting resources further.

The lack of adequate monitoring was never more apparent than at Mavinga, the site of one of the worst battles at the end of the war and a major UNITA stronghold, where there were only two people to oversee 84 polling stations. Until the minute the elections began, UNITA still controlled 53 municipalities in the south where the MPLA could not campaign freely.

This was worrying Onofre dos Santos and Marcelino Caetano de Sousa, the heads of the CNE. The CNE was housed in an immaculately restored, pale yellow colonial building which now houses the foreign ministry. I could never get through on the telephone so I'd spend a lot of time in the lobby hanging around. Right before the elections I ran into a preoccupied-looking Dos Santos there. 'Of course we're worried,' he said. 'But at this late stage what can we do? We can't postpone the elections now. All we can do is hope it turns out all right.'

The lack of observers on the ground made it difficult to properly oversee registration in areas under UNITA control and in the more remote areas in MPLA districts. Half a million Angolans living abroad were not registered because of lack of materials; only one-third were registered in the northern oil-producing enclave of Cabinda where the separatist struggle threatened to disrupt the poll. Incidents of clashes between UNITA and the MPLA were on the rise and at least 30 people had died since campaigning began in early September. On 21 September hundreds of UNITA men seized control of Cuito airport, capturing ten presidential guards. Eight died in street fighting in Luena. UNITA troops were mobilised in Huambo and there had been clashes in Malange. Propaganda, too, was growing increasingly hostile, particularly by UNITA. Savimbi repeatedly reiterated that he would only lose the elections if there were fraud.

'There is no way we can lose,' he insisted in an interview at his Miramar residence. 'We are too popular with the Angolan people. If we lose it will be because of irregularities and manipulations of the results.'

Both sides were predicting their own victory. The MPLA expected to do strongly in the capital; UNITA would feature in the central highlands. But no one could honestly foresee what would happen. How could they? In a country with such devastated infrastructure it was impossible to carry out public opinion polls. However, that didn't stop everyone from speculating. The Brazilian public relations people employed by the MPLA had done a very successful presidential campaign back in Brazil. They were convinced, on the basis of their own poll, that the MPLA would have a solid victory in the parliament and that Dos Santos would narrowly beat Savimbi.

'People are scared of Savimbi,' one of the Brazilians told me. They realised that the handsome, but wooden Dos Santos would have a tough time competing against the more charismatic Savimbi. So they marketed Dos Santos and the MPLA as a force for continuity and stability. The MPLA also appointed as its secretary general an Ovimbundu, Marcolino Moco, to try to woo the vote of the country's largest ethnic group away from UNITA. It was the Brazilians who devised the campaign slogans and a slick video with a catchy tune by local musicians. All over Luanda people hummed the tune. The heart motif caught on as well. In the markets handicraft vendors sold carved wooden and ivory hearts.

The Americans and South Africans, however, saw a clear lead for Savimbi and assured him as much. The MPLA may have had an advantage by dominating the media, but the Americans provided hefty aid to UNITA to make the transition from guerrilla movement to political party. Much of the aid took the form of 4x4 vehicles. I rarely saw these vehicles being used for campaign purposes. They were used instead to drive the leadership to restaurants and to the beach.

UNITA also employed a Washington-based public relations company, whose representative at the elections was a perky young woman dressed in leggings and body suits, as though she was on her way to an aerobics class. She and the party issued statements which seemed more tailored to external than domestic consumption. Savimbi's campaign slogan – *Calças Novas*, New Trousers – was a source of hilarity for many residents of the capital who made jokes about old underwear. The average Luanda resident didn't care whether UNITA had an economic plan acceptable to the World Bank and the International Monetary Fund; they were concerned about why people like Jorge Valentim and Norberto de Castro felt they needed to drive around with guns in their cars.

There were 11 presidential candidates and 18 parties but only two mattered, or three if you took into account the FNLA of Holden Roberto. Roberto had largely drifted into obscurity over the years but now he had re-emerged as the only viable third choice. Bespectacled and acting like an elder statesman, Roberto rarely left his suite at the top of the Meridien, where his bodyguards and henchmen sprawled in the corridors. They had all spent a long exile in Zaire and many spoke better French than Portuguese.

Because so many Angolans were illiterate, the ballots bore pictures of the candidates' faces and emblems of the parties. Later on, after the elections, the results showed that one obscure candidate had done remarkably well. Diplomats speculated that this was because his picture resembled that of Dos Santos.

Savimbi didn't look very confident at his final rally. He grimaced at the crowd of 30 000. As usual, he was late and had kept everyone waiting for several hours. Pick-up trucks and buses had brought many supporters from afar. The majority of the people in the crowd were women.

Savimbi spoke in Portuguese and Umbundu; the *Calças Novas* slogan was repeated several times. He moved his foot in rhythm with his words as he bellowed and tried to summon up fervour, but for the most part he looked profoundly unhappy. The crowd responded mechanically. On the stage behind *O Mais Velho* (The Eldest One), as Savimbi was known, Chivukuvuku and Valentim and the rest of the shadow cabinet were, however, jubilant.

'There is no way we can lose,' Chivukuvuku said, with his eye on the crowd. 'Victory is ours! We are convinced of victory.'

Mediators eager to present a calm atmosphere on the eve of the vote hurriedly arranged a summit between Savimbi and Dos Santos. It was too short a meeting to discuss anything in depth and seemed to have been stage-managed for the benefit of television. Savimbi arrived to a glare of cameras at Futungo de Belas, the presidential complex overlooking the sea on the edge of town whose enormous swimming pool and marble floors made it one of Luanda's most coveted properties. As Savimbi and his entourage left, he paused and glanced through the big glass wall in the waiting room at the large gardens outside. His look seemed to register annoyance, rather than the proprietary satisfaction of a future owner.

✛

The night before the elections UNAVEM decided to merge the two armies, despite the fact that only 1 500 of the 50 000 united armed force had been sworn in and only 8 000 had been trained. Still to be demobilised were 55 per cent of government troops and 75 per cent of UNITA's.

But the UN decided that a swearing-in ceremony was better than nothing. At dusk in one of Luanda's pink military buildings, the top brass of both sides smiled, embraced and pinned epaulettes and military decorations on each other's breasts. Ben Ben and General António dos Santos França N'dalu were sworn in as joint commanders. Someone gave a speech about brotherhood and togetherness. Anstee looked on anxiously.

Anstee danced with some of the generals at the reception which was held afterwards. The venue was an old Portuguese villa which had been converted into a restaurant and was used for functions. There was a sumptuous buffet of dishes from Angola's 18 provinces to symbolise unity – palm oil stews, beans, coconut sweets, spinachy greens, bananas and starchy porridge of several types. There was also a lot of whisky and beer. The generals from the two sides were not mixing, except at the buffet table to refill their plates. Some were getting quite drunk.

At the bar, Manuela and I approached General Cirilo Ita, who had been the head of intelligence for the MPLA military. He was in a jesting mood and wouldn't be drawn on whether this ceremony had any merit or what they were going to do about the tens of thousands of still-to-be-demobilised UNITA troops. 'Welcome to the new Angola,' he said, pouring himself another drink. 'Peace, happiness and whisky.'

✛

The two days of voting were remarkable considering the fact that nine out of ten Angolans didn't know how to read and that the country had been at war only 16 months before. An estimated 90 per cent of the electorate turned out to vote and waited in orderly lines.

Howard went off with some other photographers to get the necessary pictures of Savimbi and Dos Santos voting. Savimbi was from the central highlands and had been headquartered for nearly 20 years in Jamba in the south. But he realised that for publicity reasons it made more sense to cast his ballot in the city of his enemies, Luanda. Manuela and I drove around the *bairros*. She was very proud of her finger, which had been stamped with purple dye when she voted, and held it up and examined it several times while driving.

'I voted!' she said. 'Gave Savimbi hell!'

Others were more circumspect about their choice. We approached dozens of women and men and they all solemnly declined to reveal who they were voting for. They were separated into different lines by sex; electoral monitors told me this was to avoid any possible problems if the men got over-excited. Angolans are used to queues; now instead of waiting eight hours to buy rice and meat, they stood patiently waiting for ballots. Some were dressed in their best clothes as if going to church. Many wore the doves of peace T-shirts distributed by the CNE which were probably the freshest clothes they had. We didn't see very many UN observers.

I approached a pregnant woman wearing an MPLA T-shirt with the trademark heart, tucked neatly into a flowered cotton cloth skirt. She had wrapped a baby in another cloth around her waist and was casually breast-feeding while awaiting her turn to vote.

'Who are you voting for?' I asked.

She turned towards me slowly. 'That is a secret for my conscience.'

I pointed to the shirt. 'Your preference doesn't look like a secret.'

She remained impassive. 'It's a secret anyway.'
'What are you going to call the baby?'
'It depends who wins.'

✣

State-run radio related some amazing stories. There were quite a few poignant tales of people overcoming adversity to vote. They limped on crutches for several miles, made their X by candle-light, or they gave birth after voting and named the children 'Democracy' and 'Liberty'. The only place where turnout was poor was in Cabinda, the oil-producing province where separatists threatened to disrupt the voting and where the people have never felt part of Angola anyway.

When the second day went equally well it seemed nothing short of miraculous. Angola was seen as a successful test case for South Africa and especially for Mozambique, another former Portuguese colony which had also suffered 16 years of civil war. The Mozambican government and the RENAMO rebels signed peace accords while Angola was holding elections. It seemed to be the start of a whole new era of stability for southern Africa.

But for the most part, we had no idea what was happening in the rural areas. Most of the UNITA-held territory was inaccessible. There weren't enough helicopters and jeeps to take the 800 foreign observers to the remote areas where they were most needed. So most observers stayed around Luanda.

There were several incidents in Luanda which made me feel uneasy. UNITA armed guards prevented traffic from circulating around the residence of Savimbi. The day after the voting, police accused UNITA of attacking the nearby residence of the deputy interior minister, Armindo do Espírito Santos. Two guards were held prisoner and a third killed in the garden of a Portuguese diplomat, António Monteiro. UN officials described the incidents as 'minor'.

✢

The voting had barely ended on the evening of 30 September when the international community, including the United States and the European Community, declared that the polling had been free and fair. 'It is an example for the world,' the US liaison officer Jeffrey Millington said. 'It really has been incredible.'

UNITA didn't agree. Its verdict was that the elections had been tainted by irregularities and tampering with ballots.

I went to see Chivukuvuku the next morning at the UNITA party headquarters in São Paulo, a middle-class residential neighbourhood of Luanda. He was brooding. 'These elections have not been free and fair. I don't care what the UN or anyone else says. It is not up to foreigners to tell Angolans about their country,' Chivukuvuku said.

UNITA and Chivukuvuku's irritation increased as the first provisional results began to come out soon after. They showed a solid lead for the MPLA everywhere except the Planalto central highlands which was UNITA territory. The CNE was careful to painstakingly release only a few results at a time – at this rate it would take weeks before the final results would be known. State-run television and radio had hourly broadcasts of their own tallies, to which UNITA objected, accusing the government of issuing propaganda.

UNITA lodged a complaint with the CCPM. When it received no immediate satisfaction, the movement began to threaten the CNE, urging it not to publish any more results. 'Do it or be responsible for whatever occurs in the country,' warned UNITA's secretary general, General Mango.

✢

Meanwhile, there was no word from Savimbi. Everyone was waiting to hear what he had to say. On 3 October, O Mais Velho finally spoke.

In an address on UNITA's *Vorgan* radio station, Savimbi said in both Ovimbundu and Portuguese that he rejected the preliminary results as fraudulent. He called on his followers to be on the alert at their 'stations' and hinted at a resumption of the war.

'It is the duty of we freedom fighters, those who brought about democracy to this country through their blood and sweat, to tell you that the MPLA is not winning and cannot win,' he declared.

He said UNITA might be forced to 'take positions that could deeply disturb the situation of this country.' But he told his people to remain calm and said it was up to Angolans, not the international community, to decide the country's fate.

His voice was slurred and some diplomats wondered whether he was drugged or drunk. Most journalists interpreted the speech as a virtual declaration of war. But UNITA tried to convince me otherwise.

'You've got it all wrong. Savimbi was using figurative language which you misinterpreted. It shouldn't be taken literally,' Chivukuvuku told me one afternoon at UNITA's campaign headquarters in São Paulo.

The pert PR woman from Washington put in her bit. 'The Umbundu language is poetic. These guys are upset but they don't mean war.'

✢

At midnight on 5 October I was finishing my final story of the day when the telephone rang. It was Manuela. She sounded stricken and breathless and it took a couple of minutes before she could get out a coherent message.

'They've pulled out! This is war!'

I switched off the radio which was droning endless reams of provisional results. My stomach contracted. 'What? Slow down, who?'

'Ben Ben, the generals. They've pulled out of the army. I've just been with them. They're out.'

Ben Ben, the UNITA commander of the joint army, and several other generals had summoned Angolan reporters to their São Paulo office. There, sitting sternly behind a table in full uniform, they announced that they were withdrawing UNITA's top military from the joint army until the electoral dispute was resolved to their satisfaction.

Ben Ben blamed it on the 'deception which has defrauded the democratic process which the Angolan people so desired'. He outlined three conditions to avoid what he called 'the worst':

(1) Annul the electoral process.
(2) Stop the CNE from publishing the results.
(3) Take into consideration that Angolans were intimidated by the Ninjas while they voted.

I telephoned an American diplomat. I had to use the satellite telephone even though he was only a mile away, because all the telephone lines in the hotel were blocked. The diplomat didn't know how to read the situation and sounded vaguely in shock.

'Well, let's put it this way. If they want to go back to war they have 35 000 men ready to fight in the field.' I asked him if he thought it was a bluff. 'I hope so,' the diplomat said.

General Wambu told me many months later that the decision to pull out of the army was pushed by Savimbi's political advisers, not the military men. 'The intention was to prevent the CNE from publishing the election results. But it actually added to the tensions. From then on, a distance began to develop with our colleagues in the joint army. Many military men did not feel neutral any more,' Wambu said.

While all this was happening, no one could find Savimbi. He wasn't answering the telephone at his residence in Luanda and the guards at the door said he wasn't receiving visitors. In addition, diplomats said, Savimbi had cut off both Pretoria and Washington.

I had a good UN source with a flair for drama. He would

telephone me, often very late at night, with a useful tip and then hang up. His information was helpful but sometimes cryptic. He called me the day after the generals withdrew from the army. 'Huambo. He's gone to Huambo,' the source said. He rang off before I could ask any questions.

On the night of 7 October, Savimbi's withdrawal to Huambo was confirmed by UNITA. They hastily convened a news conference to present what they claimed was decisive evidence of electoral fraud. But the two dozen journalists like myself packed into the hot room were more interested in information about Savimbi. Huambo had been Savimbi's headquarters back in 1976 and, after being expelled by the MPLA and the Cubans, he had always vowed to return. What did this mean? What was Savimbi planning to do? Why did he not just stay in Luanda and negotiate?

The UNITA generals were annoyed by this line of questioning and kept trying to pull the discussion back to the pile of papers on the table in the front of the room which allegedly proved there had been fraud.

'Huambo is Angolan, it's perfectly normal,' General Wambu said. 'So what if Savimbi's gone there?' He made it sound as if it were the most natural thing in the world, like someone from Boston spending the weekend in New York to go to the theatre.

The vote-counting procedure agreed on before the elections was an elaborate one comprising a series of checks and counterchecks to ensure it was virtually watertight. For example, all parties were to have representatives posted at polling stations who would sign their approval on the results paper.

Most of us journalists were not convinced by the purported evidence we were being shown. The 'proof' consisted of some wrinkled ballots which allegedly had been tampered with. But the ballots had the stamps of approval of all major parties which were necessary to clear with CNE monitors before entering them into the computer. Our scepticism angered UNITA further. They slammed down their papers and suddenly everyone was shouting.

'We want proper proof!' one of the reporters yelled. 'You've wasted our time!'

'You're biased! We've shown you evidence,' shouted back one of the generals.

It was extremely stuffy in the room and the time was nearly midnight. Some of the journalists left the room either to file or to go to sleep. They were menaced with death threats by the UNITA men outside.

I went up to the front of the room to talk to Norberto de Castro, with whom I had spent time in Lisbon while we were both based there. He was normally very warm to me but that night he glared as he gathered up his papers.

'I thought you were a friend. We're very disappointed in you,' he said. And then: 'You'd better watch out.'

☩

After that news conference it became difficult to get access to UNITA. They didn't want to talk to me and when they did it was usually unpleasant. I noticed that there were now even more guards with prominently displayed arms in front of the UNITA offices and hotels around town.

Several days later I went to the airport and sat on the edge of the tarmac, waiting for one of the foreign mediators to fly in. The rainy season was about to begin and the sky was overcast with heavy grey clouds, adding to my sense of foreboding. UNITA men were guarding trucks with mortars and RPGs on the tarmac. Government troops stood by about 50 metres away, looking scared. I wondered what sort of peace accord would allow this kind of scene.

Manuela sat beside me. 'If UNITA wanted to take the airport it'd be a cinch,' she said. We looked at the outnumbered and out-gunned government troops.

'Do you think there will be war?' she asked. It was the first time I had heard someone use that word and I felt anxious, even though this was just a theoretical discussion. Manuela had been in Luanda during the first war and described the food shortages and the attacks on the electricity pylons which had thrown the city into darkness.

'This time it would be different, of course,' Manuela said.

'How?'

'UNITA never managed to take Luanda last time. This time they're already here.'

She got up to talk to someone else. I continued to sit on the kerb, feeling tired and dispirited.

How would I get out if there is war? I wondered to myself. If they take the airport I'm stuck. One of the UNITA soldiers came over and asked me for a cigarette. I didn't have one and in reply asked jokingly for the unopened Fanta he had in his hand. He smiled, handed me the orange bottle and kidded me about going back to my country with me. I gave him my standard line that he'd have to ask my parents first. I thought: 'Maybe these guys really aren't that bad. Maybe it's just posturing.'

But then I saw some movement on the far side of the tarmac and the feelings of gloom returned. Dozens of women and children were lining up in front of a plane with suitcases, cardboard boxes, plastic bags of clothes and packages of everything they could cram on to a plane out of Luanda. There were no men, just the families of UNITA men.

I rose and went over to speak to them. They looked scared and didn't want to talk. There was only one word they would say: 'Huambo.'

Savimbi was evacuating them.

✛

No one would yet say the word 'war', as though fearing that vocalising it would bring disaster. Instead, they would say 'What if?' or 'In case'.

International mediators were trying to convince Savimbi to talk to Dos Santos but he refused to leave Huambo or even accept telephone calls. On 9 October Anstee flew to Huambo to meet with Savimbi to find out what everyone needed to know: 'What does Jonas want?' She came back saying only that their meeting had been 'cordial and positive'. The following day a special UN Security Council mission arrived, comprising delegates from Russia, the United States, Cape Verde and Morocco. Anstee seemed relieved to get some support.

By now provisional results of 90 per cent of the four million returns showed Dos Santos ahead with just over 50 per cent, requiring a second round, and Savimbi with some 39 per cent. In the legislative race, the MPLA posted 55 per cent and UNITA 33 per cent in the contest for the 223-seat parliament.

At the CNE headquarters Onofre dos Santos and Marcelino Caetano de Sousa looked as though they hadn't slept for days. Every day they contended with angry delegations of UNITA officials storming in to complain. The most irrepressible was Elias Salupeto Pena, the chief UNITA negotiator on the CCPM. He was often red-eyed, seemingly from drugs or drink, and made wild statements upon leaving the meetings.

UNITA's claims grew more bizarre by the day. The latest one was that the CNE computers had been rigged in such a way that every time UNITA votes reached a certain level the MPLA's would rise accordingly. UNITA also claimed that the fax machines had been tampered with. To prove them wrong, UNAVEM called in European experts and technicians from the UN to inspect the ballots and equipment on 7 and 8 October. They flew to all of Angola's 18 provinces and inspected polling stations and ballots. They found no evidence of foul play. There were indeed cases of missing ballot boxes, spoilt or null ballots and intimidation at polling stations. But the experts felt this affected at most a few thousand votes – nothing that would sway the vote significantly either way. UNITA had 53 municipalities under its control. But the movement was silent when critics suggested that these areas were far from free.

This was too much for Salupeto Pena. I approached him as he was leaving the CNE building. 'This fraud has to stop,' he said. I asked him what Savimbi planned to do. Salupeto Pena looked at me furiously. 'I can unleash my men in Luanda without consulting with Huambo.' He got into his car and drove off.

With threats like these, the CNE decided it was better to stop issuing partial results for the time being. This was a great relief to Manuela, whose job for Reuters was to maintain vigil at the CNE to collect results as they came out. She wasn't sleeping well these days and had developed severe stomach pains. She could barely keep down any food. The Cuban doctors at the hospital said it was nerves and suggested she leave the country for a while. It was a thought Manuela increasingly considered.

It was hard for UNITA to accept that they might have lost the elections. They had been assured by the Americans and the South Africans that they would win and they now felt betrayed. Savimbi could not accept the notion that 30 years of fighting in the bush had led to such a public humiliation by the very people he believed adored him.

'Savimbi was absolutely convinced he would win. There was never any doubt in his mind. It was a total shock and he couldn't adjust to it,' said one of his aides, Honório Van Dunem.

In Luanda, the CCPM was still holding meetings but Salupeto Pena's abrasive rhetoric was not conducive to harmony. He would fly into rages outside the CNE and CCPM buildings where Anstee was calling meeting after meeting without moving nearer to a resolution to the crisis.

Salupeto Pena would not be calmed down, warning that publishing any further results would bring disaster to the country: 'Now the situation is so grave we cannot imagine a possible publication of such fraudulent results because that will be taking the country to catastrophe.'

The CNE decided to take his warnings of chaos seriously and postponed the announcement of the results, which were to have been declared publicly on 9 October, hoping that somehow the situation would be defused peacefully.

✝

Luanda is a town of rumours and periodically a story would sweep through the markets and *musseques* that the final results would be announced that day and war would break out. People would stay home from work and the streets would become deserted. Even the UN offices downtown would be empty of local staff. Usually they were back at work the following day, but nervously awaiting the next round of rumours.

Every day there were more Ninjas stationed on more street corners and more roadblocks erected by UNITA. Every day there were fewer areas where one could walk around freely in Luanda. Suddenly the foreign business people had left the Meridien and the hotel was filled instead with diplomats and journalists looking for a safe place to stay. More guards were stationed at the entrance.

In the provinces, there were reports of UNITA troop movements in Huambo, Malange and Benguela, Huíla and Luena, where government officials said they were being harassed.

Holden Roberto, the ageing leader of the FNLA, decided to revive his old alliance with Savimbi, who had served as his foreign minister briefly in a revolutionary government in exile before Savimbi formed UNITA in 1961. Roberto flew down to Huambo and he and Savimbi issued a joint statement along with four tiny opposition parties to the effect that the country would be plunged into chaos if the results were published.

✝

The first shot of the new war went off at 4 a.m. on 11 October and like most people in Luanda I slept through it. I thought I felt the floor shake in my patchy dreams but I was too exhausted to get out of bed and check. Only in the morning, when I turned the radio on as I was getting dressed, did I realise that it had not been a nightmare. I dressed and ran down to the Turismo Hotel with Howard and Paul Ames from Associated Press. We found Salupeto Pena outside, warning of a holocaust to come.

It was a car bomb, not too big, parked a comfortable distance in front of the hotel. No one had died, but the vehicle was mangled and charred and some of the front panels of the hotel had been ripped off in the blast.

Salupeto Pena seemed stoned. He was surrounded by a forbidding group of UNITA men in uniforms holding RPGs and AK-47s who eyed us with hostility as though we knew who was to blame.

'If anyone touches O Mais Velho there will be war,' he said. 'This is a very serious matter.' He kicked a piece of broken glass as the men holding the guns stared angrily at us.

Walking back to our hotel to file our stories, Paul and I debated whether UNITA itself had planted the bomb. It seemed to have been placed too far away from the Turismo to cause serious damage. An hour later I ran this theory by Howard, as he processed his film from the bomb blast. He never got the chance to reply. Suddenly RPG fire thundered out from the street. I ran to the window to see a dozen white doves flapping frantically above the tiled roof of the Turismo.

There was brilliant sunlight, the streets were completely empty and the bay was glittering; it was an oddly picturesque scene for a battle. The volleys continued as we ran down the 21 flights to the street, the shooting echoing exaggeratedly between the buildings. We tried to hail one of the Zairian taxi drivers who was usually parked outside the Meridien, but he refused to take us and instead searched for somewhere to hide. Everyone else had vanished from the streets; houses were

112

shuttered up, metal bars closed over the doors. The only people circulating were Ninjas, crouched in doorways with guns cocked. Four soldiers ran by, carrying a fifth who was moaning in pain. The wounded man's leg was soaked with blood and his trousers were ripped above the knee. They had come from the direction in which we were heading.

Howard had covered various conflicts as a photographer and I took my lead from him. He was trying to get into the streets while everyone else was trying to get off them.

As we ran past the CNE building a policeman ordered us inside. Part of me wanted to stay with the dozen other people in the sanctuary of the building. Internally I nodded as the policeman said: 'You can't go out, it's unsafe. You have to stay here.'

Howard didn't speak Portuguese so he enlisted me to negotiate our way out of this one. 'Tell him it's our job.'

'It's our job, we have to go outside,' I said in Portuguese. '*Temos que ir. É preçiso trabalhar. É URGENTE,*' I added with emphasis.

'Too bad,' the policeman said. 'It's my job to protect your safety.'

'Tell him if he doesn't let us out it will be dangerous for *his* safety,' Howard said. He was tired of this prevaricating. 'We're going,' he said and we pushed our way out towards the empty streets. The policeman didn't resist.

Minutes later we were in front of the Turismo, where several agitated Portuguese journalists were milling about. They said UNITA was inside the building holding hostage 12 policemen whom Salupeto Pena had threatened to kill. Some Portuguese journalists were inside the building broadcasting live to Lisbon from a telephone. There were shells on the ground but few holes in the building. The thing about RPG fire is that although it makes a lot more noise it is less precise than rifles. It struck me as a strange choice of weapon; if they wanted to shoot to kill they would have used AK-47s.

The Portuguese journalists outside the building explained to us that there had been a heavy exchange of RPG fire in the vicinity after a gunman in an unmarked black car fired on guards outside the building.

'Then all hell broke loose,' said one of the journalists. She was flustered and kept looking in the direction from which the car had come.

Suddenly volleys of fire erupted from around the corner where the post office was. UNITA and the MPLA were shooting at each other again. Everyone scattered; I realised that Howard had vanished. I figured that he had gone in the direction of the shooting and went to look for him.

I wasn't really thinking clearly and didn't honestly know what to do in this sort of circumstance. All I could think about was following Howard and whatever was happening. I certainly wasn't thinking about the consequences of getting in the middle of the action.

It was not the wisest thing to do.

UNITA had taken up sniper positions on one of the top floors of the post office. Government police were on the other side of the huge square, several hundred metres away, shooting back at them. Their aim was not precise and most of the shots were missing their targets. This made me nervous as I was right in the middle with only a thin sapling as cover.

There wasn't even a car to hide behind. Bullets were pinging by. So I crouched against the wall of the police station, trying to appear very small and hoping that if I looked in the direction of the snipers they'd leave me alone. I figured that they had better things to do than shoot a foreign female but I worried that with all of UNITA's anger against the UN someone might bear a grudge against whites. It's odd what one thinks about at times like that. I kept looking at the pistachio-green post office, which was a lovely example of colonial architecture, thinking what a shame the facade was being chipped by the bullets. I realised only later, when my heartbeat wouldn't slow down, just how scared I had been.

After one minute (or was it two? five? 30? I really couldn't tell) there was a lull and I ran to the end of the square, turned the corner and galloped into the entrance of the police station. The police were busy protecting themselves but found enough time to lecture me about being out on the streets at a moment like this. My calves continued to tremble and there was a sour storm of bile in my stomach. I was fretting about sending out a story and feared my news editors in London would be displeased because I hadn't filed yet. But the police were adamant that I stay inside for the time being.

'Are you crazy? You could be killed,' one of them said, shaking his head. 'I wouldn't go out there unless I was ordered to.' He looked at this weird American who appeared to have no normal regard for safety. 'You foreigners are mad.'

After about half an hour, a truce was called and I cautiously peeped outside my hiding place. Someone shouted a name, 'João!', and we all looked up. A policeman and a UNITA soldier trotted across the square and embraced. They casually chatted, guns in hand, as though it were the most normal thing to do. Except for the ammunition shells on the empty street they could have been two neighbours stopping to gossip on their way to the beach. Pleasantries exchanged, the men waved goodbye cheerfully and returned to their positions.

I didn't know what to make of this bizarre scene. Were the two sides deliberately missing their targets so that they didn't kill their friends? Where had the two men known each other? Why was this nation falling apart if ordinary Angolans didn't want to shoot each other? The oddest thing about it was that I seemed to be the only one marvelling at the scene.

✛

The skirmish was pretty minor by military standards and most diplomats dismissed it as an isolated event. At most, five people had died in sporadic battles across the city that day. It had sounded very loud because of the RPGs and the amount of firepower employed. One diplomat estimated that the ammunition used could have slain 300 people if fired properly. The fact that casualties had been so low seemed to prove his theory that the aim was to intimidate, not to kill.

'The boys are letting off steam,' was how he put it.

My editor called me from Johannesburg to get a reading on the situation.

'Do you think this is the start of war?' he asked.

Having never covered the start of a war I honestly couldn't say. I repeated the view of the diplomats.

'Fine,' he said. 'Stay on for a couple more weeks.' He paused. 'If it's war, stay on also.'

✝

For many Luanda residents, the battle, if that is the word, was a shock. Since 1975 the civil war had not spread to the capital. No one knew what was happening now. It seemed each day another section of Luanda was declared off-limits by UNITA. In São Paulo, the normally quiet residential area where UNITA had its campaign headquarters, roadblocks were set up. Barriers were also erected around Savimbi's villa in the diplomatic area of Miramar. Diplomats estimated that UNITA had maybe 3 500 to 5 000 armed men in the city. You had to negotiate with an armed man at a barricade if you wanted to pass. The men were wearing their uniforms now, in flagrant violation of the peace accords which Salupeto Pena insisted, at CCPM meetings, UNITA was still respecting. But if they wanted peace, why was fighting breaking out on the road to the president's palace, the airport and the UNAVEM complex? Armed UNITA men were roaming around the provinces. Was Luanda next?

Bombs began to go off. They were little ones, but ever closer to where the foreigners were staying. A few exploded near the

116

main UN building downtown, close to the Meridien. No one claimed responsibility but most people in Luanda suspected UNITA.

The government, meanwhile, was doing what it could to react with its limited resources. Its best defence was several thousand Ninjas. But aside from looking menacing, there weren't enough of them to take on UNITA. Everyone watched impotently as more barricades were put up.

✛

Every day hearsay, stories and conspiracy theories would circulate about what was happening in the interior of the country and even 30 kilometres outside the capital. My trusty UN source continued to telephone me when he heard an interesting snippet.

'Moxíco's fallen!' he said once, after UNITA had taken most of the municipalities in that eastern province. 'There's been a fire-fight in São Paulo!' he notified me another time. 'Listen to this: one of the Portuguese diplomats could not get to his residence. UNITA stopped him at the barricades,' was another tip. And then: 'Police had a shoot-out with UNITA in Cassenda. Four people died.'

I wanted to believe that these were all wild rumours circulated by people under intense pressure. But, disturbingly, every day a coherent picture was emerging of assassinations of MPLA officials in the provinces, attacks on airports elsewhere and mobilisations of uniformed UNITA men everywhere. By 15 October the country was effectively partitioned in half – and we didn't even realise it.

Those of us in Luanda were out of touch with the rest of the country. There was little reliable information. Most of the 400 electoral observers had left by then. The propaganda put out by the state media couldn't be trusted. Nor could assertions by UNITA. I had a vague idea that UNITA was harassing

UNAVEM personnel and government officials in the countryside. But most of this was happening in towns where the UN had no presence. By the end of October UNITA had run the local administrators out of a dozen villages in the central highlands. But everyone was too busy with events in Luanda to notice.

I, personally, was wrapped up in trying to cover endless CCPM meetings and canvassing four sets of mediators and two adversaries. I also had to monitor the regular radio bulletins, track election results and run between five embassies. I didn't comprehend what was going on elsewhere and didn't have time to think about it, let alone eat a proper meal. I ate rolls left over from my breakfast tray as I recorded the evening broadcasts. I showered with the television in the background. With everything collapsing around me I was not really detached, but was too submerged in the logistics to make sense of what was taking place.

Meanwhile Manuela's health had deteriorated and I was often operating on my own, sometimes working through the night without sleep. Except for one day-trip to Huambo, my news editor could not afford to let me leave Luanda and the satphone, which would have meant no news while I was away. My UN source was good at informing me about events, but more often than not it was impossible to verify his tips. Most of the foreign journalists had left by now and few of those who remained went outside Luanda. UNITA quietly gained territory without proper witnesses.

✝

Just when it seemed the UN and the Troika were getting nowhere in containing the situation, a sturdy man with a drooping moustache and a gravelly voice arrived in Luanda on 12 October, promising to save the day.

Roelof 'Pik' Botha of South Africa was one of the longest

serving foreign ministers in the world and certainly one of Pretoria's most resilient characters. The Americans were seen as traitors by Savimbi; South Africa was the last hope, the only foreign power deemed capable of influencing Savimbi and leading him away from the brink of war.

South Africa had refrained from publicly pronouncing on the freeness and fairness of the elections, assuming a neutral stance to avoid alienating Savimbi. What endeared South Africa further to UNITA was that several people in its government, including the Luanda embassy's defence attaché Johann Smith, were old-guard Afrikaners who had long ties with Savimbi. Smith had spent several years at Jamba training UNITA forces. He bore scars on his arms and on his forehead and dragged his leg in a limp from wounds suffered in Angola. When asked how long he had been in Angola, Smith would reply: 'Officially or unofficially?'

Hovering around Botha was Sean Cleary, a former foreign affairs official with close links to UNITA. Botha used Cleary as a 'facilitator' on this mission, shuttling between Huambo and Luanda for one week with piles of documents aimed at saving the peace process.

Botha's first visit to Huambo, on 13 October, seemed to go well. He was received by Savimbi for four and a half hours and presented a plan for a power-sharing, coalition government in the name of national unity. He came back to Luanda that night smiling.

Botha stayed on a floating boat hotel in Luanda harbour which was frequented by prostitutes and thus known colloquially as the 'Love Boat'. I'd stop by there nearly every day, as part of my reporting rounds.

Manuela and I had a seven-pronged strategy as we rushed around in cars: she'd man the CNE and CCPM meetings and follow the ministers. I'd cover UNITA, the South Africans, UNAVEM and the Americans. We split the Portuguese. Sometimes we'd have to enlist the help of another reporter or form a sort of ad hoc reporting pool. A few times Howard picked up some quotes for us. We were stretched to the limit; there was too much going on and we couldn't keep track of it all.

The best time to find Botha at the Love Boat was in the evenings, after he had finished his consultations with the other mediators. That was when he held court to the foreign press, giving informal briefings which embarrassed his aides. Botha had a dramatic style of oratory and a tendency to improvise, particularly at the end of the day.

'We South Africans will do anything to help this peace process,' he proclaimed on the deck one night, forelock hanging in his eyes and suit slightly rumpled.

His aides cringed. One of them moved forward, as though to stop him, but Botha would not be stopped.

'One thousand peace observers, if necessary. No, 5 000. If it takes 50 000 we will provide them,' Botha thundered, reaching a crescendo. He looked at us intently. We looked back, flabbergasted.

Before we could ask any questions, the aides took action.

'I think the minister has a meeting and is very tired,' one aide said, taking Botha by the elbow and steering him as quickly as possible into the interior of the boat. Botha turned and waved coyly over his shoulder.

✣

On 15 October, I finished my ninth story of the day and was preparing with Howard to shut down the satellite telephone for the night. It was just after 1 a.m. when the sound of a massive explosion ripped through the air. It felt like an earthquake was shaking our tall hotel building.

Outside the window the sky turned yellow, mauve, salmon, pink and orange as flares and rockets arched across the sky. They burst and popped in the air, illuminating the overcast night sky like neon. It looked as though the blasts were coming from the direction of the president's palace at Futungo. And it wasn't stopping.

The telephone rang: my UN source. 'It's the ammunition dump by the airport,' he said, and hung up.

I hastily filed a story to London while Howard leaned out of the window and snapped frame after frame of film. After an hour the explosions were still lighting the sky. Journalists staying in other rooms ran into ours to find out what was happening. Howard had developed his film by now and was transmitting it via the satphone.

There was an insistent knock on the door. This time it was Johann Smith, the defence attaché of the South African embassy.

'I'll take you there. Let's go,' he said. He led Howard and me as we ran down the 21 flights, through the hotel entrance, and into his jeep.

'I had one of my protective urges,' Johann said by way of explanation as we climbed into his vehicle. 'I knew you'd try to go, so I thought I'd better take you there myself. It's much safer this way.'

I followed them into the chilly night unthinking, with the blind trust that characterised my reactions in those days. I couldn't digest what I was seeing. We barely spoke during the 20-minute ride. We were tired. We didn't know what we were going to see. One boiled with adrenalin at moments like this and the pressure of work clouded one's judgement. All one could think about was pursuing the story – instead of sleeping like a normal person.

The only people on the streets were police. Few street lights were working but Johann knew Luanda well and could navigate with just his bright lights on. Several Ninjas tried to stop us at roadblocks but Johann just waved his diplomatic pass impatiently and we went through. As we neared the site of the explosion we passed dozens of women and children running, terrified and barefoot, away from the heat by the side of the road, bundles of precious belongings piled on their heads. Rockets and mortars were still going off. We dared not go too close and we parked the car several hundred metres from the explosion site and listened to the popping noise. After a while Johann drove us back to the hotel. I stayed up all night, unable to sleep.

It was only after daybreak that we got a fuller idea of the extent of the damage. Howard and I took a car and picked up some police who were hitching by the side of the road to get through security at the gate of the ammunition dump. The earth was still smouldering and tips of missiles were poking out of the brick-coloured earth.

The guards at the entrance told us it had all begun when someone, ostensibly from UNITA, fired at one of their men. Another policeman said a grenade had been tossed. About 13 people were killed in gunfire between government forces and UNITA after the explosion. UNITA denied any responsibility, but suspicions were raised by similar explosions at ammunition dumps in the provinces.

Again, I followed Howard's lead. We nonchalantly inspected unexploded missiles, unaware of the dangers buried below. We blithely pointed out Russian labels to each other and mused on the amount of money invested in such a cache. It didn't even occur to me that I could easily have lost a leg if I stepped in the wrong place. Reuters had trained me well in the ways of financial reporting, not what to do when someone blows up an ammunition dump.

Fortunately, our ignorance had no serious consequences. We proceeded safely out of the gate with all our limbs intact.

After all that risk-taking, I didn't even write a story. By the time we got back to the hotel to file, events had overtaken us. There was no time to write a description of the ammunition dump; there were election results and threats to report on.

✜

The CNE had been held hostage long enough by UNITA. The election officials decided that despite the intimidation they would announce the results. The ballots had been examined and re-examined. The CNE and UNAVEM were happy with what they saw. They weren't going to allow a bully like Savimbi to stop them. So they got the podium ready, informed the cameramen of the venue, and announced the outcome of the election on 17 October.

The final results were just what UNITA had wanted to stop: the MPLA had an absolute majority in parliament with 53,74 per cent of the vote. UNITA had 34,10 per cent. Dos Santos, with 49,57 per cent, fell short of the 50 per cent needed to avoid a second presidential round, while Savimbi won 40,0 per cent. Holden Roberto's FNLA came in third in the legislative vote with 2,4 per cent. About 4,4 million Angolans of the 4,8 million registered had voted.

Anstee declared the elections free and fair, despite some minor irregularities. Her verdict was endorsed by the Troika, the European Community and other international observers.

I was so tired that I did something that every news agency reporter dreads: I typed in the wrong numbers and sent them. This was despite the fact that the proper ones were written on the notepad next to my laptop. I quickly realised my mistake and rectified it with a telephone call to the news-desk in Johannesburg. But I later wondered whether I was unconsciously scared of what the impact of the results announcement would be.

No one was surprised when shooting broke out in the two main cities, Luanda and Huambo. In Luanda, two MPLA supporters were shot dead in the city centre. In Huambo, police and UNITA members clashed. UNITA took several police officers hostage and blockaded government buildings and main thoroughfares.

I tried to get reaction from UNITA's perky PR woman. But she had left town.

For UNITA there were echoes of the Alvor accords, signed in 1975, which had set up a post-independence transitional government comprising the MPLA, UNITA and the FNLA. Fighting had broken out immediately and the MPLA had expelled UNITA. UNITA had set up its headquarters in Huambo, the MPLA declared its own government in Luanda, and the FNLA drifted slowly away. Now UNITA, feeling robbed of what it genuinely felt was its victory, had a sense of déjà vu.

'The peace accords have never faced such a great crisis (as this). It is on the brink of a great catastrophe. It is a repetition of 1975. We no longer have confidence in the government,' UNITA vice-president Jeremias Chitunda wrote during this time.

Chivukuvuku was more succinct in another memo: 'The whites are not ready to hand over Angola to UNITA.'

✦

Things grew even more tense. A couple of CNE officials were killed in Malange and on 16 October four people died when an explosion rocked Cuito airport. Two days later UNITA restricted traffic around the Turismo, São Paulo and the streets surrounding Savimbi's residence. UNITA soldiers shot at two houses near the Swedish compound in Luanda, forcing 70 Swedes and 13 Norwegians to evacuate to Windhoek.

Meanwhile, Anstee was frantically trying to set up a summit meeting between Dos Santos and Savimbi. But Savimbi balked at coming to Luanda on security grounds and Dos Santos refused to fly to Huambo. On 19 October, the Troika sent its three top Africa experts to help Anstee – Herman Cohen, Grigor Karasin of Russia, and Portuguese deputy foreign minister José Manuel Durão Barroso, who was the architect of the Biçesse accords.

On 19 October, Savimbi assured Sean Cleary that he would

finally come to Luanda to meet with the president. N'dalu flew to Huambo with Salupeto Pena to fetch him.

Pik Botha waited at Luanda airport for Savimbi to arrive from 11.30 in the morning until 5.30 in the afternoon in the debilitating heat. As one hour stretched into two and then into three and then six, Botha's frustration increased. He occasionally emerged from the air-conditioned VIP lounge, his hair matted on his forehead, shouting at his aides about the mix-up. At one point I heard the sound of glass breaking in the lounge. Botha emerged with his aides looking chagrined.

'What is going on? Get Sean on the phone,' Botha yelled at one of his aides.

But Cleary explained that Savimbi would not receive their calls. Finally, as the sun was going down, N'dalu and Salupeto Pena returned without Savimbi. Salupeto Pena explained that security was a problem and Savimbi was worried about his safety. But he added: 'In politics there are no closed doors.'

✢

The door was apparently still open for visits. The next day, Botha flew down to Huambo. Another plane, a Hercules C-130, followed with the Troika leaders, UNITA officials and a handful of us journalists.

When we landed in Huambo, it seemed pretty clear who was in charge. The UNITA flag was fluttering from the control tower at the airport and there were no government police in sight. We were escorted in the blue 4x4 vehicles that had been donated by the Americans. I thought I saw a flicker of irritation on Cohen's face. The road leading from the airport to Savimbi's headquarters, a stately white house that had once belonged to a rich Portuguese colonial, was lined with UNITA men in uniform holding AK-47s and RPGs.

At Savimbi's residence, which everyone called The White House, Botha greeted us with an optimistic speech about how he was assured that Savimbi was committed to peace and democracy. Botha rambled on about Savimbi's beliefs in a free-market economy, which seemed a bit irrelevant when the real question was whether or not there would be war.

I waited on the terrace for several hours while the meeting went on and chatted with the UNITA guards. I spotted an acquaintance from Luanda, one of the few whites in Savimbi's entourage who had worked for the party's mouthpiece *Terra Angolana*. He was the journalist who had been arrested at the Pope's rally back in June. Once a plump man, he had lost a lot of weight and was reticent to talk, only murmuring an aside at one point: 'Things are bad, they are really bad. I wish I could leave with you today.'

Vending machines dispensed coffee and tea but no food was served. I asked if I could use the satellite telephone to file a story and the guards took me to a room upstairs which was equipped with some formidable-looking radios. One guard, after much prodding ('We don't like to waste gas'), agreed to drive me around town. There was an eerie quiet, unlike most Angolan towns. The market looked empty for a weekday afternoon. Women were subdued and hurried through the streets with firewood on their backs and their eyes downcast. MPLA graffiti was painted over with the 'New Trousers' slogan on the main street.

Huambo had suffered some of the worst damage during the war, inflicted by the MPLA and the Cubans who had evicted UNITA in 1976. Hardly a building was untouched and the rails and carriages at the train station were rusted from years of disuse. There were fresh bullet holes now and newly shattered windows.

Guerrillas in fatigues were virtually the only people around. A handful of government police stood guard in front of the governor's palace, looking as though they wished they were somewhere else.

We returned to the house just as the meeting was breaking

up. Savimbi emerged, flanked by the observers who looked grim. He was dressed in a pale blue Nehru suit. In contrast to his wild radio broadcasts over the past few weeks, he was coherent and composed.

Savimbi said he didn't know if his party would permit him to take part in the elections, portraying himself as a reasonable man surrounded by irate supporters whom he did not completely control. He repeated his rejection of the election results but said he was willing to take part in a second round.

'I do not accept it happily, but I have said that there will be a second round and this will allow a way to overcome the crisis,' he said, slowly and deliberately. 'We will try a second round. But my party does not want this.'

Savimbi took a few questions from journalists about his intentions, but the answers were all very vague. He nodded his head to indicate our impromptu press conference was over and went back into his villa.

Darkness was falling and UNITA pressed us to hurry to the airport. The sky was overcast and it was about to rain. Our plane took off in the illumination provided by the headlights of three large vehicles.

On the way back to Luanda, Durão Barroso and Cohen were ashen-faced.

'It's not looking good,' Durão Barroso said.

'There's too much tension and too many guns. There's a lot of ambiguity here,' said Cohen.

On the aeroplane I sat with UNITA's Washington representative, Jardo Muekalia, and Salupeto Pena and Chivukuvuku. Muekalia was friendly, showing me photos of his children back in the US. We chatted about monuments and museums in Washington and the advantages of raising a family there. It was hard to imagine him in the bush instead of an office.

The other two were characteristically hostile. As we landed in Luanda, Chivukuvuku asked if I could give him a lift back into town from the airport. When I agreed, he asked mockingly:

'Aren't you scared to be near a terrorist?' I said I wasn't frightened of him and that some people didn't consider him a terrorist, but a man who believed in a cause. The reply wasn't reassuring. 'Well, maybe you should be scared of us. You're not safe.'

✝

Pik Botha went back to Pretoria soon afterwards, his mission far from accomplished. 'They see us as their father,' he was quoted as saying in the South African press, describing his reception by Savimbi. But his paternalism backfired, and in fact Botha succeeded in cutting himself off as the only possible international mediator at the time.

Not only did he fail to dissuade Savimbi from war but Botha also alienated the MPLA government, which was enraged by what it saw as double-crossing by Pretoria and behind-the-scenes dealings by Cleary.

What angered the government in particular was the compromise Cleary proposed, which satisfied UNITA's desire for a strong regional government in the Planalto. It also opportunistically served as a blueprint for the type of federalist system Botha's ruling National Party was trying to promote back in South Africa. The MPLA did not like the power-sharing proposals which essentially gave UNITA a bigger weight than it was due in terms of the electoral vote and ignored the political system agreed upon under the Biçesse peace accords. It was little wonder that Botha was declared persona non grata a couple of weeks later, and Cleary was forbidden to set foot in Angola again.

The MPLA's suspicions of the South Africans, who had armed UNITA during the war, worsened with reports of flights coming into Mucusso, a UNITA base near the border with Namibia, where pilots claimed they were carrying humanitarian aid to the town's hospital. The MPLA insisted that the cargo was military. Added to this suspicion were complaints of violations of airspace by Botswana, Zimbabwe and Namibia, all of which reported mysterious flights from South Africa to Angola. There were more than a dozen supply flights from South Africa to Angola in late October, according to the Harare-based Southern African Research and Documentation Centre. The South African government's official line was that it would not get militarily involved. But diplomats suspected there were individuals acting privately who were helping the UNITA cause.

+

The mind works in strange ways when a siege mentality kicks in. Suddenly, running up and down the 21 flights of stairs at the Meridien seemed not like a nuisance but a good way to keep up my physical strength. One looks at a shampoo bottle and calculates how long the drops will last. The chambermaids at the Meridien complained that guests were hoarding packets of soap and toilet paper. Manuela and her husband had been through it before and they set up a private store of syringes, bandages and antibiotics. They also bought all the preserved food that they could find. The prices of pasta and canned goods rose in the private foreign exchange stores. So did the dollar price on the black market.

One day while out driving, Mena and I took a wrong turn and found ourselves at a UNITA roadblock in São Paulo. I had a green pass which had been distributed during the elections which said 'UNITA, free transit' but the men at the barricade rejected it. Offers of cigarettes didn't impress them. There was no negotiation; we couldn't pass.

On the way back to the hotel I asked Mena how he felt living in a city where the police couldn't maintain order and where he couldn't drive where he wanted. He used the word *prêso*, prisoner.

'Eat up, this could be our final supper,' joked Nikola.

He was a huge journalist turned restaurateur from the former Yugoslavia. Like many other correspondents from the former Eastern bloc, he had gone to Angola in the 1980s to report on the war at a time when Westerners had little access to the country. Nikola had fallen in love with and married the tiny woman who had been assigned as his MPLA minder. Now she staggered under huge trays of crabs and black beans, salads and puddings, freshly baked rolls and rice and potatoes in what was billed as a 'pre-war feast'.

In the kitchen there were bags of dried and canned goods and crates of bottled water. Nikola was not taking chances. The food smelt delicious but I wasn't very hungry. As elsewhere in the city, the talk turned to 'what if'.

'You can't escape by bay,' someone pointed out, opening another bottle of *vinho verde*. 'UNITA could easily hit the boats from the shore with mortars.'

'What about the Love Boat?' I asked.

'Not seaworthy.'

Another lunch guest noted that if UNITA closed off the road to the international airport there would be no time to get to the UN airstrip out of town.

'We're stuck, like crabs in the mud,' he said, helping himself to more shellfish and cracking open a claw.

I was American and there was no official US embassy as diplomatic relations with Angola did not formally exist. Unlike the diplomats and UN officials, I did not have a walkie-talkie. If all hell broke loose and the phones went down no one would know how to contact me. A day earlier my trusty UN source had told me: 'If it comes to that, I'll do my best to get you out. So stay at the Meridien, or somewhere where other foreigners are grouped. I can't guarantee anything, though. You're here at your own risk.'

Lots of other foreigners had moved into the Meridien for safety, including the American liaison officer Jeffrey Millington who was now travelling around with bodyguards. The hotel became like an enclave of nervous expatriates. UNAVEM personnel were being recalled from the provinces after several were attacked. Anstee received death threats on *Vorgan*. Embassies began to evacuate non-essential staff and their families. Regular scheduled international flights were being cancelled and the government had closed the February 4 International Airport more than once. The waiting lists for departing flights of panicking businessmen, who had come to Luanda just three weeks earlier hoping to cash in on a new democratic reconstruction, stretched until Christmas.

A new crowd had arrived: the merchants of war. Men wearing gold neck chains and of Middle Eastern descent who were vague about the nature of their business sat in the leather seats of the lobby, talking softly about shipments of food, arms, soft drinks and batteries – anything needed during long periods of shortage. One Lebanese man I met had just come from the chaos of Zaire, seeking to cash in on Angola's uncertainty.

'I hear there's a lot of opportunities in Angola now,' he said, handing me a business card. It only gave his name.

Manuela was no longer working at night because she was too scared to drive after dark. Like many other Angolans, she was observing a self-imposed curfew. Several clubs and restaurants had closed temporarily, complaining that business had dried up. Others shut their doors when darkness fell. Likewise, Mena went home as soon as the sun set. The journalistic adventure wasn't as much fun as before.

Even during the day, the streets were increasingly empty. The tension was almost palpable; a lot of people even stopped going to the beach. The clouds made it worse. The rainy season was coming and the sky was grey and heavy with moisture. But the clouds just wouldn't break and there was no relief from the pressure.

The pictures which Howard had put on the darkroom wall clearly depicted the narrative as it unfolded. The frieze started with the celebratory faces of young campaigners, then led to pictures of explosions and a wounded soldier, and ended with weeping hostages.

Howard just wanted to get out of Angola. He had run out of things to photograph and Luanda no longer offered a visual story. There was troop activity elsewhere in the country, but he wasn't anywhere near it.

As for myself, I was feeling quite tense. Part of the problem was that we didn't know what was going on. UNITA was still attending CCPM meetings. Officially there was peace. But until someone declared something, we didn't know what was going to happen. Reuters was keen for me to stay on; they didn't have another Portuguese speaker free to travel and it would be foolish for me to leave until the situation shifted one way or the other. I felt I ought to comply. It would be irresponsible not to follow the story through. But I was scared of being caught in the middle of a conflict without an exit.

I wanted to believe UNITA was bluffing but they seemed serious in the evenings as they passed through the Meridien lobby on their way to consultations with the Americans or the United Nations, brazenly wearing their uniforms. The talks were leading nowhere and the rhetoric was growing more bellicose.

Since I couldn't go out after dark, after filing my final story of the night I would often go down to the lobby and try to find someone who could explain to me what was going on. Chivukuvuku was often there. One time, around midnight, after proclaiming that Angola would become 'another Somalia' if UNITA officials were arrested, he grabbed my arm as our paths crossed near the elevator.

He was wearing a green safari suit sort of outfit and looked very stern. 'I think you're a nice girl,' he said. 'So I'm telling you that you ought to leave. People don't like you and you're not safe.' He increased the pressure on my arm, to make his point.

I tried to shake off his hand.

'It's not safe. Get out while you can, before it's too late.' He let me go, saying: *Tem cuidado* – Take care.'

I thought he was probably just trying to intimidate me but I figured it was worth getting a second opinion. I asked a diplomat if I needed to worry about Chivukuvuku's remarks.

'Well, you don't know,' he replied. 'They could be just bluffing. But if they feel cornered the first thing they're going to do is take hostages. A foreign journalist who pisses them off would be a good candidate. I don't want to feel responsible if you find yourself chained to a radiator.'

✦

Reuters finally agreed I should leave Angola for a short while to get some rest. I was beginning to make sloppy mistakes in my writing and was so tired I would nod off sitting in front of my laptop. If things continued as they were, I wasn't going to be much use. We had an intuition things would worsen and reasoned that, after a period of five weeks in Angola, much of it working through the night, I should have a break and then return later on.

I left on 22 October. Manuela and her little daughter came to the room to say goodbye and I felt like I was abandoning them to a terrible fate. I went through my telephone book, giving her contacts in Portugal in case they wanted to leave Angola and needed to look for work. Manuela had admired my pocket-sized short-wave radio and I gave it to her as a present. I hoped it would be useful if she needed to cover a new war.

Reuters had issued me with a plastic case of emergency

medicines and I put the contents into Manuela's eager hands for her private pharmacy. The little girl played with the boxes strewn on the bed and we had to watch her to ensure she didn't swallow anything. Some of the labels were written in English and I laboriously translated what the medicines were for and how much to take. Manuela scrawled the instructions in Portuguese on the boxes.

'This is for burns,' I said, indicating a tube of yellow salve. I peered at a box of pills. 'These are to be taken in cases of shock. I think these tablets are painkillers. And the one with the blue label? It appears to be for infections.'

There were some tampons at the bottom of the case.

'I know what those are for, you don't need to explain,' Manuela said, with a wry look. 'And you know what? They're also good for plugging up bullet holes.'

✝

The Angolan Airlines TAAG plane was delayed for several hours and I sat in the waiting room at the airport with two other colleagues fearing that we wouldn't get out. Unexpectedly, Johann Smith got through the airport guards with his diplomatic pass and came to say goodbye. He looked bereft when boarding for the flight was finally announced.

'Wish I was on that flight,' Johann said, wistfully. 'I have a bad feeling it's going to get a lot worse here.'

The plane was full and the passengers were either relieved-looking businessmen happy to be leaving Luanda or diamond smugglers. Quite a few of them appeared to be Zairians; they spoke only French. They did not appear to be professional smugglers but poor couriers instead. Someone must have advised them to wear their best clothes on the plane and they had taken it seriously. They looked as though they were dressed for a high school prom. The men wore tuxedos and the women scarlet or peacock blue satin dresses with puffed princess sleeves and big bows. They fumbled awkwardly with their seat belts. I assumed it was their first plane journey.

The girl next to me, resplendent in an emerald green outfit, insisted in impeccable French that she was Angolan but she spoke no Portuguese. I asked her in my appalling French what she planned to do in Johannesburg and she replied: 'Shopping'. The girl stuffed bread into her pockets and took my unused sugar packets and butter. She drove the stewardess mad, hitting the assistance button every few minutes to ask for more bread rolls, which by now she was hiding under her skirt. At one point something small and shiny rolled out of her sleeve. She caught it deftly and put it back in its hiding place.

Flying into Johannesburg I felt as though I had been away for five years instead of five weeks. It was dark, dry and cold compared to muggy Luanda. Howard and I dropped off our equipment at the office in town and went our separate ways. I went home feeling disorientated and extremely lonely but in no mood to talk to anyone. The house seemed overwhelmingly empty and I decided to take a long hot bath to relax. At 9.10 p.m., while I was rubbing off five weeks of grime and feeling very confused, a bomb went off outside the Meridien Hotel in Luanda. It blasted out the windows of the Banco do Comercio e Industria next door.

✛

UNITA was expelling UNAVEM from provincial towns within an 800-kilometre radius from Huambo. The UN was still trying to pursue negotiations with Savimbi, hoping that he would listen to reason. On 21 October, UNITA vice-president Jeremias Chitunda flew up to Luanda from Huambo with other party delegates and there were intense discussions at the CCPM for the following nine days. On 26 October the UN Security Council urged Savimbi to open a dialogue with Dos Santos and to respect the peace accords. Two days later, Secretary

General Boutros Boutros-Ghali put out a statement condemning the death threats against Anstee on *Vorgan* and expressing frustration over the fact that she could not reach Savimbi by telephone.

Back in Johannesburg I felt dazed and flat, unable to concentrate on much, like a deep sea diver coming out of compression. I had grown accustomed to living in a small hotel room and the space in my large suburban house and garden seemed overwhelming. Despite being away for a while, I only contacted friends who had some link with Angola. I camped out in the living room and virtually didn't venture out of it, listening continuously to news bulletins on the short-wave radio. There was little news about Angola but what broadcasts there were described thousands of UNITA men marching towards Caxito, capital of Bengo province, 90 kilometres north of Luanda.

Then, on Saturday 31 October 1992, Luanda went to war.

✤

The first news was sketchy. The report on the short-wave radio from Angola was that fighting had broken out around Luanda's airport and in Huambo. It was only later that the details emerged. According to the state media, if it was to be believed, early in the morning of Saturday 31 October, about three dozen UNITA men took up positions around the airport. They tried to get to the cargo terminal at around 2.20 in the morning but were repulsed. A Hercules C-130 was riddled with bullets, an underground fuel tank was hit by a shell and 14 cars were ruined.

Earlier, in the poor neighbourhood of Cassenda near the airport, 13 people were killed, including three Portuguese who were shot dead by UNITA on their way out of a discothèque near Chivukuvuku's house.

The incident followed a charged CCPM meeting. UNITA

had been planning to hold a rally in central Luanda, its first since the elections. But the government refused to authorise it and Salupeto Pena called the gathering off. The discussion at the CCPM meeting centred on confrontations in Huambo that had occurred during the past two days. UNITA had shelled the government police station and tried to take several government buildings, including the governor's palace and the radio and television stations. Houses had been sacked in the Benfica neighbourhood and UNITA took several prisoners, including an army general and two colonels. UNITA also surrounded the town of Lobito and occupied Cacula, Jamba-Mineira, Balombo and Chipinda.

Pressed by the MPLA side, Salupeto Pena insisted at the meeting that he had no information. 'There was a battle. In battle there is death, there are captives. Therefore I don't know,' was all he said.

+

Whether or not UNITA actually attacked the airport, the people of Luanda had had enough of bullying. A confrontation was probably inevitable and all they needed was a provocation like this. The MPLA let its men loose and ordered its supporters to kill every UNITA man, woman and child they could find.

Manuela's telephone had gone dead. The diplomats had gone into hiding. The reports coming over the BBC were of a full-scale battle for the city.

'Of course you don't mind going back?' my news editor said. More of an order than a question.

Of course not.

Willingness was one thing. Logistics and reality were another. All international flights were cancelled. It was impossible to get to Luanda via land. So Reuters and several other news groups chartered a Beechcraft ten-seater. The satphone took up most of the weight allowance.

'Don't let anything happen to it,' ordered my news editor. 'It costs a fortune to replace.' I wondered what I would do with it if we were suddenly under fire at the airport and had to run.

✣

I didn't get there to find out. While pandemonium was breaking out in Luanda, I was stuck in Rundu on the border between Namibia and Angola.

We had stopped in Rundu to refuel, as it was half-way to Luanda. But by the time the pilot had filled up the tiny plane and we had strapped on our seat belts and risen into the air, the fighting in Angola had increased to such an extent that the Luanda air controllers wouldn't let us land.

The pilot, a South African who claimed he used to fly for Savimbi, asked me sit up front in the co-pilot's seat in case something came over on the radio in Portuguese. The other journalists sat in the passenger seats in the back. We were a third of the way from Rundu to Luanda when the message crackled over that we should turn back.

'You can't land! UNITA has shot up another three planes. The government will shoot you too!' the voice said. It spoke in two languages just to make it clear.

We turned back in the air, the red earth of Angola below us.

✣

In Rundu, the pilot found us a room at the house of one of his friends. The six of us shared it, covering the floor with mattresses. We set up the satphone on the well-cropped lawn outside, hoping to find out what exactly was going on in Luanda.

I still couldn't get through to anyone. Our only news came from the hourly broadcasts of the BBC. The radio station had reached Nikola, the Croatian correspondent, who was one of

138

the few foreign journalists in Luanda now.

He reported a battle across the city on the Saturday and Sunday, like spontaneous combustion. Nikola had a panoramic view from his tall apartment building near the Meridien overlooking the bay. What he could see and hear was intense fighting as it swept from one UNITA hotel to another like brush-fire. He said the Turismo Hotel was completely raked by RPG and machine-gun fire. It had been reduced to a shell with bodies strewn on the stairwells and corridors, and its front facade was blown off in the mêlée. Smoke was rising all over the city.

✢

We didn't know it, but while we were trying to land UNITA was besieging the American compound. Diplomats were hiding under the containers, praying they wouldn't be shot. Anstee, meanwhile, was holed up at the British ambassador's residence. Everyone who had one was communicating on walkie-talkie radios.

One American diplomat maintains that what saved them were the radios they gave to a local commander who handed them over to Salupeto Pena and General Paulo Gato.

'Salupeto Pena was completely out of his mind, he seemed like he was high on something like coke,' the diplomat said. 'He was raving.'

UNITA men entered the American compound and told the Americans they wanted to escort them out 'to protect us'. They refused, fearing they would be taken hostage.

According to one of the diplomats trapped there: 'We knew we'd be in the soup if we left. We convinced them it was not a good idea to force themselves into the compound. On Sunday the firing grew worse and incoming rounds were coming in. So we moved under the containers, about a metre and a half of crawling space, to get protection from the mortars, and taped

139

the windows. We then lay on the ground and listened to the mortar rounds. There were occasional lulls but fighting basically continued into the night. That night UNITA tried to get in again and set up a defensive perimeter around the gate with a rocket launcher. They used the containers as cover. At about 1 or 2 a.m. the UNITA men took off in their convoy.'

UNITA officials insisted later that they had no plan to seize the city. Their version was that the MPLA used the alleged airport assault as a pretext. What was clear was that rogue elements were operating on both sides. Also evident was that UNITA was ill-prepared for the ferocity of the MPLA response. The MPLA and its supporters were bent on expelling or exterminating the invaders at any cost. The MPLA did not have an intact army but it had thousands of civilians who knew how to shoot and were happy to do so.

According to UNITA's economic chief, Fátima Roque, the fighting began at two in the afternoon at the Turismo Hotel, two hours before the CCPM meeting broke up. She said she had been warned that something was afoot and decided to remain in her hotel after the lunch break in the meeting. Roque said that by late afternoon on the Saturday, the fighting had spread to the *musseques*, and to the other hotels and offices used by UNITA. Similar fighting, but not as fierce, had broken out in the provincial cities of Malange, Lobito, Benguela and Lubango.

✢

By Sunday Nikola's dispatches were getting repetitive; there was a limit to what he could see and hear from his vantage point. What he didn't know was that from Friday 30 October, the government had called in civilians and had handed out thousands of guns to impromptu militias. The civilians reported to police stations and private houses. In some *bairros* they registered the weapons on laborious lists. In other areas, they simply handed them to any willing individual or went from door to door handing out guns.

My frustration at being stuck in Rundu was equalled by a feeling of trepidation about actually getting to Luanda and seeing the carnage myself. I worried about Manuela and her family but figured that she was probably safe, being street-wise and having a well-stocked private pharmacy and a food supply sufficient for a month underground.

The bonhomie and gung-ho-ism of my travel companions was beginning to grate on me. For them it was just another war, after a long string in Central America, the Middle East and Africa. 'What a great story. We'll be the first in,' one of them remarked. They'd just do a week or two in this conflict and move on to the next. They didn't know anyone who might be killed in Angola.

I walked along the river and looked at Angola on the other bank, being careful to stay on the shore because of the crocodiles. On the other side of the river was a ruined village whose small houses had been shattered a long time ago in a war which was officially over. At night I saw cooking fires burning; townspeople in Rundu said they were made by UNITA.

I thought what an odd place Rundu was for a stopover. It had been a base for the South African Defence Force during the time when the apartheid regime was fighting SWAPO rebels, the same rebels who now ran Namibia. It was also used as a refuelling stop for planes heading to Jamba. In those days Rundu was replete with troops and intrigue. Now it didn't have much besides two bars, a pool table and lots of Windhoek Special lager.

The locals were a bit suspicious of us at first, but they knew our pilot well and warmed up after a few beers at one of the bars. I asked one man what he thought of a new war in Angola. He looked at me blankly.

'But it's peace, man. It's all changed. Those days are over,' he said.

That Saturday night, UNITA's leadership was practically wiped out. Thousands of its members were hunted down in the *musseques* – chopped, shot, clubbed or sliced. People armed with kitchen knives, pistols, clubs and machetes went from door to door massacring anyone they suspected of belonging to UNITA. They killed as they shouted '*Kwacha, Kwacha*', the pejorative name for UNITA. Many victims were easy targets because, expecting to attend the cancelled rally, they were wearing baseball caps and T-shirts with Savimbi's picture or the letters UNITA. Those who could escape fled through sewage drains. Others shot their way out of town, hiding in the bush until they made it to safe houses 80 kilometres away. Others stole government army uniforms.

When they saw the Ninjas, armoured vehicles and militiamen advancing up the hill to Savimbi's house early on the Sunday morning, UNITA vice-president Jeremias Chitunda, Salupeto Pena, Ben Ben and Chivukuvuku decided they'd better flee. They formed a three-car convoy, hoping to escape the barrage, and they took as hostages two foreigners, David and Eleanor Chambers. The pair had hidden in the garden of the Swedish embassy next door, trying to escape the UNITA men. But they were found and escorted to Savimbi's house, where they spent a frightened night. When the convoy took off, police opened fire, killing the driver as well as most of the passengers including Chitunda and Salupeto Pena. The car in which the Chambers couple was travelling rolled over, but they miraculously survived.

Ben Ben was thought to have been killed also. Chivukuvuku's legs were shattered and he couldn't run. He was found by police who took him to the military hospital where he was held in custody.

Later that Sunday police and militia made their way to the Trópico where Fátima Roque, Honório Van Dunem and about three dozen women and children, including the family of Jaka Jamba, were hiding. They fled next door to the Tivoli and Carlos Amorim, the Portuguese hotel manager, stood in the entrance and prevented the police from taking them captive.

'The police burst in and stuck an automatic rifle in my stomach and demanded that I hand them over,' Amorim recalled. 'I refused. Fátima handed me her radio and I communicated with the UNITA colonel who was inside the Trópico. It took a lot of persuading; initially he said he was prepared to die defending the cause. But ultimately he agreed to surrender his weapons so that the police would not attack the people hiding here in the Tivoli. I was not going to allow blood to be spilled in my hotel.'

Amorim, who had his own network of walkie-talkie radios, helped evacuate Portuguese and South African citizens trapped in his hotel and elsewhere, an action for which he was later awarded Portugal's highest honour.

At 8 o'clock that night, UNITA's General Wambu made radio contact with colleagues who informed him that Ben Ben, Chitunda, and Salupeto Pena had been killed. Wambu was now effectively in charge and he called the government's General N'dalu on the radio to arrange a truce.

'He told me that if I could convince my men to stop fighting it would help. So I called Mango on the radio. He asked: "Are you sure N'dalu is sincere?" I said: "I know him. He is a serious and responsible man." So N'dalu agreed they would stop firing if they could get word out. I convinced Mango he should stay put until the combat stopped. But Carlos Morgado (Savimbi's doctor) told me there was disagreement about the matter among the men. In less than ten minutes we heard shots. My last communication with Mango was at 23h40. He said: "I cannot convince my colleagues." The radio went dead.'

On the Sunday morning, while the UNITA men were fighting for their lives, we tried to get to Luanda again. The pilot shooed away the long-horned cattle sauntering on the Rundu landing strip as I packed up the satellite telephone. My stomach was sour with anxiety.

I sat in the front again. To pass the time, the pilot told us stories about when he flew for Savimbi. The passengers in the back swapped anecdotes, cheerfully spurring each other on with accounts of being beaten up in Iraq, mock executions in El Salvador and kidnappings in Somalia.

'We always went at night, flying just over the treetops. Man, we got to travel!' the pilot said. In the back someone was saying: 'And then they blindfolded everyone and put guns to their heads.'

'What did you think of him?' I asked.

'A gentleman. Charming.'

From the back: 'Then they cocked the rifles and said: "We'll shoot if you move."'

I asked the pilot his opinion of the Luanda clashes. 'What do you think about what's going on now? Do you think Savimbi was responsible?'

'It doesn't make sense,' replied the pilot, turning up the radio to communicate with Luanda air control.

The message from Luanda was the same: It was too dangerous to land.

'We have to turn back,' the pilot said.

The air was dry and there were no clouds to obstruct our view of Angola. The pilot pointed out Huambo below, prompting calls for parachutes from the back of the plane.

'Let's go for it. No one is going to kill a bunch of white journalists,' someone said.

'Yeah, we can make it by lunch time,' another said.

'Not a chance,' the pilot said. We swung back towards

144

Rundu.

On the way back I felt that familiar mixture of relief and dread. 'A reprieve,' I thought, but didn't say as much out loud.

The pilot drew my attention to a conversation on the radio.

'That's a South African plane. It's flying into Mucusso,' he said. Mucusso was a UNITA base with a hospital that in the old days had been serviced by South Africa. It was close to Jamba.

'What would they be doing there now?' I asked.

The pilot fixed his eyes on the African sky ahead of him, and pushed a couple of buttons.

✛

Johann Smith was on the Love Boat, docked off the Ilha, looking at the mayhem from afar. I finally reached him on the satphone on the Monday, 2 November, while he sat in frustrated refuge with hundreds of frightened Portuguese citizens. It was still unsafe to drive around the city but he could view the fighting up at Miramar and reported APCs crashing into Savimbi's residence, backed by heavy artillery. UNITA tried to fire at the bay several times with mortars but missed. Johann sounded confused. He had fought for his country with UNITA in Jamba and had been very close to Jeremias Chitunda. Now his friend was dead.

'They've killed Jerry,' he said. 'Christ, they've killed Jerry.'

I could barely hear him because of all the gunfire in the background. At times he was completely drowned out by the sound.

'Those who aren't fighting are looting,' he said. Another boom went off.

I asked him if he was safe on the boat. 'UNITA tried to fire some mortars but they didn't reach the bay. It's like a refugee camp here. People are camped out all over the deck.'

Johann said much of the fighting centred initially in Miramar, where the embassies and Savimbi's house were located. The cemetery down the road became a battleground, with people using tombstones as cover. Many people hid in their houses; bodies were left on the sidewalks to rot because no one wanted to venture out. They could smell the putrid decay all the way to the Ilha.

By now, Monday morning, government tanks and armoured vehicles had moved into the final pockets of UNITA resistance. On Tuesday 3 November, police escorted the stricken Americans and stranded UN officials to the Meridien, which was beginning to resemble a luxury displacement centre.

The MPLA got rid of the bodies en masse, piling them into trucks or ditches. The city smelt like an open-air morgue. There were so many dead that they were thrown unceremoniously into mass graves or burned with the rubbish in the streets.

✤

We still couldn't get into Luanda.

After five days in Rundu, Reuters felt that spending thousands of dollars on a plane which was going nowhere and a reporter who wasn't filing anything was reason enough to call off the mission. We went back to Johannesburg, with me feeling mainly disappointed.

✤

By the time I finally got to Luanda – on Saturday 7 November on a UN cargo plane from Windhoek, a week after the fighting had broken out – they had removed most of the corpses from the streets.

I flew in with half a dozen other journalists, most of them specialists in war reporting. Because we were with the UN, the customs officials waved us through. There were no other arrivals.

The detritus of the battle was still fresh at the airport; there

146

were some new mortar holes and charred vehicles. A few stricken planes with bullet holes were paralysed on the tarmac. The streets were empty. Before finding a hotel we went to the UN office downtown, where the staff were still unshaven and dishevelled after the week's traumas.

People had been isolated in different parts of the city, but as we collected their accounts we began to get a fuller picture of what had taken place.

The tally of the dead was anywhere between 4 000 and 10 000. Even during the day the streets were empty, apart from the occasional military convoy, and a night-time curfew was in place. The windows of shops were boarded up, broken glass from the looting lay unswept in the streets. A shaky cease-fire agreement was under way in some major areas like Benguela and Lobito, and the UN was trying to negotiate with UNITA who had seized the giant Kapanda dam and had taken foreign hostages.

UN offices across the country had been sacked for food, medicines and other supplies like tents and vehicles. Looters had sacked the Turismo and taken beds, crockery and furniture. Eight UNITA generals and six brigadiers were in government custody in hotels or at the defence ministry. They were among the UNITA top brass – Generals Peregrino Wambu, Adriano MacKenzie, Junior Benguela, Jeremias Njahulo, Zacarias Mundombe, Andrade Chassungo Santos and Artur Bumba, and Brigadiers Renato Campos Mateus, Norberto de Castro, Aluaro Lutukuta 'Luwawa', Diamantino Kaluwawa, Malheiro Lohoca, Madaleno Tadeu and Colonel José Pombo Vilinga. Fátima Roque and Carlos Morgado were also in government hands. General Mango was dead. It was a huge coup for the MPLA.

Hospitals and morgues were filled; flies and dogs hovered around the bodies that had been hastily buried in public roads. Occasionally we'd drive by a mound in a traffic island or in front of a house and smell the stench of death.

In Viana cemetery, grave-diggers knocked down a wall

because they were running out of space to bury the bodies. Townspeople whispered of 'clandestine' mass graves and pointed to big mounds in the earth. At least these victims had been buried. At another cemetery, Camama on the edge of town, the overpowering smell of a decayed abattoir rose 200 metres outside the perimeter walls. The bodies of maybe 30 people had been thrown into a garbage pit and soil had been hastily bulldozed over them. The earth was covered with ordinary litter, like scraps of paper and juice cartons and bits of UNITA camouflage uniforms. Blood was still smeared on the brick-coloured earth. A UNITA baseball cap lay where the victims had been shot. At first glance it appeared the ground was covered with piles of excrement. Closer inspection revealed that the mess was from boxes of Nestlés cocoa which had been rotting in the rubbish dump, presumably from before the executions.

+

I booked into a room at the Hotel Meridien. There was no problem finding an available hotel bed. The hotel had a spooky, abandoned air and there were only about five guests spread between the 25 floors. The European management had fled and the local staff were unaccustomed to being in charge, handing guests the wrong keys for their rooms and allowing them to make international calls for the price of local ones. Room service and cleaning had stopped. My travel companions moved to the house of a British diplomat who had been evacuated. I needed a hotel with good communications because I was filing so much and decided to move to the Tivoli where the UNITA people were still being held captive and where armed guards stood reassuringly at the entrance.

The government propaganda machine was working overtime. It rejoiced in the humiliation of UNITA, publishing graphic pictures to serve as reminders. Huge photographs showed men sprawled on the tiled floor of what appeared to be a restaurant, face down in pools of blood, presumably after summary executions. Their trousers were pulled down to their knees, perhaps to stop them from running and to humiliate them further. Maybe they had been raped first. No caption was needed. The picture said it all: 'Don't fuck with us again, UNITA.'

The one thing the propaganda got wrong was the death of Ben Ben. The television news repeatedly showed images of a watch and a skull which were allegedly his, retrieved from the ill-fated UNITA convoy on the morning of 1 November. But he had escaped alive and walked the 95 kilometres to Caxito, dodging ambushes and sleeping in the bush. In Caxito he joined Generals Gato and Begin, who had also escaped the Luanda massacres, hiking for a couple of days in a long column of other UNITA members who had escaped. Waiting for them in Caxito was General Abilio Numa of the now fractured joint army. Ben Ben resumed command of UNITA's army and Numa went north to lead a new campaign.

✢

We went to the press centre shortly after visiting the UN office. The centre was normally the first port of call. In the past the building had buzzed with people trying to get the telexes to work or simply hanging out for lack of anything else to do. Now there was an empty quiet. Like most of the city, the press centre wasn't really functioning.

Four of the staff were sitting in the dirty leather chairs, in soiled clothes which reeked of perspiration. They said some of their colleagues had been trapped in the building during the siege weekend. Others had been in the *musseques* when the massacres began and were too scared to go outside. They were still quite shaken.

I felt shy about asking sensitive questions. But one of the men sidled up to me and volunteered some information.

149

'The killings are still going on in the *musseques*,' he said.

'I thought it had ended,' I said.

'No, they're still going on. It's nothing on the level of the previous weekend, however,' he said. He paused, looked at the floor and added: 'There doesn't seem to be a limit to how many more people they can kill. The streets were filled with soldiers. A lot of innocent people died. They didn't understand what was happening. They went to the market as normal and were shot along the way.'

He was whispering as though he feared someone would overhear him. The centre was run by the MPLA. None of the disappearances and ex-judicial killings he described had been mentioned by the state-run newspaper or radio. Were the massacres actually orchestrated by the authorities, and not a spontaneous eruption of rage as was being portrayed?

The previous war had been divided roughly along ethnic lines: the FNLA had the support of the Bakongos in the north, UNITA the Ovimbundu of the south and central plateau, and the MPLA the Kimbundu and *mestiços* of Luanda. But that was an oversimplification. There were members of all ethnic groups in each of the movements.

Now, however, according to this man from the press centre, there wasn't just a strong ethnic component. The way he described it, it was outright cleansing.

'They're targeting the Bakongos and the Ovimbundu. At first they killed everyone whom they knew were UNITA. But then it got out of control and they went after anyone suspected of being UNITA. Anyone who had the wrong accent got this,' he said, making a gesture like a cleaver coming down on a neck.

A couple of days later I ran the information by an acquaintance who was a card-carrying MPLA stalwart. He, too, told a similar chilling tale of slaughter. Normally he was happy to show me around the *musseques*, which were like dusty mazes of concrete houses that went on for miles. But now he didn't want to accompany me and warned me against finding another guide. Was it for my own safety, because I was white and might be mistaken for a UNITA supporter? Or was it because there was something he didn't want me to see?

It was strange to feel that the *musseques* were suddenly sinister places which I couldn't comfortably visit. In the past months I had spent endless hours there and never felt menaced. This new situation reminded me of South Africa, where many of the townships had no-go areas where an outsider had to be escorted by a local guide. Suddenly, now the *musseques* were inaccessible.

There was another thing which reminded me of South Africa: my acquaintance's impassive delivery. It was the same when you went to a township after a massacre or a necklacing and people stood around with that empty expressionless air about them.

He must have been a witness, I thought. How can you live in a crowded place where your neighbour's house is a metre away and not hear the sounds of a crowd knocking down his door and the baying for blood? How could you know they shouted 'Die, *Kwacha*, die' without seeing the murder? Maybe the truth lay in what he left unsaid. How could he not have participated? How could I expect him not to? Yet maybe he hadn't.

People like my acquaintance had survived the 1970s when thousands of MPLA supporters died in party in-fighting. They had remained quiet and kept their heads down. Was this any different?

Out of a sense of delicacy I didn't ask too many questions, in case he had lost someone he cared about. I didn't press him to describe what he had seen or heard. I felt it only polite not to reawaken the trauma of loss.

But it only struck me later that he wouldn't have lost anyone close. His family, being MPLA and Kimbundu, wouldn't have been killed.

I did, however, ask him if he joined in.

151

'No,' he said.

But I thought he hesitated a little too long before replying.

✤

At the press centre bar a lone figure was drinking – Mena. He had gone to the airport every day while we were stranded in Rundu, encountering army convoys and bullets as he waited in vain for our arrival.

'What do you think, Judite? Will I make a good journalist?' he asked. I pretended to punch him and told him he was a loyal fool.

In Mena's block of flats, where the MPLA had handed out weapons to all able-bodied men, red-eyed drunken activists with AK-47s and machine-guns had pounded on his door demanding to be let in to look for UNITA supporters. According to Mena, they seemed more interested in looking at his stereo system and short-wave radio. They decided that he, being white, must certainly be a UNITA supporter and returned on several consecutive days to question him at gunpoint.

'I don't even think they were soldiers,' he said. 'They were just kids on the block who were given rifles.'

Mena had a nice line of empty brandy glasses on the counter and looked like he hadn't changed his jeans and button-down shirt since the massacres. He insisted that what he had seen was nothing compared to 1975 when tens of thousands of Portuguese had fled.

'I don't believe in politics. No one can accuse me of anything or touch me,' he said. 'I stayed last time. I will stay this time. They will not force me to go. They will not break me,' he said resolutely.

✤

152

News travels quickly in Angola.

After I got back from visiting Benguela I didn't have to tell Manuela about the businessman whose paint factory was vandalised by UNITA, the magenta, indigo and ochre paints flowing outside the cracked building like a bitter parody of Jackson Pollock. I didn't have to tell her about the villager named Rosa whose house was shelled by the MPLA for supposedly being a UNITA member, where a row of graves adorned only by bits of broken glass marked where the MPLA supporters came in and slaughtered them. I didn't have to describe to Manuela the children with pus-infected artillery wounds who were too scared to go to hospital in case they were identified as UNITA.

I didn't have to tell her about the whites who were rounded up in Huambo and Cuito and shot in the head, or about the houses which were occupied and the cattle which were stolen. For Manuela, the echoes were all too strongly those of the violations she had suffered in 1975 when thousands of her countrymen left the country and she decided to stay behind.

Manuela hid in her house for a week after we arrived in Luanda and even when her phone was restored the lure of making money could not get her outdoors.

She had been assaulted in Uíge in 1975 and the Luanda massacres were a vivid flashback which evoked everything she had managed to bury. Even well after the shooting had stopped her three-year-old daughter continued to scream and didn't want to be separated from her mother.

They left shortly thereafter, to live in the back room of a crowded apartment in Porto with distant relatives. She made the wrenching choice to leave her husband Bento behind. Bento ran the bar at the press centre and had various other business ventures which he didn't want to abandon. This was a lifetime's work and investment.

Manuela and I had a fraught farewell. I gave her a hug and I knew this time it was a final goodbye.

'I'm getting out,' she said, holding the big-eyed child close to her for her own comfort as much as for the girl's. 'I can't live through this again. I should have left last time when I had less to lose.'

✛

I told Mena about Manuela's departure while we driving to Panguila, which was the nearest front line to Luanda, a mere 60 kilometres away. He insisted that he would never leave Angola.

The area around Panguila had fallen to UNITA a couple of weeks before and the road was deserted except for Mena's big white van and several tanks barely hidden in the tall grass by the side of the road. We had heard that UNITA had blown up two bridges and mined the road closer to Caxito and weren't sure how far we could go. A couple of days before, UNITA had robbed a five-car convoy of Portuguese and British journalists of thousands of dollars worth of cameras when they got to the spot we were heading towards now.

A woman clutching a tiny infant which must have been born a week before the elections suddenly ran out of the bush and stood in the middle of the motorway, frantically flagging us down. She climbed in, stinking of excrement and distress and covered with dirt. She said she had walked for three nights from Caxito, sleeping on the ground during the day. She had nothing but her little daughter with her and kept her hand over the baby's mouth to muffle its cries.

We reached a blown-up bridge. Four men jumped out of the grass, waving rusty AK-47s in our faces. Their eyes were bloodshot, and their uniforms were from the old MPLA army. Mena pulled out his tattered identification papers, but all they cared about was searching the car for food.

'Bread, bread?' one of them demanded as he went through the van. He even checked under the seats and inside the engine.

I had half a pack of cigarettes and a roll of peppermints which he grabbed. They waved us on, after kicking the van and telling us to turn back.

Mena did a U-turn and we turned back towards Luanda.

'There should be a third choice,' Mena said, slamming his heel into the accelerator. 'That's what's wrong with the country.'

Something was wrong. His face was red and tears were streaming from his brown eyes. I think Mena had met one soldier too many. He was reminded of the vigilantes who had demanded his television and accused him of being something he wasn't. I should have anticipated it coming. I was worried we wouldn't make it as he gripped the steering wheel and began sobbing.

We returned past the tanks hidden in the trees in the ancient grove of baobab trees that had witnessed the arrival of his ancestors 500 years before. We drove past the derelict tyre factories which had been deserted in 1975. All the way back the silence was punctuated by Mena's repeated murmurs: 'Both of them are as bad as the other. There has to be a third option. There has to be another way.'

The woman with the baby gestured for us to stop at the outskirts of Luanda. We drew up in front of a shuttered restaurant and she left in silence.

When we got back to the press centre Mena parked hurriedly and ran to the bar. He was still muttering: 'There has to be a third option. There has to be a third way.' He ordered one brandy and then another. When Mena was well into his fifth brandy, I walked back to the Tivoli past the Ninjas guarding shops whose displays had been emptied by looters. It was getting late and I wanted to be back before dark.

That was a Thursday. Mena didn't show up for work on Friday, Saturday or Sunday. On Monday, when he still hadn't appeared, I called his house.

In Portuguese some verbs are passive. When you fall or collapse or terrible things happen they use the passive – *se caíu*, something made him fall. You never just fall by yourself. When I telephoned Mena's home, whoever answered the telephone said that Mena had been sitting in the apartment staring in front of him, refusing to talk to anyone. They decided to take him to hospital. The person used that Portuguese passive phrase which eloquently described Mena's state: '*Se caíu.*' And then: '*Foi a confusão.*' He broke down from the *confusão*.

5

The War of the Cities

I

It is 23 January 1993 and something is terribly wrong. Nausea sweeps over me as the big UN cargo plane I am travelling in spirals and twists with speed down into Luena. The pilots are agitated and mutter anxiously in Russian. Only when we touch down do I realise what the problem is. UNITA is shelling the airport and we are landing in the middle of their missile fire.

The crew shout at us to keep our heads down as they throw open the Antonov's doors to a cacophony of panic and automatic rifle fire. Dozens of inert bodies lie amidst the potholes of the asphalt runway, patches of red and brown against the grey. Those who can move are running towards the plane, waving their arms, running on top of the sick and the wounded lying on the ground.

Those who can run shove everyone else. I see a man push a pole attached by a tube to a body on the ground and an intravenous drip bag flies into the air. The wounded on the tarmac are moaning but their complaints are drowned out by the yelling of the strong. Those who can, clamber up the ladder into the aircraft. Many are empty-handed and are pushing each other. Some don't even know where the plane is going but they don't care. They didn't have enough time to pack when they heard the plane overhead and ran to the airport to take their chances.

This was supposed to be a routine food drop to a town cut off from the world during a two-week bombardment by the rebels. The city is surrounded by land-mines and the only access is by air. UNITA had promised not to fire but reneged at the last minute, lobbing artillery at the landing strip from 15 kilometres away as we descended. All formalities are suspended in the rush to get the wounded aboard. The crew hurl sacks of beans and rice to the ground, oblivious as to whether they are being picked up by civilians or military. We have to get out quickly and this is not a moment to sign forms or ask for names.

The Russian pilots are still shouting, bellowing, for people to hurry when space runs out in the unpressurised cargo section. I count about 50 wounded, 23 bodies bleeding on stretchers. There is not much room and the passengers are leaning on each other like in a crowded bus. Most of them lie there stunned by the pandemonium. A woman yelps when someone accidentally lurches on to her bandaged stump; someone else gestures wildly at an infant left on the tarmac which she says is hers. She screams: That is my baby, someone bring me my baby! The air is foul from adrenalin and untreated flesh wounds. Most of the injured were hurt in the shelling during the past two weeks but the airport attack has reaped its harvest too. My last sight before the crew close the hatch is of a pair of crutches lying on the tarmac.

There are no ambulances waiting when we get back to Luanda with our human load. Everyone who has a vehicle drives the wounded to the hospital. The passengers look dazed as they struggle slowly out of the plane. Now out of Luena, they are orderly and are politely assisting each other. I wait until the very last one leaves the waiting station which is the tarmac. Then I go back to my hotel and wipe the blood of strangers from my forearms. The blood in the basin matches the brown water from the corroded taps and I keep the water running a long time until I am sure it has all been washed down. I take a white washcloth and scrub my wrists and palms and knuckles and fingertips although I know they are already clean.

Then I sit down at my desk and file my story.

+

The next day it was as though nothing had happened. There were no records of the incident in the Angolan media. Reuters had hundreds of clients but there were no immediate signs in the play reports that anyone had published my dispatch. The article had been sent out on a Friday evening; every print journalist knows that Friday is a black news hole where stories disappear like ships in the Bermuda Triangle. Angola was not Bosnia or Israel; editors apparently didn't deem the story worthy of holding for the Sunday newspapers. As far as the world was concerned, nothing happened in Luena on 23 January 1993.

✢

Some newspaper, I think it was British, coined the phrase 'The Forgotten War' to describe Angola. There have been many Forgotten Wars over the years. Sudan is one. Casamance was another. However, what made Angola's situation seem particularly pernicious was its abrupt abandonment by the very countries which had contributed to its instability in the first place. The Cold War was over, so Russia and the United States had turned their attention to matters elsewhere. The UN had botched its poorly conceived plan for Angola and was more concerned with the debacles of Somalia and Sarajevo. Angola was no longer strategic enough to hold centre-stage.

'The international community has to wake up to the fact that it has a responsibility in this matter,' Foreign Minister Venâncio de Moura complained in an interview we held around the time of the Luena incident. Newspapers and news magazines from around the world lay on the coffee table in his office. He pointed at the covers with an angry jabbing finger. 'Bosnia, Bosnia, Bosnia,' he said. 'Where is Angola? Where? They can't just leave their dirty laundry with us.'

✢

Part of de Moura's problem was convincing the international community that Angola's situation was grave and would fester further if unattended to. After the 31 October 1992 massacres in Luanda of 10 000 suspected UNITA supporters when the rebels were run out of town, many embassies had either closed temporarily or evacuated staff down to a skeletal level. Those diplomats who remained were trying not to exaggerate the extent of the dangers.

'It's not a war. It's only a conflict,' British ambassador John Flynn said at a November 1992 news briefing in Luanda. It was imperative to speak to Flynn; he was one of the very few people in Luanda in telephone contact with Savimbi, who was hiding in Huambo 800 kilometres to the south. A group of us from British and American publications had flown into Angola after hearing reports of vicious renewed fighting. Flynn admonished us for not making the distinction between war and mere conflict, reminding us that technically the 1991 Biçesse peace accords were still in place. He looked at us intently as he reiterated his point.

'There is still dialogue going on. There have been clashes. This is a conflict.'

Everyone took notes. I looked up at him inquisitively. 'It is not a war,' he repeated.

✛

I had never covered a proper war before, but it seemed like one to me.

But then again, I never expected to be in a situation where I had to make that distinction. I had stumbled on this war, conflict, clash, whatever you wanted to call it, by pure accident.

It was the first week of November 1992 when I arrived back in Luanda and the city was slowly returning to life, dazed and in slow motion, after the massacres which had resembled an animal cull. Riding through town I would turn a corner and smell a decaying stench; bodies bulged from traffic islands where they had been buried because the cemeteries had run out of space. People were only now emerging into the sunlight after staying in hiding during that devastating week.

The MPLA government had firmly won the battle for the capital. But across the rest of the country it was a different story. Within a few weeks UNITA had expelled government authorities from 70 per cent of the countryside and occupied two provincial capitals. It had seized the diamond fields which the MPLA government depended on for one-tenth of its budget. Thousands of UNITA troops were roaming on military alert through the Planalto, or central highlands, in full uniform in violation of the peace accords. UNITA had sacked UN warehouses containing medicines, tents, water containers and food worth millions of dollars. They had also seized the peace observers' radios and jeeps and were using them to conduct manoeuvres. Several UNAVEM personnel had been shot at or menaced and many of the 57 stations in the provinces were being closed due to the dangers. The argument from New York was that they only had observer status and were not mandated to shoot in their own defence.

Whatever the diplomatic semantics, the government couldn't officially declare war because it didn't have the means to defend itself, let alone go on the offensive. The MPLA was starting from a virtual military zero, a slate that had been wiped clean as stipulated by the peace accords. Like a good student, the MPLA had done as it was told. Now it was caught by surprise; having demobilised its army as agreed with UNITA, the MPLA government now had only 20 000 armed men, mainly riot police and militia volunteers. Across the country the government was calling civilians to arms and handing out old assault rifles and grenade launchers at police stations. But this was no match for UNITA's well-disciplined 60 000 troops who were primed for a messianic crusade of honour.

The MPLA had a navy and air force in name only. Many of the planes had become inoperative from disuse and, besides, the MPLA had relied heavily in the past on Cubans and other foreign pilots to fly missions. Its own pilots couldn't bomb straight, its men were notoriously undisciplined, deserting their posts at the height of battle. Every night in Luanda I heard gunfire and saw flares arching through the dark streets. It wasn't UNITA on the attack again; it was drunken government soldiers firing into the air or, worse, at each other.

General António dos Santos França N'dalu, the government's military commander, had gone on a shopping mission in Europe which seemed to have been successful; planeloads of arms were being unloaded at Luanda airport. But with an official arms embargo on, the government was competing against a number of planes reportedly leaving Zaire for UNITA territory, loaded with supplies, and mysterious flights leaving South Africa in the direction of Angola. The government may have had 650 000 barrels per day of oil, but UNITA had some of the best quality diamonds in the world.

To make matters worse for the MPLA, it was hard to convince Angolans exhausted by war that they had to start all over again rationing food, handling cartridges, worrying about children playing near land-mines and converting basements into bunkers. Men who had fought 1 500 kilometres away from their families for the duration of the war didn't want even to think about making the same sacrifices again.

This was worse than if the war had continued, they said, because the hopes which they could not allow themselves for 16 years had flourished during the 16 months of peace. They had repainted their houses, plugged up the bullet holes in their walls and grown new gardens. Suddenly it was war again.

Benito, a former soldier who was now working as a waiter, was stuffing bread rolls and sugar packets into his pockets from the restaurant table I was sitting at.

'Just in case,' he explained, with a sorry attempt at a wink.

+

While diplomats debated the semantics of strife and UNAVEM tried to organise peace talks, Savimbi was on a military high. City after city, town after town was falling across the 18 provinces and it seemed no one could do anything to stop him.

For the first time in 30 years of war he broke one of his cardinal rules: don't concentrate on the cities. This time, in what ordinary Angolans were calling the Second War, he closed road access routes to the north, where the oil and diamonds were, and opened his own supply lines from Zaire. Meanwhile, he consolidated his gains in the central plateau, where his Ovimbundu people and provisional headquarters at Huambo, the country's second city, were located. Jamba in the south was no longer strategically important, but Savimbi held on to the huge expanse of UNITA territory in that region to facilitate supplies coming in from South Africa. The coast and the rest of the south he left alone.

In hindsight, my notes read like a chess match of unequal partners:

UNITA:

- Caxito, capital of Bengo province, falls in late October 1992.
- By 21 October all Bie province towns are occupied except the capital Cuito.
- On 28 October UNITA occupies Cubal, Bocoio and Dombe Grande in Benguela province.
- By 30 October UNITA occupies half the 13 municipalities in Huíla province, 10 of 16 in Uíge province, all of Moxíco province except the capital Luena, 6 of 9 in Cuando Cubango, 2 of 10 in Cuanza Norte and the majority in Benguela.
- By 1 November local authorities have been run out of 75 per cent of the countryside, including the Lunda diamond area.

- N'dalatando falls soon afterwards.
- Uíge, capital of the province of the same name, and the nearby Negage air base are taken on 29 November.
- Malange, capital of the province of the same name, is besieged in November. The provincial capitals Cuito, Luena, Saurimo and Menongue are encircled in January 1993.
- M'banza Congo, capital of Zaire province, falls in January as does Soyo, the country's main onshore oil centre.
- By February, 45 of 67 UNAVEM observer stations are closed down.

MPLA:

- January 1993: Police and civilian militias fighting street battles expel UNITA from Benguela, Ondjiva, Namibe, Lobito and Lubango. Hundreds of people die, most of them UNITA members. A tenuous cease-fire established in November 1992 breaks down.

✝

I sat in the container which served as the American liaison office on the top of a hill above the bay, looking at a huge map of Angola. Angola is a large country and looks even bigger when it occupies the space of a wall. One of the diplomats was taking me through the 18 provinces, pointing at what UNITA controlled and what it didn't. It seemed to hold most of the country. The MPLA had virtually only the coast and several cities like islands in the middle. The diplomat explained that 75 per cent of the area described as being under UNITA control was more like a no man's land.

'UNITA actually captured few towns in the conventional military sense; instead it chased out the local MPLA authorities and made the places so unliveable no one would want to come back,' the diplomat said. I must have looked puzzled. He nodded and continued. 'It's a new strategy – a break from the hit and run attacks of the first war.'

It seemed clear that Savimbi was playing straight by the rules of his Maoist training in China in 1964. Strangle the cities, one by one.

The pattern was the same from east to west, north to south. UNITA would surround the town, peppering govern-ment buildings and all able-bodied men with bullets. Surviving villagers not sympathetic to UNITA would flee into the *mata*, the bush. Then UNITA would systematically rip the wire cables from the walls, tear the metal pipes from the bathrooms and seize all working vehicles. If the vehicles weren't functional they'd remove the tyres. Then they'd stuff corpses down the wells and shoot out the light bulbs.

When I flew to Uíge in January 1993, two months after UNITA occupied the city, almost the only people I saw were rebel cadres. Uíge looked like a movie set for a war film. Many townspeople had fled into the fields. The stores were empty. The buildings had entire walls and planks of wood missing. They were so stripped of furniture that it was hard to discern which of the shells had been houses, offices or shops. Most of the crops had been eaten. You couldn't really call it a city any more because there were practically no people or commerce.

The people who remained told me that the rebels came with trucks when they invaded Uíge. They loaded up all the furniture they could find, tore door-frames out of houses for firewood, and drove off with the computers and files of aid workers. 'They even took the paper clips,' said a Norwegian UN employee who had been evacuated. Practically all that was left intact was the bishop's palace, and a handsome Alsatian which belonged to the Norwegian. For weeks the dog had the empty streets to himself, running barking past the splintered buildings looking for his master. He grew progressively thinner as food ran out.

Sometimes I felt that the only people who had a remote idea of what was really going on were the Russian pilots, who flew everywhere. But they didn't speak English and I didn't speak Russian.

The day after I returned from the ill-fated Luena flight on 23 January, I went to the government-run press centre, that musty building where the smell of cooking oil and blocked toilets had grown more oppressive. There were no journalists around, just some policemen drinking beer at the bar downstairs. The radio droned on about some Portuguese football scores. Since no one cared about the Luena incident there was no need for other reporters to file; besides, the electricity had been cut off for the sixth time that week and the telexes weren't switched on.

As journalists, and there were only a few of us correspondents stationed there continually at the time, it was extremely difficult to get a true reading of events in the hinterland and even more problematic to get the news out. Most diplomats were forbidden by their embassies to leave Luanda for security reasons, so their information was generally second-hand. The national media was run by the MPLA so one had to sift through thick layers of propaganda. International humanitarian organisations were increasingly withdrawing their staff from the provinces because of the dangers there, so we couldn't rely on their radioed reports from the interior.

Most major roads had been destroyed or mined or were manned by UNITA who were hostile to the media. The only feasible way to travel was by air. The military rarely allowed journalists to accompany flying missions so I relied on the aid organisations, particularly the World Food Programme whose country director, Frenchman Philippe Borel, was eager for news to get out. I would usually fly in and out in a day, to avoid getting stranded if sudden outbreaks of fighting resulted in airport closures.

For an African country in conflict, it was remarkably easy for a small white woman to walk on to the military section of Luanda's airport, stride past the camouflaged attack helicopters and MIG fighters and thumb a ride on the tarmac. After a while the guards recognised my creaking rented brown car and would wave me in. Normally I would arrive at the airport between four and five in the morning and trot between the Antonovs and Beechcrafts looking for a lift. Even at that time of day the air was oppressive. The destinations were completely dependent on where there was fighting that day. Flights were often arranged or cancelled at the very last minute. I'd usually board as dawn broke, sitting alone in the huge cargo section with the sacks of grain and the smell of diesel.

After the Russian pilots discovered my surname was Russian, they insisted I sit in the cockpit like a mascot. Many had been in Angola for years but they barely spoke Portuguese and during the flight would repeatedly give the thumbs-up sign and say, smiling with stained teeth, 'Good! Friend Russian! Peace!' That was about the extent of what we could communicate and I never found out how they felt so far away from Georgia or Moscow in a collapsing sweltering African country where their daily routine was flying into someone else's war. They wore sweaty old clothes, flew with plastic sandals and passed around bottles of vodka en route. I hoped they knew what they were doing.

No matter how many trips I took, I never exorcised the anxiety about landing. I was less worried about dying in the air than about what awaited me upon descent. It got worse after the Luena airport incident. But even before that I was always filled with nervous anticipation in the transcendence of being airborne. I asked myself silently every flight: What would I find?

The scene was invariably similar once we reached our destination. We would descend in rapid spirals to avoid possible missiles. Whether it was UNITA- or MPLA-controlled territory, men with guns met the aircraft. If it was UNITA they pointed their weapons at you. If it was MPLA, they demanded to see your papers. If it was a government area, civilians would press around the pilot and beg for a ride out, pulling at our arms and not letting go. In Malange police had to keep the crowds back with batons and a barbed wire barrier for fear they would attack the crew. The workers would throw the bags of food on to the tarmac with unnecessary force so that loose grains of rice would spill out which they could then pocket. Once I saw small boys roll under the plane and lick powdered cornmeal from the ground as the provisions were unloaded. They ran away only when a policeman kicked them and threatened to shoot them with his pistol.

The crews tried to hand over the sacks of provisions and boxes of medicine and cooking oil as fast as possible. But generally there was a long enough stop to hitch a ride to town with the local militias or aid groups and get a sense of how things were. No matter where we went, we seemed to see a repetitive succession of amputees with bloodied stumps who sat listlessly outside hospital wards because there were not enough mattresses. There was an endless panorama of buildings without walls, and of women in reeking rags begging me for a seat on a plane which I didn't own. Their sense of helplessness was infectious and I had no defences against the debilitating despair.

Back in Luanda, I would hurriedly write and send my story via satellite telephone from my room, number 602. I'd open a couple of cold Portuguese beers from the mini-bar, step into the air-conditioned cocoon of the Hotel Tivoli's lobby, and even go out for a seafood dinner with friends at an open-air restaurant on the beach. Then The Fragmentation would set in. I'd have spent the day with people who would probably be killed the next, and I'd seen eighteenth-century architecture which was so badly shattered that it was indistinguishable from a construction site. Now I was eating grilled calamari and sipping *vinho verde* on a beach.

There was one time in particular which bothered me. I went to dinner on the Ilha, the sandy peninsula which juts out from the city, where the best seafood and grilled chicken are served. I was with a group of Angolan friends, most of them MPLA supporters, who were gossiping cheerfully – there wasn't much else to do in a town like Luanda. I had just been to Uíge where I knew at least one of them had family. I didn't want to be asked to describe what I had seen earlier in the day and see their faces as I told them about their destroyed towns.

So I toyed with a parsley sprig and thought about the fragile world I'd been to hundreds of miles away. I ran the conversations I'd had and the faces I'd seen over the weeks through my mind, back and forth like a tape. (This from an old woman: 'Three grandchildren, five sons, two brothers – they've all disappeared. Our house was burned.' This from a newly-wed: 'UNITA raped my wife in front of me.' This from a six-year-old boy: 'I found my father in the well with wire around his throat.') I wrote it all down and then left them, knowing that the destruction would resume soon after our take-off. But they had followed me in my head to Luanda and I didn't know what to do with the responsibility.

I spoke about it with a friend; we had been through all the arguments before. You knew it wasn't your fault, it wasn't your country and there was nothing you could do. But that didn't stop the old women and legless kids and bandaged masses from stampeding into your mind late at night.

What made my sense of impotence worse was that I rarely heard what happened to the people I met. There were so many of them. It was impossible to ask the man from the Red Cross: 'What happened to that woman in the pink torn dress with the daughter who stepped on a land-mine and lost her foot?' Or 'What about that skinny boy whose back was stripped clean of its flesh by the mortar?' There were too many and they became a blur of nameless phantoms.

One exception was a priest I met on a flight to Uíge, to

which he was returning after UNITA had occupied the city. He was apprehensive and reluctant, but a sense of religious duty recalled him to his parish in that occupied town.

'Are you scared?' I asked. The lush fields of Uíge, which years before there was war made Angola one of the world's largest coffee producers, lay fallow and mined below us. It was starting to drizzle and even from the air you could see the gaps in the roofs of buildings which had been bombed.

The young priest was trying not to look out of the window, as though by ignoring the scene he could delay disembarking. He seemed to be torn between his faith in God and an instinct for self-preservation.

'I must go, I must be there with the people,' he said simply. I wondered if he knew how many of the people had fled.

Months later in Johannesburg, I received a letter written in immaculate Gothic calligraphy from my travel companion. He wrote chattily about the rains which had finally come and plans to celebrate Easter Mass. There was no mention of the war or the door-to-door witch-hunts that had taken place. I was no wiser, nor was I reassured. I never heard from him again.

✣

My own sense of powerlessness was probably nothing compared to what the UN special representative Margaret Anstee must have been feeling. An angular, intelligent woman, Anstee was being blamed by many for the UN's failure to put a brake on Savimbi. In her defence, Anstee had a limited mandate with limited funds. Hers was an observer, not a peacekeeping mission, which had been pared down dramatically. There were no sanctions to back up pressure on Savimbi and the only thing she could do was urge him to talk. She couldn't threaten him with arms embargoes. Powerful, policy-making minds at the UN were concentrated on crises elsewhere. Angola was an embarrassing nuisance everyone hoped would go away and

Anstee was the unfortunate person stuck with it.

Anstee had a particular problem with Savimbi: she was a white woman. For a patriarchal man whose movement relegated women to bush housewives, a sexagenarian British woman who wore pearls and flowered dresses was not what he called a proper adversary. She may have had an impressive curriculum vitae, but he was not going to negotiate with a woman who walked through the rubble of a city in high heels. UNITA's *Vorgan* radio sneered at Anstee, calling her a prostitute and saying she was carrying Dos Santos's baby. UNITA threatened to kill her. Anstee would wait for days for Savimbi to grant her an audience in Huambo. Upon arriving there, she would wait for hours to be received. He often did not bother to return her telephone calls.

I felt much sympathy for Anstee, isolated at the complex of containers on the edge of town which comprised the UNAVEM headquarters, swimming dozens of laps a day in the pool there to cope with the stress. In retrospect, she was too soft on Savimbi. Indeed, she may have looked incongruous walking at the side of the generals to inspect the detritus of war. But as a woman I winced internally every time my male colleagues made fun of her blue eye-shadow. I could understand the need to preserve appearances in the most male of circumstances. What did they know about a woman trying to do a man's job?

I certainly wasn't going to tell the men about the small yellow vial I packed into the medical kit that Reuters issued in case of emergency. There, among the syringes and burn ointment and dehydration tablets, nestled the tiny bottle of lotion which my mother had given me. 'Here, take it for business trips,' she had said, as though going to Malange was like visiting a trade convention in Chicago. I never opened the vial, which contained enough cream for one hand. But I carried it around as a talisman of another, softer world, where mothers took their daughters to school instead of to hospitals to have their legs amputated.

Nevertheless, the peace process fell upon Anstee's shoulders. With other mediators out of the question, UNAVEM was the only force driving negotiations. After his electoral defeat Savimbi felt betrayed by the Troika – Portugal, the US and Russia – which was the guardian of the 1991 peace accords. UNITA's radio station *Vorgan* regularly put out broadcasts calling the Portuguese dogs of war who were no better than Cubans. The US had lost its clout, now that it had withdrawn military aid from UNITA. UNITA commanders inspected their troops while driving the blue 4x4 vehicles donated by the US to help the movement transform itself into a political one. Washington had created a Frankenstein which mocked it. Besides, American government policy was directionless between Bill Clinton's victory in the November 1992 presidential elections and his inauguration in January 1993. This was not a time for Washington to take decisive action.

South Africa, too, had lost its influence over its former proxy. Pretoria could not dictate to Savimbi now that it no longer armed him. To make matters worse, the MPLA government, which had never trusted Pretoria, suspected double-dealing. The Luanda government had declared Pik Botha persona non grata on 6 November 1992 and thereafter South African diplomats complained they had little access to the Angolan government. The embassy closed on 3 December for security reasons.

Johann Smith, the defence attaché who had been so helpful to me during the Battle of Luanda, came to the Tivoli bar for a final goodbye beer. He was hurt and confused by the MPLA's spurning of South Africa. He had been wounded serving his country in southern Angola in the 1980s. He had dealt then with the enemy, the MPLA. He had stood on a boat and watched as his friends from UNITA were killed on a distant hill. As a diplomat he had not protested. Now he was being told to leave, without ceremony.

Pik Botha and the Troika had basically given up trying to

mediate after their failed mission in Luanda in October 1992. After the high-level presence following the elections, the UN Security Council went home and wished Anstee good luck. Occasionally an important person would come to lend help, such as UN peacekeeping chief Marrack Goulding who arrived on 12 November and Jeffrey Davidow, Washington's number two Africa expert, who met Savimbi in Huambo on 12 December. But they, too, failed to persuade Savimbi to change his course.

There was an added problem: following the October 1992 massacres most members of UNITA's negotiating team were either dead or in custody. It took a while for Savimbi to name a new delegation. But Savimbi never regained his trust, if he ever had any, in negotiations with the enemy.

Ironically enough, the MPLA military commander, António França N'dalu, was the only man in the government who had a modicum of Savimbi's respect. A compact man who rarely lost his temper, he exuded integrity and calm authority and seemed to rise above the corruption rampant in the government.

During peacetime N'dalu had forged a superb working relationship with General Ben Ben, his counterpart from the UNITA army. Savimbi respected N'dalu's military prowess and considered him an honourable man. N'dalu was reputed to be a reasonable negotiator who was able to convince his adversaries that their position was being considered with the utmost respect.

During much of October and November 1992 N'dalu was in regular contact with Savimbi. But N'dalu was tired of war and, as a moderate, was becoming increasingly isolated in a government where hardliners were in the ascendant. When he suddenly went to Europe for 'health reasons', the way was opened for hawks to come in. N'dalu was replaced by hardliner João de Matos when the government announced a new cabinet in December to confront the threat of renewed war.

Anstee had no choice but to try to keep dialogue flowing

with Savimbi so that he did not become completely isolated. But she erred in that she treated him as a reasonable man who acted in good faith. The fact that he had lied to her and that his people had threatened to kill her did not inhibit Anstee's determination to negotiate. She kept pushing for a meeting between the UNITA leader and Dos Santos, naively believing Savimbi might acquiesce. She miscalculated, not understanding that Savimbi was a man who operated by force and responded only to force.

Savimbi's ability to manipulate Anstee and the UN's misguided trust in him was never more obvious than at Namibe on 26 November. There, in that pretty coastal city on the edge of the southern desert, senior MPLA and UNITA members met to revive the Biçesse peace accords.

Just several days before, on 18 November, Savimbi wrote to Marrack Goulding saying that he accepted the result of the elections, although he still considered them rigged, and would accept a presidential run-off vote. Many diplomats dismissed the letter as a way to buy time but Anstee, desperate for optimistic signs, took it seriously enough to go ahead with the Namibe meeting.

Savimbi and President dos Santos didn't attend the meeting, which was held in a stately Portuguese building which must have been the residence of a colonial governor centuries back. Instead, they sent their lieutenants. At the airport where the UNITA delegation flew in, a row of a dozen military aircraft was parked, meant presumably as a show of force by the government. One of the first to step out of the UNITA plane was Jorge Valentim, one of Savimbi's closest aides.

While the enemy delegations met, sitting in a big horseshoe formation in a dark hall, I strolled around town with several Angolan and Portuguese journalists. Someone commented on how unusual it was to see an Angolan provincial capital where the buildings were intact and well painted. We sat at an open-air café in the main square and ordered Fantas and stale cheese sandwiches.

While we debated whether anything could really be accomplished, the café owner sat listening, elbow propped on the counter.

A customer walked in and asked for some coffee. 'What's going on? Why are there so many people here?' he asked.

'Peace talks,' the proprietor scoffed. 'Peace – it's all talk. Tell them we want to talk to Savimbi ourselves.'

We walked back to the palace just as the curtains parted. The meeting was breaking up. Someone read a short statement in which UNITA solemnly pledged 'to fully accept the Angolan peace accords as the only solution to the Angolan problem and to reiterate and effectively apply the cease-fire in the entire country and immediately cease all offensive movements'.

Anstee looked grim, but said mechanically: 'I'm optimistic.'

I asked a Portuguese diplomat what he thought. He shrugged. 'Who knows with these people.'

Then the members of the two delegations ostentatiously embraced, got into their separate planes and flew home.

Three days later UNITA invaded Uíge and nearby Negage, the country's most important air base in the north.

✢

By January 1993 Savimbi was enjoying the biggest military gains in his entire career; none the less, these were difficult times for him. Diamond wealth was paying for planeloads of supplies from Zaire, but he knew his stockpiled weapons would not last for ever and he could not depend on help from the outside as before. Supply routes through southern Africa were becoming more difficult, with complaints of air space violations by Zimbabwe, Namibia and Botswana who were pressuring Pretoria to end these clandestine flights. Plus, he knew the political transition gaining pace in South Africa meant his former apartheid backers would eventually be replaced by the

MPLA's ally, the African National Congress of Nelson Mandela. Savimbi was running out of time.

With many of UNITA's senior men dead or held in detention in Luanda, Savimbi was distraught and obsessed with security. He rarely slept in the same place two nights in a row and sometimes moved four times a night. He was particularly bereaved over the death of his nephew, Elias Salupeto Pena. Savimbi increasingly got his counsel from hardliners like Valentim. Ironically, it was military men like Ben Ben who had to be coaxed reluctantly, some say forced, back into the struggle. They had developed a good rapport with their counterparts in the MPLA army, and with it a certain empathy. Having lived with the deprivations of the bush for so long, they no longer wanted to continue fighting.

Savimbi didn't appear much on the front line to animate the troops as he had in the first war, leaving this task to others. His villa in Luanda had been destroyed by tanks during the battle for the capital in October. His house in Huambo, called the White House, had been bombed by government air raids in January. Savimbi wasn't going to take any chances.

When the new war resumed, Savimbi staged his longest disappearance yet from the public view. Often he would refuse to answer the telephone when Anstee or other mediators called. Once adept at manipulating the press, he had grown hostile towards the foreign and local media after losing the elections. Savimbi rarely granted interviews any more. How different it was from the Jamba days, when he flew reporters up from Pretoria at huge expense, plying them with whisky and beer.

Now Savimbi had to conserve his strength and resources. He left the public relations to Valentim, who periodically dialled the BBC in London on his satphone from Huambo. It was rarely switched on for incoming calls, partly to save energy and partly for security reasons. It was never clear whether the unpredictable Valentim was acting autonomously or under orders from the top man. One never knew which persona one would get – the smiling Valentim who suavely insisted he was for peace, or the belligerent Valentim with glittering eyes who justified the occupation of Uíge as a reasonable revenge for the loss of Luanda.

Jamba was abandoned as a military base although civilians remained there, including families of men taken captive in Luanda and fighters in the field. The relatives were not allowed to leave Jamba; and fear about their welfare kept many a man from defecting. Part of what disturbed Savimbi the most was that some of his cadres, after tasting 16 sweet months of peace after 16 bitter years of war, had lost the conviction that *O Mais Velho* knew best. Many just didn't want to fight any more.

✛

Face pressed against the window glass, Honório Van Dunem sat in the lobby of the Hotel Tivoli, looking out at a world he couldn't touch. Most Luanda residents would gladly have stepped into the cool quiet of the city's premier hotel. But Van Dunem was a prisoner in a luxurious purgatory, sipping cup after cup of bitter black coffee as he pondered his fate.

It was December 1992. Two months earlier Van Dunem, UNITA's former shadow interior minister, sought refuge in the hotel with 60 women and children when government police rounded up all the UNITA leaders they could find.

Now, restricted to this surreal, elegant prison with little to do but reread the government newspaper and take saunas, Van Dunem had endless idle hours for contemplation. He was most worried about what Savimbi was doing 800 kilometres away in Huambo. Van Dunem was isolated from the other imprisoned UNITA leaders, who were held in custody across the city in other places. He needed guidance but didn't know where to seek it.

The Americans periodically called on Van Dunem to urge him to denounce Savimbi's new war. Van Dunem was a portly, well-dressed man who favoured tweeds. He came from one of Luanda's most prominent intellectual *mestiço* families aligned to the MPLA; one relative worked for the BBC and one was a foreign minister. Honório was the only one who had joined UNITA. Now he was thinking of co-operating with the MPLA, but his immediate family was in Huambo and he was worried about what would happen to them.

We spent a lot of time talking, since we were staying in the same hotel. Every time I returned to the hotel from a reporting assignment, it seemed he was waiting at the door. He'd take my arm, guide me to the soft armchairs in the lobby and ask me what I had seen and heard. Often he sought me out at the breakfast buffet, asking my advice in a low voice over the pineapples and croissants.

'It is not a matter of choosing between two options,' he said during one crisis of faith, lapsing into English and French as though he had forgotten who he was. 'I feel like I have no choice. But I'm scared of the consequences. *C'est tres difficile.*'

Eight generals and six brigadiers from UNITA were scattered across the city, undergoing similar self-doubts. On the one hand was the lure of comfort, money and protection from the government. On the other was the abandoning of something they had believed in and fought for, for more than a decade.

Three people were steadfast. Savimbi's shadow health minister and personal physician, Carlos Morgado, never wavered. Likewise, UNITA's shadow finance minister, Fátima Roque, who was staying at another of Amorim's hotels, the Império, never denounced Savimbi. Due perhaps to her white skin and a strong lobby in Portugal – she was a respected economist there and was married to one of Portugal's richest businessmen – she was released on 4 February 1993 and allowed to fly to Lisbon.

Another loyal cadre was Savimbi's foreign affairs chief, Abel Chivukuvuku, who was interned in Luanda's military hospital, his elegant long legs shattered after escaping the ambush in which other UNITA leaders had died when the government expelled UNITA from Luanda. He told visitors he opposed war, but always stopped short of criticising Savimbi.

Telephone contact was allowed between the prisoners and Huambo but Savimbi was suspicious of the detained generals, believing that they had been tainted by contact with the enemy. The government media and interrogators seized upon this. Feeling isolated, the UNITA men in custody began to crack.

On 3 February 1993, at a military installation in Luanda, five of the detained generals, one brigadier and UNITA's deputy information chief Norberto de Castro held a news conference at which they announced their decision to rejoin the government army which they had left when Savimbi resumed his war.

The generals – Peregrino Wambu, Andrade Chassungo Santos, Zacarias Mundombe, Adriano MacKenzie and Artur Bumba – and Brigadier Renato Campos Mateus wore civilian dress and proclaimed that the war was not in anyone's interest. However, they were evasive about how they had been treated and were careful not to condemn Savimbi outright. De Castro insisted: 'I do not want to judge Dr Jonas Savimbi.'

I approached them afterwards, as their escorts prepared to take them back to the defence ministry. Would they fight for the government side if asked to? There was a long pause. They looked at the door and said nothing.

When Van Dunem finally made his decision he was more forthright. 'Savimbi is a psychopath,' he declared. 'I don't understand why Savimbi is making the country suffer with more war.'

Having made his choice, and having obtained financial and security provisions for his family, Van Dunem assumed the role as the country's leading UNITA dissident and held court to the foreign and local press. On 15 February 1993, Van Dunem took his seat at parliament along with nine of UNITA's 70 elected deputies. He wore his best brown tweed jacket and tie and ventured out hesitantly into Luanda's fetid air.

✜

Each time I left Angola people who weren't journalists would ask me, 'What is it like covering the war?' I suppose they wanted to hear about glamorous intrigue and torrid romances on the battlefield. I promptly disappointed their notions with an automatic instinctual reply: 'Rush, no time, and logistics.'

So much of agency work – for news and television – is just gathering and disseminating the information. I lurched from deadline to deadline, eye on the clock as much as on content. In a place like Luanda where most telephones don't work, where rumours are rampant and so many sources lie, much of what one does is race from office to office, barracks to ministries, trying to find someone to confirm or deny something someone whispered to you over coffee. Sometimes I'd get so frustrated trying to phone another part of the city and would be so tired from the debilitating heat, I'd pick up the satphone and call down the road for $10 a minute. If I had film to ship I'd have to go to the airport and find a human 'pigeon' to hand-carry it to Johannesburg. Hopefully, the human pigeon would call my office and deliver it. Often he didn't.

I suppose I used the logistics problem to avoid thinking too deeply about what I was, or wasn't, witnessing and how I was powerless to make an impact. Unlike the visiting correspondents who could fly in for a week, get a sense of the place and then disappear, I was getting too immersed in the story to maintain my objectivity. Most of the time I was also too busy to think about the larger implications.

Life in a small contained space in an intense decaying environment makes reality at home seem distant. Telephone calls to Johannesburg or New York were exorbitant; I used the price as an excuse not to call. It would have been too complicated to try to explain to people outside what it was like, let alone where Angola even was. For six months I didn't fax or call anyone outside except my news-desk.

During that time there was nothing cementing me much to another world. The postal system didn't work, so occasionally visitors from Johannesburg would bring letters or packages of my vice, sugarless gum. I didn't have pictures of loved ones in my hotel room. The room was sterile, as though I planned to leave at any moment. There was something refreshingly simple about living with four changes of clothing which wore out after a couple of months. The only personal adornment was a clay figurine of an angel sent by the man I had left in London before I moved to Lisbon. It was a peace offering of sorts. In return, I sent him a *Pensador* statue carved from dark ebony wood.

Promiscuity and *pregos*. People's patterns of behaviour change in a situation like this. And living in a hotel gives one a sense of impermanence or transcendence. I knew people who were normally staid and strait-laced who suddenly had wild affairs with the most unlikely people. One woman who hated the army took as lovers a succession of military men. My fix was steak sandwiches; a strange choice for someone who rarely ate beef. The more I visited towns which were running out of food, the more I would eat my compensation: *pregos*, those juicy steak sandwiches of the Portuguese-speaking world.

Covering Angola for a news agency like Reuters, the central points of your life become your room and your car because you spend so much time in them. They were the only constants and, unlike most things in Angola, they generally worked.

Let's start with my room in the Hotel Tivoli. It was three floors above the lounge where the UNITA prisoners sat looking desolate in big chairs in front of the elevator which rarely worked. My room, always 602, was near the top so that I could hang the cable of my satellite telephone from the roof through the window. Even if I stayed away for a while, the management would reserve my room upon my return. There were always cut flowers in the dining room, whose menu faithfully kept the Portuguese heritage alive. The hotel was almost Alpine in design, temperature and cleanliness. It was so different from The Outside World where teenage prostitutes urinated on the street corner, and orphans rifled through rubbish bins looking for something to eat. The white floor tiles would remain cool even when the air-conditioning went off, which was often. You could stare at the pine panelling and not know where you were, until you looked out of the window. The view at a distance was a pretty pink and blue one. But below was a courtyard belonging to missionaries; and the front, like most buildings in Luanda, was pocked with bullet holes and decay.

There were a few regular characters living in the hotel – Van Dunem, two melancholy Portuguese journalists who were based in Luanda for temporary secondments like myself, an Israeli dealer in something suspicious, a Portuguese banker who was following an economy which really didn't exist, and a South African who frequented the diamond areas.

Now the car. Angolan cars are a phenomenon in themselves. Bits and pieces are held down with tape and the wires sprout from the inside like flowers. Most of the cars lack intact windows. Forget about working lights. Anyway, no one ever signals. The car I rented was a beaten dark brown Mercedes, the colour of chocolate if you were charitable and mud if you weren't. It also had a windshield – a veritable luxury in a country where there was no window glass. Those who could afford it attached metal clips on the edges to prevent thieves from taking the windows. Those who couldn't enjoyed natural air conditioning.

The brown car was owned and driven by one of Luanda's most amiable citizens – João Martins, a stylish, smiling Bakongo from the north who had endless patience and who had spent much of his life as a refugee in Zaire. He was always polishing the car, even though the inside stank of several generations of perspiration. He lived in the *musseques* and knew which streets

182

became swamps when it rained. He wanted better for his wife and kids, and treated me as his personal emissary to the world. If we drove to the Portuguese embassy for an interview he'd ask: '*Mana Judite,*' please check on that visa application for me.' If it were the interior ministry he'd have a special message about the treatment of the Bakongos. At the Zairian embassy, one time, he paused. 'Tell them I don't need to go back.' He was a man of eternal hope.

✢

As the war grew worse, my Angolan friends complained that I neglected them. 'All you do is work,' was a regular refrain. It was true that to some extent I was using work to avoid telling them about what I had seen of their ruined country. It was generally easier for a foreign journalist than an Angolan citizen to travel around the country. The United Nations would not take Angolan reporters on its flights in order to maintain its neutrality. So when I came back from a trip to the interior people would drop by the hotel for information. I dreaded those encounters when they asked me to describe their home towns or the schools they had gone to, which were now little more than rubble.

But also there wasn't much time to socialise. Right after a trip like the one to Luena, I'd rush back to my room to make the 'sked', which has to be attended to several times a day like a nursing child. I had a numbing routine which was fuelled by seven cups a day of Portuguese espresso coffee called *bicas*: rise at 6.45, listen to the morning propaganda on radio, run down to the street and get a paper from one of the street vendors, run back into the hotel and skim enough over two croissants to think of something to write, then run upstairs to my room and hook up the satphone and somehow come up with a story. The day was consumed by checking in at the press centre, making visiting rounds at the defence ministry and embassies and the

UN, and maybe taking a day trip to the provinces. A story was produced at midday and another after the 11 p.m. final radio news broadcast, and sometimes others in between. I'd normally be free some time around midnight but most of my Angolan friends didn't have cars or wouldn't want to be on the streets at that hour.

The one time I had free was Friday nights when I didn't need to file. Then we'd visit the few clubs which were open and return just before dawn. It seemed that as the war worsened Angolans in Luanda partied harder than ever.

One club was aptly called Pandemonium; gunfire often erupted outside between the civilian militiamen who still hadn't handed back the weapons they had been supplied with in the Battle of Luanda. There really wasn't much else to do except party if you wanted to unwind. The cinema was closed because of irregular electricity supplies and the owner didn't want to spend the money to import films. The two museums, of slavery and of war, were shut. The one theatre and the art gallery which had opened before the elections had now shut down too. Browsing in the two bookshops meant looking at a handful of out-of-print Portuguese translations of Karl Marx or poetry by Neto. The animals in the game park near Luanda had been killed by hunters and in any event there were too many ambushes on the road. One could go to the beach or to a restaurant with friends, and I did that a lot. I couldn't catch up on much-needed sleep because I felt caged in my small hotel room where I spent so much time.

The only excursion remotely described as 'out of town' which was accessible was to Kilometre 19, an open-air crafts market supplied mainly by Zairian traders of contraband ivory. But even the market was a reminder of the war. Most of the goods came from the north where there was fighting. The looted treasures of the ancient Angolan kingdoms and of museums now ended up at Kilometre 19, sold by people who didn't know their worth. You could chart UNITA's progress by what was missing or what was available. After several months of war the vendors ran out of the dark ebony wood from which they traditionally carved the *Pensador* sculptures and substituted a lighter-coloured less valuable wood. A large regal chair adorned with exquisitely carved skulls and animals was on offer, obviously pillaged from a museum. There was an abundance of rare grey parrots, chimps, leopard skins and ten-foot-high piles of ivory. Anything that was illegal could be sold with impunity. There was a war going on and international environmentalists were not going to police Angola.

✠

After about two years of flying back and forth between Angola and Johannesburg, Reuters gave me a handbook that had been distributed to cameramen in areas where wars had been officially declared. From that pamphlet I learned that I had been doing a lot of things wrong: travelling alone, not watching my back, and driving on the soft shoulder of the road where land-mines might be buried.

I had, however, learned some other things which weren't in the book, such as always to carry cigarettes for roadblocks, although I hadn't smoked for seven years. I learned that satphones blow up when power surges when the generator switches back on – and that when they blow up it can cost $10 000 to fix them.

✠

During my various trips outside Angola someone invariably asked THAT question: 'What is it like doing that work as a woman?'

It was in the same sort of tone as they might ask 'What's it like to walk on hot coals?' People always wanted to know what I wore (FYI: T-shirts, jeans, sneakers in the field; occasionally skirts in Luanda).

I would assert, maybe too defiantly, that it was no different for a woman. I could run fast and be very nasty. I went to the same places as men, rode in the same jeeps and employed what I hope was the same acute analysis.

But sometimes I wondered; maybe there were differences. Maybe, I thought, we women had different responses from men. Maybe we felt more powerless.

✢

I don't remember the exact date that M'banza Congo fell to UNITA, but I can describe how it felt to wear a flak jacket for the first time.

It was some time in January 1993 and everyone was trying to get to Benguela where about 560 people had died when the government tried to expel UNITA from the town. I was doing the odd bit of translating for a newly arrived BBC crew, which had come to Angola like everyone else to get images of the conflict, now officially a war. In those days UNAVEM for safety reasons wasn't taking journalists on flights so we would all queue up for the few available seats on WFP planes.

The visiting BBC correspondent, the late John Harrison, was a proactive man who did not wait for things patiently. He had put himself or other members of his crew on the waiting list of every flight, to the annoyance of other journalists. Somehow Harrison convinced, persuaded, cajoled and possibly bullied the UNAVEM leadership, who were British, that the BBC should have special access. We were sitting in their office when suddenly a call came through on the radio that a helicopter was being deployed to evacuate three UNAVEM peace observers who had been held hostage by UNITA in M'banza Congo. UNITA had given them a pledge of a 15-minute truce to enable them to fly in, collect the men and get out quickly.

'OK, that's it,' John said, turning to me as the news crackled through. 'Looks like we've got ourselves a good story.'

The UNAVEM man was somewhat taken aback but John had a forceful way about him that was very effective at such times. 'Don't worry, we've got permission from the top,' he said, closing his notebook. John gestured to the crew to pick up their gear. The UNAVEM man looked unsure but gave his OK.

We raced to the airport and jumped into the helicopter waiting in the military section. The UN men there lectured us about the dangers, saying there was no guarantee we would get in and out alive. They handed us robin blue flak jackets. I had never worn one before and it pressed down on my breasts, hurting them. It was manufactured for a normal-sized man and I am what is often described as a petite woman. The jacket came down below my thighs, which didn't make moving very easy. The sound-man wasn't adding to my enthusiasm. 'These things are lightweight. Any AK bullet could pierce them,' he said. 'The ones we use in the townships in South Africa are much more effective, and even in those you can be killed.'

Suddenly one of the UNAVEM men turned to us. 'Does anyone speak Portuguese?' In their haste to get to M'banza Congo they had forgotten to arrange a translator. I proudly put up my hand like a student who knows the answer, wanting to show these battle-hardened men how useful I was. I instantly regretted it.

'Wonderful. You get out first and talk to the UNITA commanders and make sure everything is fine.' He gave me a list of things to say, such as 'Don't shoot, we're from the BBC'. As we prepared our descent John clapped me heartily on the shoulder. 'Thanks, old girl.'

I've often wondered how the UNITA commanders must have felt, seeing the chopper land and a female person the size of a child with an armoured vest down to her knees struggling to get down the stairs. The welcoming party, if you can call it that, consisted of six men who pointed their assault rifles at the aircraft as we landed. Even before I could say '*Bom Dia*' – Good Day – they lowered their weapons and simply stared. They knew the head of the UNAVEM mission was a woman but sending an emissary like myself was apparently going too far. The mighty men-folk, meanwhile, remained inside the helicopter until I shook hands with the commander and then waved them on. I noticed there was a look of relief on the commander's face when he saw some men coming out and his finger happily stiffened a bit on his trigger.

Our mission explained, the commander took the journalists for a tour of what remained of M'banza Congo while the UNAVEM men located their very relieved colleagues and led them, weeping from their ordeal, to the tarmac.

M'banza Congo was Portugal's first Catholic settlement in Africa. It was settled 500 years ago and was once a fine example of colonial red-tiled architecture. The UNITA men were proud to take the town, but there wasn't really much to see – homes whose roofs had been shot off by the government's MIG air attacks; the airline office with a bullet hole like a bull's-eye through the head of the sable antelope emblem. I didn't see any ordinary people, just goats and guerrillas and the hostages being released. The cinema was pocked with bullet holes and streaked with dust and smoke.

Suddenly there was a boom from the lush jungle surrounding the town. That was the signal that the truce was coming to an end. Our tour guides escorted us to the helicopter and bade us a polite goodbye. The commander looked as though he wanted to say something to me, and finally found the words he was searching for. '*Que faz aqui menina?*' It was the equivalent in Portuguese of 'What's a nice girl like you doing in a place like this?'

No one spoke during the flight back to Luanda. The three freed hostages were too overwrought to say anything. They had embraced a cold cement floor for three days, a live mortar hanging unexploded in the wall above them. Bullets whizzed just one metre above their prone bodies; one went through someone's trousers which were hanging on the laundry line. UNITA wouldn't let them leave the building for their own security. Even if they had, there was nowhere they could have gone. UNITA had taken their jeeps and radios.

Now one man cried quietly, stroking the cheeks of his rescuers. The other two smiled, positively beamed, during the entire wordless journey until we touched down in Luanda.

✝

Dominga Manuel sat on a floor in Menongue with her left leg blown off below the knee and wondered how her faith had brought her to this. The 17-year-old mother of one didn't understand why UNITA had denied them food during a nine-month siege. Like most people in the city she had voted for the movement in the elections. She had supported them and this was her punishment. She had chosen not to go into the hills when Savimbi called them to battle. Now, in August 1993, she was paying the limbless, hungry price for staying behind.

When I met her, she was sitting with a row of other listless women with that glazed, vacant look I had come to recognise so well. What set her apart was a large cross around her neck. The chain hung so low it swung between her breasts. She was struggling to nurse her baby, but with the stump that ended at her thigh and the hard metal cross she was having difficulty manoeuvring into a balanced, comfortable position. Like the other women in the ward her face registered no expression, not even pain, when what remained of her bandaged leg bumped on the hard floor. The stump and the baby were the same length, both swathed, and for an instant, in my tiredness, I had the macabre thought that she was cradling her lost leg.

I crouched like a voyeur in front of her asking my routine journalist questions, the proverbial W's: 'What happened? Where did it happen? When? How?' When I got to 'Why?' I stopped.

For a movement which had always prided itself on the support of its people, UNITA had little shame in choosing soft targets like Dominga. The very people who voted for Savimbi were being bombed by him if it so happened that the MPLA was in charge of the city administration. For the very first time, Savimbi was losing the hearts and minds of his ethnic group, the Ovimbundu.

As 1993 progressed, food became the main weapon of the war. Savimbi's strategy of trying to take the cities had not worked so he had switched to starving them. He held a few provincial capitals – N'dalatando, Caxito, Huambo, Uíge and M'banza Congo. Those he didn't hold had become like MPLA islands in UNITA territory. Malange, Cuito, Luena, Menongue were like Angolan Sarajevos, the front line just miles away. But the big difference was that they were suffering a far worse humanitarian crisis. The war had reached an unprecedented level of ferocity which Angola had never seen before and which was difficult to depict as a writer.

Bananas and corn ripened in the fields but only the desperate ventured out to pick them because of the mines which had been planted by both sides – by UNITA to keep the population in and by the MPLA to keep UNITA out. The population had to rely instead on occasional air drops. Stalks of corn grew in the front gardens of people's homes and in public squares. Only rarely could relief planes get in with emergency supplies, and only after UNITA agreed to a quid pro quo – one plane to UNITA territory, one to MPLA. The WFP knew much of the food in UNITA areas was probably going to rebel soldiers rather than civilians but felt it worth overlooking this to save lives.

Compared to the inertia of UNAVEM, Philippe Borel's WFP team looked like heroes. The UN Security Council was vacillating about taking firm action, but Borel's team operated on its own, sticking pins in a big map on the wall: 'We can go here, we can't go there.' WFP Angola had a commitment which was rare for UN agencies that I've seen anywhere since. Part of it had to do with the fact that Borel's deputy, Fritz Zander, grew up in Angola and another team member was engaged to a woman from Huambo. The flight operations chief had also been raised in Angola. The team's motivation was also due to Borel's own personal dynamism. The WFP staff flew food to places UNAVEM was scared to go to, because they knew people they wanted to save. But there were casualties of their bravery. Planes carrying food aid, like the one I flew in to Luena, were targeted repeatedly. We were lucky. Three months later Russian flight engineer Victor Nestrenko was not. He died stepping on a land-mine when his plane crash-landed in Luena after being hit by a missile.

Someone in the UN coined the phrase one thousand deaths a day. No one really knew if that was a proper estimate; most of the wounded never made it to hospitals or morgues. As one British diplomat confided: 'Sure it may even be higher. We truly have no idea.' But the phrase was catchy and would periodically lure foreign camera crews and correspondents from major newspapers to fly in to try to capture images. But it was invariably impossible to get to the worst fighting and they flew out again, taking with them only the vaguest memories of the Forgotten War.

Savimbi wasn't doing a very good job of winning the hearts and minds of the international community. The UNITA chief was viewed as the big spoiler. The fact that he gave so little access to the media made it harder for UNITA to call attention to the MPLA's sins. The government had the moral high ground by being perceived as acting in self-defence. It also was more amenable to peace talks than UNITA.

Several rounds of negotiations were held in 1993, swivelling between Addis Ababa in January-February and Abidjan in April. UNITA failed to show for further talks in March, and those that took place yielded no conclusions. Having the military advantage, UNITA was only using the talks to gain time. Savimbi was never present, sending amongst others the loyal

Valentim and a young moderate, General Eugénio Manuvakola.

If the MPLA had had a good public relations sense it would have exploited the situation and brought along photographers and television crews to the front. But what would they have filmed? The government bombing its own cities. Pilots who needed to fly with the coast as a guideline because they were unable to follow maps. Soldiers who would rather drink and whore than fight. Thirteen-year-old children press-ganged into the army. A pathetic inability to wrest towns from UNITA. So the government practised what it thought was damage control – and the world saw no scenes of combat or tragic sieges like they saw of Bosnia. There were a few poignant humanitarian tales of hungry bedraggled refugees but no truly horrifying television images to galvanise the world.

There was one place in particular which was shocking, which every correspondent wanted to get to but couldn't. Huambo.

✢

As the government slowly rebuilt its army, the military's main efforts were concentrated on expelling UNITA from Huambo. Huambo was once the country's second city, with a population of about half a million people. It was once the country's breadbasket, poised on the now crippled Benguela Railroad on the central plateau. Huambo had been Savimbi's headquarters in 1976 and when he was driven out by the MPLA and the Cubans in February of that year he vowed that he would win the city back. Now he had.

The MPLA's General João de Matos knew Savimbi would be demoralised without his headquarters, which was more important psychologically than strategically, although the city was located right in the middle of the country. The ensuing battle for Huambo made its people the war's first big martyrs, a symbol of the determination of both adversaries to win at whatever cost.

Residents today refer to the 55-day battle merely as the 55 days. Others say it was 56 days. While it was happening, many people in Huambo lost track of time and the days of the week. When I went back to Huambo, many months after the battle, it was difficult to get a vivid picture of the impact from residents who had been rendered inarticulate by loss, shock or fear of reprisals.

Most would use a simple word like 'bad' or 'sad'. The vocabulary to express their trauma eluded them. Many had stayed indoors for most of the siege and could not describe what had happened outside their one-room refuges. Indeed, when the very first film footage came out of the siege many viewers were disappointed. There were only scenes of some street clashes and women giving birth on the exodus from the city. The true horrors were the inner ones.

One of the very few who could articulate what he felt was Jorge Ntyamba, who wrote a disturbing account entitled 'Huambo: 56 days of Terror and Death'.

As Ntyamba tells it, troubles in the city began in October 1992 when Savimbi withdrew there after the elections. Several thousand rebels in uniform joined him in the city, lining the boulevard running to the airport and standing guard around his white villa. By November the city was divided in half. UNITA occupied the Baixa, or downtown section, maintaining roadblocks to prevent pedestrians or police from entering without permission. People without passes were shot on sight. The government was restricted to the high part of the city, but because police were nothing more than a formality UNITA could circulate freely there too.

Certain streets gradually became impassable. Then, inexplicably, suspected government supporters began to disappear, even during the day. White and *mestiço* businessmen and supporters of the MPLA were favoured targets. They wouldn't come home for dinner; they were shot going to watch

TV with a friend. Their bodies were found floating on the surface of the river Kulimahala, which residents used for washing and drinking water.

Thousands of inhabitants began leaving the city. Some said it was for a holiday on the coast. Others said they had relatives they wanted to visit in Luanda. Some inhabitants, remembering when Cuban troops rolled in in 1976 to expel Savimbi, hoped someone would come to the MPLA's aid this time too. Many of those who remained expected a confrontation over Christmas. They relaxed when New Year passed peacefully.

Many were thus caught off guard when, on 9 January 1993, the government took the initiative. Police shot at Savimbi's White House and tried to take the airport. UNITA repulsed them and the streets boomed constantly with mortars for nearly two months thereafter.

There was no way the MPLA could win from the ground, seeing that they were pinned down on the equivalent of ten city blocks. The best the government troops and armed civilians could do was shoot from the opposite side of the street. UNITA, however, was easily supplied by land from the towns it controlled on the periphery of the city.

General João de Matos had no alternative but to order air attacks. UNITA responded with more artillery from the ground. Civilians caught in the middle were subjected to relentless shelling by both sides. 'Some days I counted more than 400 missiles falling,' said Ntyamba, who was there for the battle's duration. According to American diplomats who scanned satellite pictures, parts of the city were pulverised to dust.

Ntyamba said civilians who were handed guns for the first time in their lives didn't have time to think about the consequences of their actions. People grew matter of fact about ammunition rounds and cartridges. One friend of Ntyamba who was inexperienced with explosives accidentally stepped on a mine he was setting up. Ntyamba watched the man fall, his legs suddenly shortened to the knees. The man looked impassive as he struggled to get up.

The city moved downwards as people progressively sought more secure shelter. First the top floors and roofs were abandoned, then the third and second floors, until everyone camped on the ground floors of apartment buildings, ultimately establishing bunkers in basements and cellars. There they would huddle during the barrages with 70 to 100 new neighbours at any one time. Ntyamba was amazed at how harmoniously strangers got along with people they had nothing in common with in the intimacy of that cramped space.

Maybe one reason tension was so low was because every tenuous reserve of energy was concentrated on survival. People were dazed by sleeplessness and anxiety. Every sense was under assault: the smell of excrement from blocked drains and the reek of corpses made the air noxious; pounding cannons hurt the ear drums and interrupted dreams; dust from the crumbling ruined buildings irritated the eyes. As Ntyamba put it, people were reduced to an existential 'state of petrifaction'.

Rarely did he venture outside and when he did he ran between street corners, seeking shelter behind burnt-out cars. One time the only movement in the street was a dog gnawing on cadavers. During the siege he was too scared to bathe, fearful he'd become a magnet for artillery fire 'akin to the way the heat of aeroplane motors attracts anti-air missiles'.

Nytamba likened the macabre situation to that of caged wild animals. People grew delirious in their sunless confinements. 'Some expressed the desire to be birds and fly,' he said.

Finally, at the beginning of March 1993, the government admitted in a tersely worded statement issued in Luanda that its objective had failed and that its troops were carrying out a 'strategic retreat'. A column of 4 000 civilian refugees left the city under the protective cover of the soldiers withdrawing towards Benguela on the coast. About 500 died on the way. Women gave birth and then stood up and continued walking.

Mothers left their dying children behind. Many of the refugees walked 300 kilometres shoeless, sleeping in the cold mountain air without blankets or jackets.

I asked one American diplomat in Luanda whether perhaps Savimbi's victory of Huambo was Pyrrhic. What was once Angola's second city of 500 000 inhabitants was reduced to rubble and broken masonry. About 10 000 people had died in the siege and more than 400 000, some of them former UNITA supporters, had abandoned the city. Surely it wasn't worth it?

The diplomat differed. 'It may look like Dresden but this is Savimbi's finest moment. He's been fighting for this for 30 years and was expelled from there in 1976. Huambo has always been his spiritual capital.'

Savimbi, with his customary hubris, proclaimed on *Vorgan* on 9 March that for all the destruction, the taking of Huambo was 'a question of honour' for the people of the Planalto. All his hurt pride and childhood hatred stemming from the humiliations inflicted by the Portuguese and then the *mestiços* of Luanda, swelled to the surface. Savimbi articulated the two motivations which had driven him for 30 years: anger against northern domination, and nationalist defence of his Ovimbundu people. He had tried to set up a capital and was invaded by foreigners and whites – Cubans. He vowed that Huambo would never again fall into the hands of the MPLA, even if the war lasted many years.

'It is aimed at enabling us to unequivocally demonstrate that weak people, that people considered weak, have the strength to react to and to win when their cultural values and their traditions are attacked . . . in their own land,' he declared in Umbundu, the Ovimbundu language.

Then he reminded them: 'During this period of joy after the liberation of Huambo, it is equally important to speak about our bitterness, the humiliation that we have endured since the colonial period, how we are divided by *Luandalandia* (Luanda) as if we were a showroom.'

One dawn in January 1993, while lying half asleep in bed, I felt a vibration like a hum, first in my throat, then in my stomach, then in the room. It was a MIG, heading north-east. Was the government bombing Caxito? Another thundered past, going south. Huambo? For the next few weeks, these ominous rumblings accompanied daybreak. But none of the flights was ever mentioned in the newspaper.

Instead, we read a lot about women's sports. The *Jornal de Angola* newspaper would often have absurd diverting headlines on the front page, usually about an obscure match. Just when UNITA was taking town after town, readers could find out about Angola's competition with Zaire in women's basketball or how women's handball was faring in the African games.

Maybe it was meant to divert people, like escapist films made during World War Two. No one I knew had ever attended these games or heard of these athletic girl heroines. Most people I knew in Luanda were solely preoccupied with the war.

The oddest headline was about unemployment rising 10 per cent from 1990 to 1991. This in a country where one-third of the population was now living in refugee camps and no one really knew how many were alive!

The only sense one really got of the enormity of the tragedy was in the daily radio broadcasts listing people seeking news of missing relatives. The names were read by a woman with a monotone voice, for example: 'Mrs Maria Elena Gonçalves seeks information about her brother Mario and his wife Maria Paulinho who were last heard of in Huambo on November 28.' 'Zé Maria Moco from Andulo please contact your parents in Luanda.' The announcer's bored voice never evoked the anguish of the families. As the months went on the broadcasts got longer and longer. A friend from the radio station told me they rarely received responses.

✢

Savimbi had recaptured his beloved Huambo but another big prize eluded him: oil. Oil was the government's Achilles' heel. The 650 000 barrels per day production accounted for 90 per cent of export earnings and was mortgaged years in advance. Without oil, the government could not finance its fight. Oil meant victory.

During the first war, UNITA never had success attacking the northern oil fields. This time they did better. They captured Soyo, the country's second main oil centre which accounted for most of the onshore oil output and one-third of total production. Defended mainly by Ninja riot police, Soyo was ill-prepared when UNITA struck. Witnesses told a pathetic tale of police and soldiers hiding in the sand or escaping on boats when the enemy approached. The installations of multinational companies, Petrofina of Belgium and the American Texaco, were razed.

Soyo subsequently changed hands several times. In March 1993 the government recaptured it, but lost it again in May to UNITA. By the time the government firmly recaptured Soyo in 1994 the complex was completely devastated.

But UNITA never succeeded in major strikes against the main prize, Cabinda, which was just north of Soyo. Cabinda was the main offshore oil centre and accounted for the other two-thirds of production. It was run by Cabinda Gulf, a subsidiary of Chevron.

The enclave, separated from the rest of Angola in a sandwich between Zaire and Congo, had remained virtually untouched during the previous war except for some minor attacks by Cabinda separatists. This time, too, it seemed unlikely Savimbi would stage a successful assault. He lacked the boats and long-range missiles necessary to damage the offshore facilities. Plus, the Americans made clear to Savimbi that he shouldn't take them on. This would escalate the war to a level which he knew he would lose. As long as American facilities and civilians were untouched, Washington would stay out of the war.

But war fever spread to Cabinda anyway. UNAVEM observers dug trenches at their onshore compound. Cabinda Gulf pulled out 200 non-essential expatriate oil workers on 23 January and drew up contingency plans for a controlled evacuation if disaster struck.

In case Savimbi had any doubts, US ambassador Edmund De Jarnette flew up to Cabinda in February to make clear the US position. He took me and another journalist along as he addressed several hundred oil men, just to make sure the message got across. The ambassador looked vaguely like John F Kennedy and on this occasion resembled a handsome young senator at a campaign rally.

'Hands off Cabinda, Dr Savimbi,' he proclaimed to the oil men's applause. 'See what happens if you touch Cabinda.'

Savimbi never did.

✛

Like Cabinda, the capital was immune to the martyrdom of the provinces. But UNITA took malicious satisfaction in menacing Luanda and keeping its residents on perpetual edge. Although expelled in October 1992, UNITA hovered only 90 kilometres away in Caxito. From Cacauco on the city limits you could see smoke rising in the bush. That was too close for comfort for those of us who remembered the roadblocks and bombs in October.

The government propaganda machine only fed the hysteria. The high point came on 11-12 November, when the state-run daily *Jornal de Angola* published the so-called Chitunda diaries, which included an alleged UNITA plot drawn up on 7 October to paralyse Luanda.

The grand plan was to attack and paralyse electricity, the port, water stations. Then UNITA would unleash 2 500 men on the capital in an assault on the president's palace at Futungo de Belas. Access to the airport would be cut off.

There was also a detailed plan to evacuate the UNITA wounded and an ominous three-year-old list of leading whites and *mestiços* in the MPLA. They included N'dalu, General Higino Carneiro and the now head of the military, João de Matos.

This apparent hit list and the other documents, hand-written by senior officials like Jeremias Chitunda and Carlos Morgado, were dismissed by some sceptics as fraudulent. (Later, senior UNITA officials confirmed to me that they were authentic.)

But for the people of Luanda who had kicked out UNITA and were afraid of the bogeymen returning, the Chitunda diaries fed fears of something sinisterly imminent when in January and February 1993 UNITA cadres destroyed water pumps and electricity pylons on the outskirts of town, plunging Luanda into parched darkness. What was coming next – poisoning the water supply? Cutting off the airport? UNITA had been in the city months before and knew the lie of the land. Was the grand plan coming to fruition?

✝

Aside from the psychological pressure, the sabotage made life distinctly uncomfortable, especially for those living in the *musseques*. The rich at least had generators. They could hire trucks to carry tanks of water from the river 90 kilometres away or pay $10 a bottle for mineral water (the price tripled in a week and was more than for beer). At the UN compound, the Russian pilots shaved in the pool. One UN agency loaded up a routine supply flight to Namibia with dirty clothes to launder in Windhoek.

It was a different story for the poor, who lacked plumbing in their shacks anyway. Since independence in 1975 they had coped with periodic shortages due less to UNITA sabotage than to deteriorating infrastructure. But after the 1991 peace accords life had improved greatly and this was a frustrating setback.

They were reduced again to bathing in the already dirty sea or using toilets which were filled to the brim, lit by candle or paraffin light. Cholera was breaking out.

My own deprivations were limited. I had convinced Reuters I had to stay in a hotel with a generator and emergency supplies of water.

When the plumbing crisis struck I suddenly became extremely popular among waterless acquaintances. Sources suddenly wanted to hold interviews in my room, and then would ask casually where the 'facilities' were. I even caught someone taking a surreptitious shower. My bathroom became a Mecca.

I was feeling pretty grimy, none the less, rationing the brown river water which was brought in by truck and refilled in my hotel bathtub every few days. It left a dubious 'tan' on my skin. The women of Luanda put on a glamorous front against adversity. I once asked my friend Rosa how she and her friends managed to appear impeccably fragrant while going three weeks without a bath. That day she was wearing a turban, ostensibly to cover her unwashed hair, and her skin looked luminous.

'Vodka,' she said. 'Cleanse your face with it. It's very good for the pores. Then you wash your hair with beer or tonic water, which gives it a nice shine. Use dark nail polish to hide the grime. Wear black clothes which obscure the dirt. And splash on perfume. Lots and lots of it.'

✢

Luanda residents felt under siege and in their impotence vented their rage on the first ready targets. Savimbi was increasingly using ethnic rhetoric, talking about Ovimbundu nationalism and broadcasting menacing messages against other ethnic groups. Indeed, UNITA had targeted these groups in witch-hunts in Benguela, Cuito, Lobito and Huambo. The desire for revenge exploded when the government alleged that Zairian troops had backed UNITA in their capture of Soyo. Within 24 hours on 22 January people in the *musseques* went on the rampage and slaughtered more than 60 Zairians and French-speaking Angolans.

Bakongos and Zairians were called the Jews of Luanda for their entrepreneurial streak. They ran many of the stalls at the open-air markets. Now other ethnic groups and have-nots were getting their revenge.

I first heard about the reprisals from the driver João Martins. João lived in a Bakongo section of the *musseques* – a prime target for the mob. He was from the northern Uíge province. During the first war he sought refuge in Zaire, where he learned to speak flawless French and took the name Jean. Luanda is a city of virtually no public transport or taxis; there are only a handful of private cars waiting at the airport to provide taxi services but you can't hail one down in the streets. There wasn't much competition, but João, or Jean, made much more money with his brown Mercedes than most other taxi drivers because he worked harder and took the initiative to wait outside hotels. He also spoke French, which was an asset for picking up foreign customers.

João rarely came upstairs to my hotel room, where I worked. He'd phone me from the lobby instead. I was surprised, therefore, to hear a knock on my door, an insistent, staccato knock, and find him standing in the passage. The back of his shirt was wet as though he had been sitting in front of a fountain. I realised only later that it was soaked with fear.

João said he was going to 'keep a low profile' for a couple of days until the frenzy died down. It wasn't safe to be driving around the streets for the time being.

'They're all over the place, big groups of them. They went into Roque Santeiro (the market), looking for all the Bakongos. They went to my neighbour's house and tried to break down the door.' He spoke quickly, winding the key chain tightly around his fingers until there were marks where the blood seemed to stop.

'They tore off the clothes of the women, even elderly women,' João said. 'One girl was allegedly raped more than 30 times. They say the police just stood by, guns in hand, and did nothing. They even smiled.'

I asked him what he and his family planned to do. The last time this had happened, during the October massacres, 200 Zairian citizens and many more Bakongos and Ovimbundu were slaughtered as the gangs went from door to door in the *musseques*, hunting them down like antelope. Those who survived barricaded themselves inside their homes. I offered him money so he could manage until things calmed down, but João declined.

He got up from the chair he was sitting on and headed towards the door. He looked tall and very proud. 'It's OK, *Mana Judite*. I've seen this before. We'll get by.'

✛

Someone, presumably a member or members of the staff, was taking medicines from the clinics and selling them in the markets. At the city's main hospital, Graça Machel, doctors complained that someone had stolen antibiotics and swabs. One of the nurses said the medicines weren't even being delivered to the hospital; government officials were selling them directly on the streets.

I went to the market once with an Angolan friend who wanted to buy antibiotics for her daughter. We walked among other worried mothers searching the stalls, where individual pills were laid out according to type. Some of them couldn't read and bought the wrong type. I felt worse for the victims who had flown up from faraway places like Menongue. They'd lie alone, in a strange city where they knew no one, groaning in pain on a mattress stained with a stranger's blood.

Trauma counselling was out of the question in a country

where there was no anaesthetic for amputations. Most people resorted to 'natural healing'. A particularly ghoulish centre, run by a religious man named Papa Kitoka, was set up in the *musseques* for the mentally disturbed. The mad and the infirm were chained to tyre hubs or poles, gangrene setting in around their ankles where manacles dug into their flesh. Some patients had dents in their foreheads from banging them against poles as they rocked back and forth with their inner demons.

✛

Anyone who had access to a speedboat would go to Mussulo, a peninsular bar of white sand across the bay from Luanda, to escape the sweltering weekends. A palm-fringed sanctuary, the biggest worries there were jellyfish stings, sunburn and how to keep the prawns fresh and the white wine chilled.

The only reminder that there was a war were the fighter planes thundering overhead on their way to strafe Huambo, mirrored in the seas below where expatriates were perfecting their water-skiing.

Diplomats and foreign UN personnel needing to unwind would accept any opportunity to go to Mussulo. I accompanied one evacuation drill by Texaco and US embassy staff, which was coupled with a trip to the beach. In a leisurely fashion we piled into a speedboat, carefully positioning the wine coolers and pâté, and sped through the harbour past the rusting hulks of sunken ships towards a waiting boat. There we clambered up with great alacrity to complete our mission. Speed was of the essence; we had to get to Mussulo fast, before the food warmed up.

As we embarked at the pier, I ran into General Cirilo Ita getting into a boat. He was dressed in plastic sandals and Bermuda shorts and was carrying a basket which looked suspiciously like it might contain lunch.

'Hey, there's a war going on. Shouldn't you be with your

troops?' I joked. At that moment, another MIG screamed overhead.

He shrugged, pushing the edge of the boat with his foot. He looked slightly irked. 'They can fight. I'm going to the beach.'

✦

Frivolities aside, UNITA was seen as the spoiler and the MPLA was gaining more credibility on the diplomatic front. In May 1993 six weeks of talks in Abidjan were suspended after UNITA refused to sign a compromise political settlement and cease-fire. The MPLA's reward was diplomatic recognition from the Clinton administration later that month. The embassy in Luanda was inaugurated officially on 21 June, the first formal American diplomatic presence in Angola in nearly 20 years of independence. It was just a row of trailers with the Stars and Stripes hoisted above in the stagnant air. But it was the beginning of a new political era and further isolation for UNITA.

Margaret Anstee had meanwhile had enough of Angola and asked to leave. Her replacement, Alioune Blondin Beye, arrived on 29 June 1993 and announced that a cease-fire would be his main priority.

A former foreign minister of Mali, Beye was a heavy-set, assertive man who had no qualms about summoning ambassadors at one in the morning for consultations if work needed to be done. Savimbi felt Beye was more his match – he was a black African man. However, this didn't stop Savimbi from mocking Beye's traditional garb, to which the UNITA leader referred derisively as a 'dress'.

Gaps were appearing to allow emergency food and medicine into besieged cities. Cuito was still being denied supplies but in August UNITA agreed to short truces to allow shipments into Menongue.

By then, the city of 60 000 had lost a tenth of its population to hunger, fighting or disease. Those who survived were terrified of attacks. Descending from the WFP plane, I had to leap over mortar holes on the tarmac which reminded me that the UNITA trenches were only 15 kilometres away, uncomfortably within firing range.

Like other besieged cities, Menongue was full of idle people. There was little to do all day, with the mined fields untillable and the markets bare. People were numbed by artillery fire, grief and malnutrition. They stayed close to their homes or the trenches on the city's edge in case the shelling resumed suddenly. Just sweeping the debris outside their homes was too much effort. The only time I saw a renewal of energy was when UN food flights thundered above. Then everyone hurried on foot or piled into pick-up trucks to get to the airport to seek nourishment, news or escape. Suddenly the apathy would give way to shouting, jostling and running. The dogs would bark.

✢

Two pony-tailed photographers from London who had flown down to Menongue on the same plane as myself were desperate to get to the scenes of the fighting, obsessed with capturing images of battle.

'Gotta get to the front, man,' the dark-haired one kept muttering.

To pass the time, they joined me on a tour of the hospital, which was filled with legless children with the malnourished silhouettes of grasshoppers – skinny arms and legs and swollen stomachs. We had come down on the first aid flight in weeks and the nurses were desperately urging their weak charges to swallow a watery gruel to restore their strength before the supply flights were cut off again.

Land-mine victims were moaning on the urine-stained

concrete floors while they waited for attention. Amputees dragged themselves on their stomachs for lack of wheelchairs, on dirt-encrusted tiled floors. Stretchers piled up outside served as reminders that many hadn't made it this far.

The clinic had long ago run out of anaesthetics. Operations were conducted without painkillers or antibiotics. The medical staff would tie wailing patients to the beds to keep them from writhing off while they sawed at mangled limbs.

The clinic's only doctor, Domingos Aguiar Vicente, exhausted after months of working in such conditions, noticed the photographers weren't taking any pictures.

'This is the war,' he said gently. 'You don't need to go further to see it.'

✧

I often think of the five months I was away from Angola, from March to August 1993, as an exile of sorts. It was to a large extent self-imposed; when everyone was flying to Angola to get to Huambo, I was trying to get out. I was exhausted after working six months without a break and needed to get away for a while to regain my perspective on life. But from the moment I left that claustrophobic environment I felt disorientated. Suddenly I had time to process what I had seen, but I didn't quite know how to sift through the experience.

I must have appeared rather hollow-eyed and gaunt because my boss in Johannesburg took one look at me and ordered me to have a month's leave, which just about compensated for all the days off which I never took in Angola.

I went to New York to visit my family and stopped off in Portugal to see some friends. It was like seeing colonialism in reverse. Everything was in an Angolan context; I couldn't view things for what they were. I was seeing the blue and white tiled friezes depicting Portugal's lost maritime empire and the architectural seashell motifs as echoes of Luanda instead of the other way around.

I went to my old haunts, the African night-clubs where everyone had celebrated the Biçesse accords in May 1991, madly drinking beer and toasting the future. But now some of the UNITA guys were dead or jailed and the MPLA went to different spots. The UNITA acquaintances still in town didn't want to talk to me; they just glared and said they didn't mix with traitors.

I asked some of the Angolans about my friend, the singer Waldemar Bastos, the former muse of the MPLA. They said he had stopped writing music since the war resumed and was depressed.

'He's cut himself off completely since then. He's in a big gloom,' one friend said.

Waldemar and I went out for a Chinese meal; he was no longer talking to his family back in Luanda who accused him of joining UNITA. He drank heavily and swiftly while we ate and called me an MPLA supporter.

'But Waldemar, I don't take sides,' I said, rebutting the accusation.

'How can you live in Angola and not take sides?' he insisted, jabbing chicken with his chopstick, practically knocking over the beer.

'It's your war, not mine,' I said.

'No, it's gone beyond that,' he answered.

I didn't reply because I was so angry. But later I thought about what he had said and wondered if perhaps he had a point. I had lost my objectivity by now and was too emotionally wrapped up in Angola to maintain a safe distance.

✥

My 'exile' coincided with the MPLA's great moment – the military balance began to tilt in its favour in August and September 1993. The government had by then built up its numbers to 50 000, almost matching UNITA. The government pilots, who had missed their targets miserably in the beginning, had vastly improved their aim. The MPLA army was gaining experience in counter-insurgency, the area in which it had previously been most deficient.

The Angolan government was also getting help from the most unlikely of sources – former South African soldiers who had fought for UNITA. A Pretoria-based company, Executive Outcomes, had signed a $40 million contract with the Angolan government to post about 350 South African veterans as military advisers. At first they helped guard, or defend, oil installations at Soyo.

Later the South Africans were spotted elsewhere and were credited with a major role in the retaking of Huambo in November 1994. The men frequented expatriate bars in Luanda, looking like caricatures of Afrikaners in khaki shorts, loudly discussing rugby scores. Some of them spoke Portuguese, learned from the time they had served in Jamba. Diplomats said they were nothing more than glorified mercenaries, but both the company and the Angolan government insisted the men were merely providing security and training and were not engaged in actual combat.

Months before, I had seen the MPLA's military comeback being plotted in the lobby bar of the Hotel Tivoli. The characters swirling around the marble floors and potted palms could have served as models from central casting for a Hollywood spy movie – from the Lebanese traders moving cargoes of 'import-export' to the muscular Israelis who knew about diamonds. They huddled over the cashew nuts, with occasional clinks of frosted beer mugs punctuating their whispers and murmurs.

The wealth of the country was often divided and sold in that lobby. Angola's riches attracted intrigue unparalleled in neighbouring countries. Actors changed sides easily, indifferent to the ideology of their funders, depending on the financial gains involved. South African pilots and soldiers who fought readily in defence of UNITA under apartheid later switched to the MPLA's more lucrative side.

On slow news days I would simply sit in the lobby, a bottle of Portuguese Sagres beer in hand. Sooner or later someone would sit down at the next seat and boast about a deal I shouldn't have known about. It was at the Tivoli that Executive Outcomes first negotiated its agreement to provide security for the MPLA. A smooth, cigar-smoking Englishman and a South African in shorts sat at the hotel bar for hours every day with the head of the state oil company Sonangol, working out details and payments.

There were other characters who gave cryptic responses when asked about the business they did. Even Otelho Saraiva, the great fallen hero of the Portuguese revolution, had a minor role. For weeks on end he dined in the hotel restaurant, always accompanied by a silent dark woman. Those in the know said he was there to negotiate deals in arms, construction and food.

✛

On the diplomatic front, the UN Security Council was finally asserting itself with UNITA. After a series of tepid threats, on 26 September 1993 the Council imposed an oil and arms embargo against Savimbi, with an implicit warning that more sanctions could follow. The UNITA leader tried to head off the embargo by declaring a unilateral cease-fire on 20 September. But this time no one was fooled.

The sanctions were largely symbolic at first, but they were an added psychological blow as the government forces advanced across the scrub-land between Benguela and Huambo on the hilly central plateau. By September, the MPLA army had recaptured Cubal, Bocoio and Ganda and two columns of around 4 000 soldiers were moving in a pincer movement towards Huambo. They were about 130 kilometres from their target.

During those six months which I think of as my exile, John Liebenberg would call periodically to keep me informed of things back in Angola.

Liebenberg was a freelance cameraman from Namibia who was what is known as a good operator. He had wiry, uncombed blond hair and a good rapport with kids and the military, who affectionately called him 'General John'. He didn't speak any Portuguese except for the words written on the back of his ripped salmon-coloured jacket: 'Don't shoot, I'm the piano player'. He went to places no one else did, at times when no one else was there. He was as hooked on Angola as I was, probably more so because he had been going there since the 1980s. These days Liebenberg was always popping in and out of Luanda. Reuters sometimes hired him for shoots.

'It's getting very bad. They're starving the cities,' Liebenberg said in June. The next month he called to say that things had deteriorated further. And then another time: 'They've got South African mercenaries stationed in Soyo.'

Each time I suggested to my employers that I go back to cover one of these stories Reuters reminded me that South Africa was my main responsibility, as well as one of the world's top stories. But then in August John called on a crackling and echoing line from Luanda: 'It's completely changed. The military are breaking through towards Huambo.'

Reuters finally said, 'OK, go back to Angola. But only for a short one this time.'

✢

Flying into Luanda was a homecoming of sorts. João, the driver with the beat-up brown Mercedes, was at the airport and we caught up on news. Lots of journalists had come through and he had made enough money to buy a new car. But we took the rusted old brown one for good luck. I barely stayed in Luanda, though. Liebenberg had arranged a flight on a diamond cargo plane to Benguela, the city on the coast where the military flights were being co-ordinated for Huambo.

Liebenberg had briefed me in so much detail about the advances of the government on the Huambo front that we didn't have much time to discuss Benguela. I wasn't fully prepared for the deluge of refugees, tens of thousands of them. It seemed one-third of the country was living on the beach in plastic tents donated by the UNHCR, refusing to go home even though the government had 'liberated' their villages.

In fact, only half a million refugees had converged on the city over a staggered period of time. None of them had money, houses, intact families or clothes other than the rags on their backs. Most of them had diseases, wounds and terrible memories of what UNITA had done to them. It was seven months since I had last been in Benguela and the city then still had much of the charm which had made it a favourite retreat during colonial days. Now it was practically unrecognisable.

We stayed along with two other colleagues at the house of some friends of Liebenberg's, a gracious hospitable family who had had a lot of money in times past. I couldn't figure out why they had stayed, but the husband, a Portuguese businessman, mumbled something about its being too late to leave. My three travel companions were relegated to sharing a one-roomed cottage outside the main house. I was assigned one of the daughters' rooms – a little girl's room of dolls and lace and Snoopy stickers in a house with no water. I wasn't very bothered where I stayed but the woman of the house was protective towards me. 'You can't sleep among those men. Stay in the house. You'll be safe.'

The next day we went to see the commander about flying to the front. He wasn't enthusiastic about a woman coming along. The first thing he said was: 'Where is she going to sleep? She can't sleep with all those men around her.' It was definitely a problem being a woman in Benguela.

We began a round of delicate negotiations at the barracks at Catumbela military airport, a flat building surrounded by orange helicopters. Liebenberg looked at them longingly when they took off, muttering 'We've got to get on one of those.' We handed out 16 packets of Marlboros to anyone in a uniform who'd shake our hands. We had papers issued by the military command in Luanda with some very impressive stamps, but the problem seemed to be lack of flight space available and helicopters breaking down.

There was another problem, apparently. The commander kept bringing up the fact that I wasn't a man, whispering it to Liebenberg in my presence as though I had cancer. Arguments that I was as mean and tough as the guys and that they would ensure no soldier sullied my virtue did not convince the recalcitrant commander. Liebenberg was adamant, less probably out of loyalty than because he was scared of losing my skills as a Portuguese translator.

'If she doesn't go, I don't. And if I don't, no one gets to see pictures of your progress,' he said. The commander just dug into the pack of Marlboros we had given him and frowned.

We had deadlocks and apparent progress, stalemates and advances, only to return the next day to the barracks to find out that things really were '*dificil*'. I suddenly had insight into what peace negotiators must have experienced at the talks in Lusaka. We engaged as mediators two local journalists, Jaime and Nito, who had spent time with the commander on *O Frente*, the Front. They assured us that with a bottle of vodka and a chicken everything would be OK. But Jaime did ask, one time, 'Where is she going to sleep?'

For ten days we sat in Benguela, eating peanuts and cheese sandwiches and drinking beer at the little bar across the street from the house. Being in limbo for so long and a high level of alcohol intake was making our little group irritable. On the verge of a breakthrough, our fragile arrangement was almost upset by our American colleague who entered into a drunken argument with Nito. Discussion led to a Portuguese journalist who was close to the commander and was learning to use guns.

'So what?' Nito said nonchalantly. 'We carry arms out to *O Frente*.'

The American was outraged. 'How can you guys do that? That means you're taking sides.'

Nito looked at him as though he was daft. 'Of course we take sides. We work for the government media. UNITA kills journalists like us. We're not like you. We don't just fly in and out.' He got up and went to his jeep, slammed the door loudly and prepared to drive off, revving more than was necessary. He leaned out of the window, shouting: 'We don't have an embassy to protect us.'

Fortunately the altercation didn't spoil our plans. I think the commander was so tired of our badgering that he finally relented out of sheer exhaustion.

'You can go now,' he said wearily, 'but only if there's a spare place on the chopper. The wounded and soldiers get preference.'

He looked at me and started to say something but then stopped. I was expecting him to say: 'Women go last.'

✛

There were no soldiers or wounded to compete for seats on the way to *O Frente*. On the contrary, most of the other melancholy-looking people on the helicopter were civilians who had been away from their villages during UNITA's ten-month occupation of the area and were finally coming home to reclaim their land.

Among them were the town fathers of Ganda, which had recently been liberated. It was the closest town to the front line that we could visit. Ganda was 120 kilometres west of Huambo and among the very first towns occupied by the rebels in October 1992. The men were animated on the ride, talking about what it would be like to see their homes again and get back to work after being in limbo for so long.

'We must open the schools soon,' said administrator Mateus Franco. 'Those children must get back to school.'

He seemed oblivious, in his high spirits, to the dangers below – UNITA. The pilot flew the helicopter low for security reasons, hovering just over the treetops. Liebenberg motioned with his eyes to a plane which had been shot down recently, its charred carcass just a few hundred metres below us. Usually people run out and wave when helicopters pass overhead, but the huts had been burnt out and emptied of their owners. Unifying the ghost villages was the fractured spine of the Benguela Railroad which had linked Angola with Zaire and Zambia and on which Savimbi's father had served as the first black station master.

When we landed on a dirt patch outside the town and walked towards the buildings, Mateus Franco was silent too. Every building had bullet marks and every shop was closed. There were hardly any people. The school, where he wanted his children to learn multiplication and proper grammar, had no desks or chairs. The only things on the stripped cement floors were some corn husks and excrement deposited by the occupiers before they withdrew.

We left Franco at his home, or what used to be his home. Now it was a bare building with bullet holes the size of golf balls and empty walls with brown smears.

'My house, my house,' he said in soft lament, touching the walls where a picture used to hang, walking through what used to be a parlour in which to play cards and have Sunday dinners. 'My house, my house.'

His colleagues waited quietly for him to finish his inspection so they could start their meeting to plan their new administration. But Franco sat for a long time, just looking at the metal frames which used to have doors.

Outside, Liebenberg had set up his camera to film but was

215

frustrated by the deserted panorama. Even at the market everyone seemed too tired to move. They were offering onions that should have been as big as baseballs but were the size of pebbles. But he couldn't get them to hold out their wares with sufficient animation. 'I need some life for proper images,' he complained, brusquely folding up his tripod in front of the closed bakery where only one shard of glass hung in the window-frame. 'This is too static.'

✝

On the Ganda front, MPLA Colonel José Manuel de Sousa sipped some chocolate milk out of his rations and stretched his legs in the springtime sun. A mortar pounded somewhere in the distance, maybe a couple of miles away, but he wasn't too worried. He was more concerned that one of his men might step out of line, literally.

'Mind your feet,' he called out jauntily as someone went to check the generator at the back of the camp. Along the periphery was buried, with delicate care, a necklace of land-mines to keep the enemy out.

De Sousa was in a bouncy mood. Sure, he and his men had been dug in for several weeks. Sure, just in front of them were rocky hills which comprised the most difficult terrain left to their objective. But they were half-way to Huambo and well supplied. Morale hadn't been this good in months.

The men were preparing lunch and digging more trenches. Most were Ovimbundu and had been born somewhere between Benguela and Bie on the Planalto. All of them had lost family in the war. They were all MPLA sympathisers and said they hated Savimbi.

Another boom went off in the background and someone made a joke about Savimbi farting.

'Yeah, O Mais Velho has a big ass,' one soldier said, opening a can of peaches.

'*O Mais Grande*, The Biggest One,' another said.

'The biggest ass in Africa,' another soldier said. 'Hey, hand me some of those peaches, will you. I've got an appetite.'

The peaches and chocolate milk were from Portugal. I couldn't see the labels on the men's uniforms but could tell they were new – crisp, that bright green before they fade to dull olive from the sun and washing on river rocks.

In Luanda the diplomats told me the MPLA was doing better now. The Troika by now acknowledged that the Biçesse accords were dead. In July 1993 the three countries officially allowed the Angolan government to acquire arms. Israel was offering military equipment and technical assistance too.

De Sousa wasn't giving me too many details about his next move or where supplies came from. ('This is a war. It is a secret.') But like any man proud of a job well done, he hinted at fresh advances planned in the near future. 'Come back in a couple of months,' he said cheerily. 'We'll see you in Huambo then.'

✢

On the flight back to Johannesburg from Luanda I sat next to a little girl of about eight years and her mother. The girl had deep scars from knife cuts on her forehead and cheeks. I thought it odd; tribal scarring is not common in Angola, especially with women. On closer inspection, I realised she was unwell, her breathing laboured. Her face was abnormally puffy and her eyes were swollen shut. The girl and her mother were dressed in old and worn clothes, which was unusual; most people who rode on the twice-weekly Luanda-Johannesburg flight were diamond smugglers or members of the MPLA elite going on shopping sprees in South Africa.

The mother asked me for some help filling out the immigration forms in English and we began talking. She told me the girl had fallen very ill six months before with what appeared to be an eye infection. The problem was, they couldn't

217

find the proper medicine in the markets and the doctors in the Graça Machel hospital said they didn't have the means to treat it. They suggested she take the girl to Johannesburg, but she didn't have enough money at the time. As the infection festered, the girl's face swelled with pus and she lost her sight. To relieve the pressure, they cut her face with a kitchen knife to drain it. It took a few months, but finally her family and friends raised enough money for two plane tickets. Now they were flying to a country where they knew no one and barely spoke the language.

When we got to Johannesburg I telephoned an acquaintance who worked at one of the township hospitals to see if we could arrange free medical treatment. The mother spoke some English but the girl spoke only Portuguese and I was afraid that they would be exposed as foreigners instantly. The doctor listened gravely to the story and said it sounded like major surgery was necessary to prevent the infection from reaching her brain. He suggested they pretend they were from Venda, a region where comparatively few people spoke English.

'But it's a risk; there may be a nurse there who speaks Venda herself and then their cover will be blown.' He paused and asked me to repeat the symptoms of the sick child. 'It's a terrible shame; it could have been treated easily in the first week with a simple dose of antibiotics. I doubt she'll see again.'

The mother never tried to go to the hospital or pretend to be from Venda. She was too scared they'd be found out and expelled as illegal aliens. The last I heard she had taken her daughter to the barren Free State to seek the help of a priest someone had recommended.

✝

Our footage of Ganda and Benguela was well received. However, the place I felt I needed to get to was Cuito. But no one could get in. Cuito was the worst battle, Angolans said, and it became a symbol for the lack of testimony to Angola's silent agony.

Once a pretty town in the breadbasket of the central highlands, Cuito had eclipsed Huambo as the symbol of martyrdom in the new Angolan war. The battle of Huambo lasted 55 days. The siege of Cuito lasted nine months. Those nine months, Angolans said, were worse than the 55 days in the battle for Huambo. In Huambo the dogs ate the dead people in the streets. That happened in Cuito, too. But then the people ate the dogs.

The chunks of broken masonry which were left in the city bore no resemblance to the affluent colonial town with two swimming pools which had been favoured by the Portuguese.

The human disaster which had been under way in Cuito had reached mythical proportions because no outsider could get there. The lone voice of the state-run radio correspondent, his voice crackling and barely audible in his daily dispatches, served as the only source of information for outside. The correspondent catapulted from obscurity to become a national celebrity. People in Cuito sheltered him as he shifted between safe houses, knowing that his transmitter was their only link with the world.

As the military pressure and sanctions took their toll on UNITA, the movement relented and decided to let the UN bring in emergency supplies to Cuito, in return for supplying UNITA areas.

It was a Thursday in October 1993 when the WFP's Fritz Zander called me from Luanda. I was at my desk in Johannesburg editing a story about Zambian mining. The line was fuzzy but the words 'Cuito' and 'Dante's Inferno' got through clearly enough.

'. . . maybe 30 000 dead' . . . 'city a virtual cemetery' . . . 'smell of gangrene everywhere' . . . 'corpses in the river . . . no clean drinking water . . .'

And then: 'We'll try to get you on a flight.'

I was in Luanda a couple of days later. The WFP had reserved every last inch on the cargo planes for food and drips and medicine. Only when the emergencies were taken care of would journalists be given space. I was at the top of the list to go in once the crisis was attended to. But then things went wrong. A WFP spokeswoman went on a walkabout in Cuito and gave an interview on state radio about how awful the conditions were there. UNITA was furious and closed the airport. She was stranded there for two days and flights were suspended for a while.

When she returned to Luanda, a picture began to form of what had happened in Cuito. It was an apocalyptic vision which seemed so awful that I had to go for myself to see it. After following Cuito's agony for months I wanted to be there at the liberation.

The WFP spokeswoman reported that there wasn't even an aspirin or a band-aid left in the hospital. Patients dragged themselves on their stomachs into the clinic's backyard to chew grass. Amputations were conducted at home with kitchen knives.

Snipers from both sides were separated by just a few hundred metres. Every building had been touched by the fighting; some still had unexploded mortars sticking out of the walls. On the main street, which served as the front line, the entire front facade of an apartment building had been blown off, balconies jutting out tenuously and living rooms exposed targets. Everyone was recruited for the war effort. Amputees propped themselves up on sacks, women and young boys of eight who could barely hold their weapons strapped cartridges around their chests as they crouched behind window sills to take aim.

They knocked down the walls between apartments and houses for safe passage along an entire building or street, keeping ropes handy in case someone ventured out into the streets and got caught in crossfire. They buried the dead wherever they could – on the roofs, on verandas and in backyards. They went weeks without sleep, against a backdrop of relentless artillery and the stench of blocked toilets. They lost the desire for sex, even for food. They ate cockroaches, their children's cats and dogs and roots and grass. When all these provisions were eaten, they'd organise large groups, called *batidas*, which comprised hundreds of men and women, some with babies strapped to their backs, to shoot their way out of the destroyed town to forage for cassava leaves, mangoes and rats and to collect water from the river.

This was compelling stuff, but Reuters had lost interest in Angola by then and they could not afford to wait a couple more days.

'We need you to work the night-shift, we're too short-staffed,' the editor in Johannesburg said. 'Get on the first flight back.'

I did. Four days later the first journalists flew into Cuito.

My frustration at not joining them was not purely professional, although I was indeed angry that having come that far, we had needlessly missed a story. It was also that I had to see Cuito for myself to put into context everything I had heard. I could only describe Angola with gaps, and this was a vital piece of the puzzle missing. I fumed in Johannesburg, feeling as though I had been denied a visit to an ill friend in hospital.

I finally visited Cuito more than a year later. I walked gingerly with a friend on the main street which had been the front line, careful not to stray off the road because of the land-mines planted in the grass. The hospital was filled with women whose legs had been blown off while they were planting corn in the fields on the edge of town. We saw grenades sticking out of the buildings, which were roofless and so wrecked with huge holes that it was questionable whether they could still be called buildings. People were camped in the ruins. They had nowhere else to go.

My friend was silent during most of the visit. As we got

ready to return to the airport to fly back to Luanda, he turned to me.

'This is worse than Bosnia. Why didn't anyone write about it?'

✣

After the aborted Cuito trip I stayed away from Angola for a long while. My new exile extended into 1994 and lasted that entire year. It was a crucial year for Angola – a year of consolidation, misery and, remarkably at the end, a peace accord. It was also the year of South Africa's first multiparty elections.

About 800 foreign correspondents converged on the country for what was considered to be the year's top international story. There was no way Reuters was going to release me during such momentous events to go to an African country no one really cared about. In South Africa white minority rule was being buried, civil war was being threatened, history was being made. South Africa was part of the grand scheme of a new world order and I was privileged to be there.

But all I wanted to do was go back to Angola.

I found it hard getting used to working in a proper office with regular hours and pot-plants. I was also actively offering to go out to the townships with the photographers in the East Rand or KwaZulu-Natal where there was an undeclared civil war going on. It was odd behaviour for me; I never used to volunteer.

Now I was deliberately pursuing misery and danger as an echo of something else. In my confusion, I was seeking out situations which reminded me of Angola without realising why I was doing it. I rarely talked about it; certainly not with others in the office. They seemed to deal with the violence with jaunty cynicism and I didn't want to be seen as a weak woman.

'The day isn't complete without a stiff before breakfast,' someone once joked, picking up a flak jacket on the way to the car.

'It was a good day; lots of bodies,' another would say returning to the darkroom.

Those were turbulent times in South Africa. Three hundred people were dying every month – I calculated that was about one-third the number in Angola on a good day. The violence was taking its toll on the journalists too. It seemed each week someone else was killed or beaten up on duty. Juda was walking around with his arm in a sling after being shot. Frank and Mark were badly beaten. Ken was shot dead, Willie barely survived. John Harrison, my travel companion from M'banza Congo, died in a car crash. Some people had received threats from right-wingers and guards posted outside our office building checked our cars for bombs before we entered the parking lot.

The year 1994 was when the dream first happened. At first I didn't realise I was having it; others discovered it first. My screams would wake up whoever was around. One time a guest staying on the opposite side of the house ran and knocked anxiously on my door, thinking I was being attacked. Other times my two wolf-like dogs howled protectively from the garden outside when they heard me shriek. Apparently it was a scream out of a Hitchcock movie. But I couldn't recall what the dream was about and I would wake at a loss for an explanation.

There was only one person I mentioned the dream to. He was one of the photographers, a disturbed individual who pursued violence in a manic, drugged fashion. He was an unlikely confidant, his insight blurred with Mandrax, coke and grass. He had smashed his car, lost his job, his best friend was shot dead, and his girlfriend had left him. We had endless discussions while driving around in his red pick-up truck, comparing notes about what professionals would probably call post-traumatic stress. We didn't put a name to it. After I told him about the dream he took me to a shooting gallery in a suburb of Johannesburg. It was next door to a diaper service and a dry cleaners and matrons shot rounds there between errands.

'See how it feels to hold one,' he said handing me a handgun, as though that would serve to exorcise the dream. It didn't.

The dream only seemed to come alive when I was awake, and suddenly then I would get an inkling of what it was about. One time on patrol in a township in KwaZulu-Natal I caught a glimpse of a youth manning a roadblock against a backdrop of corrugated tin huts. Something about the scene, maybe it was the red rich earth or the boy's face, reminded me of the *musseques* in Luanda.

Then at the end of April 1994 the elections were held in South Africa, and bombs planted by white rightists started going off. In Soweto I stood interviewing people who were voting for the first time in their lives. There were long queues of people, women with babies tied to their backs, who were rejoicing in their liberation. I had a sense of déjà vu. It deepened when a friend with a cellular telephone shouted that another bomb had gone off.

'Was it near the Meridien?' I asked someone.

'Pardon?'

They obviously thought they hadn't heard right. And they hadn't; I had forgotten where I was for an instant.

It got worse as the year went on. The photographer with the red pick-up truck committed suicide in July. He took the hose-pipe from my garden and attached it to the exhaust of his truck. At the morgue I noticed that he had a tattoo on his upper arm, of a map of Africa. I looked at the dark spot on the cold flesh for a long time, and was transported back to another country in Africa. A place where the morgue stank from lack of electricity, where they piled the bodies up in the streets and burned them because there was not enough space in the cemeteries.

The day of the photographer's funeral my dogs tried to kill each other. The bitch threw herself on the male and, like her

Alaskan wolf ancestors, pinned him to the ground with her 40 kilograms. He struggled in a foam of blood and excrement but couldn't get up.

I screamed, screamed worse than in any dream I didn't remember. The dogs were going to die and there was nothing I could do. I threw buckets of water at them, until I finally managed to haul the bitch by the neck away from the runt.

Then I went to the funeral with dog blood on my stockings.

The vet later said my confused state of mind had destabilised the animals. Separating them would do no good; they'd try to kill each other again. I decided to get rid of the bitch because she was the aggressor. I delivered the trusting dog to a new home, silently apologising as I stroked her silver fur for the last time.

I thought a lot about my father during that time. He had experienced some of the worst fighting of World War Two when he was still a teenager and spent most of his adult years trying to figure it out. During three years as an infantryman he had lost most of his company in some of the heaviest fighting of the war. He had fought in the liberation of Prague and Normandy and was in Germany at the end during the dismantling of the concentration camps.

There was not a movie about the war he didn't see. My parents' living room had a wall of books, a huge wooden bookshelf which held hundreds of books. Many were about the war. My father collected paperback pot-boilers and academic textbooks. He never spoke about the war but he had visual evidence and memories he could return to over and over again.

It was different with Angola, where so much of the war was insinuated or left to the imagination. There was nothing about Angola in the Africa section of the bookshops in Johannesburg. There was plenty about safaris in Kenya or South Africa's conundrum, but nothing about Cuito. I went to the video-shop and saw a similar gap on the shelves. There were movies about Vietnam but nothing about Angola. I didn't have reference points or outlets to pinpoint what I had seen.

+

Sometimes during that year people telephoned from Luanda at night when the lines were clearest to tell me what was going on. They said UNITA was being squeezed by the UN sanctions and was running out of fuel and food. People who visited Huambo in March 1994 reported that everyone seemed to be riding bicycles and suffering from tuberculosis or malnutrition. The situation worsened as the months went on.

The 1994 military scoreboard in my notebook had changed dramatically. All the gains were on the MPLA side, it seemed. In January the government recaptured Ambriz, in May N'dalatando, in June new positions in Cuito and in July further positions in the northern diamond areas. In August UNITA lost position in Huíla and the government launched more air strikes against Huambo on 31 August. And UNITA? Nil.

There was a strange see-saw of peace talks, military advances, negotiations and battles. With every military defeat the peace talks in Lusaka gained momentum. UNITA was backed into a corner and Savimbi knew it. The two sides agreed on provincial and cabinet posts. They agreed on the make-up of a new joint army. They agreed on everything except a final cease-fire. By November the government was a mere 80 kilometres from Huambo, practically savouring its bitter victory. This was the very first time the MPLA could claim a decisive military victory against UNITA. The men were already talking about the women and houses that were theirs. General João de Matos was not going to stop here. There would be no cease-fire until he had expelled Savimbi for good.

Many people believed that a peace accord this time would be different from the 1991 accords. 'One reason why the last one didn't work was because there had been no clear military victory beforehand,' one diplomat said. 'That was unprecedented. Normally someone wins, or is on the verge of winning, so that the loser is willing to give way. But it was inconclusive in 1991 and both sides felt denied victory.'

On 9 November 1994, the day before the Lusaka peace accord should have been signed, the government announced absolute control over Huambo. Savimbi ran out of town and hid in the village of Bailundo, which was where his grandfather had been so humiliated when the Portuguese colonial army put down a 1902 revolt. UNITA's last gesture was to loot Huambo of all its goods and steal at gunpoint everything from cars to toilet seats from foreign aid organisations.

The last week before the cease-fire was finalised was full of typical Angolan uncertainties. Everyone was asking: 'Will Savimbi sign?' The UN, as with the ill-fated 1991 Biçesse accords, was not going to let this one slip out of their hands, having got so far. They primed 7 000 peacekeepers, this time outfitted with guns and blue helmets, to come in to supervise the new peace. But the headlines on Reuters during the last week reflected the confusion and precarious nature of the process:

NOV 14 – UNITA TEAM ARRIVES IN LUSAKA, SAYS
        LUANDA BROKE PACT
NOV 14 – ANGOLAN ARMY CHIEF SAYS WAR GOES
        ON AGAINST UNITA
NOV 14 – ANGOLAN FOES POSTPONE PEACE
        PACT INDEFINITELY
NOV 20 – ANGOLAN WAR FOES EYE CEASEFIRE
        WITH GUARDED HOPES
NOV 20 – ANGOLAN WAR FOES SIGN PEACE
        ACCORD BUT DOUBTS REMAIN
NOV 21 – ANGOLANS HAMMER OUT CEASEFIRE
        DETAILS
NOV 22 – CEASEFIRE DECLARED AFTER 19 YEARS
        OF WAR IN ANGOLA

NOV 22 – UN HAILS ANGOLA PACT BUT WORRIED
FIGHTING GOES ON
NOV 22 – LUANDA FEARS ATTACKS DESPITE
CEASEFIRE

And then, on 30 November:

FIGHTING RAGES IN ANGOLA DESPITE CEASEFIRE

The final accord signing was a farce. Savimbi refused to attend, citing security preoccupations. Dos Santos was already there waiting, looking slightly foolish, like a stood-up date. So their lieutenants signed the accords. Beye looked relieved but everyone else looked tired or nervous. This time the church bells didn't ring out in Luanda.

I watched the Lusaka peace accord being signed on CNN, sitting in a hotel in Maputo recovering from malaria. I was listlessly flipping the remote through the channels and sprang to attention when the word Angola came up. Mozambique had just held elections and RENAMO rebel leader Afonso Dhlakama had tried a Savimbi-like manoeuvre, withdrawing to his provincial headquarters, claiming that the elections had been rigged and hinting at war. But this time the script had changed. South Africa, under its new post-apartheid leadership, gathered together neighbouring states for a unified stance. They summoned Dhlakama like an errant schoolboy and told him they would intervene militarily if he didn't get back into line.

Dhlakama, perhaps mindful of all that Savimbi had lost, was not planning to take it as far. He conceded defeat gracefully and took up his role as the head of the parliamentary opposition. Dhlakama had studied Savimbi's example and it hadn't worked.

6

The Man

The first time I interviewed Jonas Savimbi, he went through all the gymnastic permutations of his various personae within the space of two hours. It was April 1992 in Luanda, and he was back from the bush after 30 years of war. He was on the defensive, off his own territory, and in certain quarters suspicions were high that he was responsible for the deaths of some of his senior henchmen.

The interview started calmly enough as he assumed the veneer of the revolutionary populist. Supplicants entered Savimbi's grand villa overlooking Luanda's bay, asking protective favours of their chief. We journalists were kept waiting two hours while he sat imperiously in his stuffed armchair, holding court surrounded by bodyguards.

When Savimbi deemed the time right to begin, he summoned us to a hall and switched to the urbane statesman, telling anecdotes in French, German and English which showcased his ironic wit. He had just met with the IMF and they liked his proposed programme.

By the time he got around to talking about his election platform, his demeanour had hardened to an inflexible shell. Savimbi would lose only if there were fraud. The people loved him. They already called him The President. There was no doubt that he was the only man who could lead Angola into a free and democratic age.

Like a chameleon jumping from a rock to a fern to red flowers, Savimbi suddenly took on another colour, evolving into an irrational man. I inadvertently provoked the change by asking about the murder of his former protégé, Tito Chingunji, and his entire family. I asked: Was it a mere coincidence that ten people of the same family had all died mysterious deaths in UNITA's Jamba headquarters?

Savimbi stirred in his chair, fixed bulging eyes on me, and with the same finger that had ordered 60 000 men to the front told me to stop right then and there.

'No! No! These things happen. There is nothing strange. It is a coincidence.'

I couldn't get in another 'But'.

'No!' Savimbi bellowed. 'I said, No!'

The interview was over.

✝

If you wanted to understand Savimbi you had to go to Jamba, people said. I had been going to Angola on and off for a few years and still hadn't been to that place near the border with Namibia which the Portuguese had called The End of the Earth. It was there that Savimbi, with the help of South Africa, had moulded a resilient army and his own legend as well.

So when the chance arose in 1995 to catch a ride on an aid flight, I went. I was eager to see this place where Savimbi had perfected the myth of himself as the indefatigable freedom fighter.

Jamba was not quite what I expected.

By the time I got there, its founder hadn't been there for three years. The man who single-handedly shaped Angola's history for 30 years was hiding in a tiny village 800 kilometres away with just a few changes of clothing and using toilet seats stolen from foreign NGOs.

During those three years he had lost the presidential elections and nearly all his foreign support. He had suffered some of his worst military defeats ever. But for the people of

Jamba, left behind in the bush camp which had been his headquarters, Savimbi was still their most valiant chief.

For them, Jamba was still that amazing place which had impressed visiting American congressmen and South African military advisers with its parades and factories. Journalists were given stamps in their passports at Jamba International Airport as though it were a separate country.

Over ten years, Savimbi created out of nothing a showcase military base which was like a guerrilla theme park. When he arrived there, trekking more than 3 000 kilometres with a few hundred supporters after the Cubans invaded Huambo in 1975, only wild animals inhabited this promised land. It was christened Jamba, the word for elephant, for the herds that thundered through the desolate scrub-land. With the help of South Africa and several other countries he set up landing strips, bunkers, schools, clinics, radio transmitters and a village where he could pioneer his utopian vision of a free Angola.

But what I saw when I landed on the dirt air strip was a Jamba stripped of illusionary grandeur. It was just a cluster of reed-thatched rondavels.

A motley collection of people met my plane, an Antonov carrying food aid because Jamba could no longer feed itself. Visitors were rare these days and they were curious as to why I'd come. The welcoming party included a white Portuguese colonel who had joined Savimbi to found Jamba, and some solemn children and soldiers. None knew how long they would be there. Although it was officially peacetime, they didn't feel free to leave. They were waiting for instructions which would probably never come.

An affable young man named Aurelio attached himself to me. He found out I had come from 'the north', as the people of Jamba called the rest of the world outside.

'Have you seen Savimbi?' he asked, as though I might casually bump into him at a restaurant.

I told him I hadn't seen the chief for a long time.

Aurelio couldn't hide his disappointment. Nor his faith. Was he coming back soon?

Again, I had to admit I didn't know.

The only signs of the man who had created Jamba were the photographs and wall murals, which also pronounced that Victory is Ours! Everyone talked about Savimbi's return, as if he had been away only a weekend. He had given a voice to people who were voiceless and put them on the world map, in a corner of Cuando Cubango province. And now he had abandoned them there with his dreams and theirs.

Aurelio, who was assigned as my minder, took me on a tour of UNITA's former capital. We had to wait a while for a vehicle; petrol was hard to come by these days and UNITA used it sparingly. We drove several kilometres along a dirt road through silent bush where not even a bird cheeped. We arrived at a circle of huts surrounding a round plaza, where a lone amputee sat in a wheelchair.

'Freedom Square!' Aurelio announced proudly.

We drove around the other sights, which were nothing more than huts with the doors shut. 'Everything is closed now that the war is over,' said Aurelio.

I thought about accounts by people who had been flown in during the days when Savimbi strutted around with his cartridge belt slung around his waist and presided over rallies that lasted all night. He was a conjuror who could turn the fly-blown hut which was the clinic into a sophisticated hospital capable of curing all ills. He showed visitors munitions factories with rusted and broken AK-47s which had allegedly been captured from the Cuban enemy. The visitors weren't shown the Stinger missiles and long-distance cannons donated by UNITA's benefactors. But they imagined them.

I couldn't imagine anything now. The place looked like a museum or an off-season safari camp. Without its creator, I could see Jamba for what it was: a circle of thatched huts in a remote part of the world. Aurelio could declare 'Victory!' with all of his enthusiasm but all I could see was a woman sweeping leaves from the dirt plaza because she didn't have anything else to do.

There wasn't much to do. I met some of the local commanders who eyed me suspiciously. They fed me a sparse lunch of limp pasta and beans and then escorted me to a 'hospitality' hut so that I could rest, even though I insisted that I wasn't tired. I waited there alone for several hours until the plane taking me back to the north finally came and I was driven to the airport.

In the bush you hear the Antonovs before you see them. As the aeroplane descended the people of Jamba ran towards the landing strip. Aurelio accompanied me to the plane, which had brought more grain from the aid organisations. He watched silently until every bag had been removed and the engines started up for take-off. No one got off. The pilot waved at me to board and I bade goodbye to Aurelio. He slowly walked back to his camp of phantoms and resumed the long wait for Savimbi.

✢

The closest anyone has come to documenting the facts behind Savimbi's mythology is the British journalist and author Fred Bridgland. His book *Jonas Savimbi: A Key to Africa* is widely recognised as the most definitive work about Savimbi's early years. Bridgland wrote it, by his own admission now, when he was an admirer of the UNITA leader. Bridgland spent more time with Savimbi than any other Western correspondent. But with time Bridgland grew disillusioned with UNITA's totalitarianism.

What upsets Bridgland in particular is the lack of clarity about the murder of his beloved friend, the senior UNITA official Tito Chingunji. (He half jokingly refers to a chapter which deals with the deaths of Chingunji's family as his 'first work of fiction' because of the untruths spread by UNITA which were accepted as gospel at the time the book was written.)

Savimbi typically provokes strong emotions. As a journalist, I followed Jonas Savimbi for nearly ten years. I cannot recall anyone who claimed to know him well. But people seemed either to detest or love him.

Savimbi was one of Africa's most enduring guerrilla leaders and one of its most inscrutable. For 30 years this son of a railwayman with a grudge against the Portuguese built up an army whose fanatical loyalty helped destroy one of Africa's potentially richest countries. Savimbi could shell his own people and send thousands to the slaughter in quixotic battles.

Yet no matter what setbacks he suffered, Savimbi always bounced back like a rubbery cartoon character. He lied to the US State Department and broke UN embargoes. But everyone took him seriously, even after he lost all the territory he had gained. Like the Iraqi leader Saddam Hussein, Savimbi wooed and fooled the West. Washington created a Frankenstein which it couldn't control.

Savimbi's supporters called him *O Mais Velho*. The highest sign of veneration, it means The Eldest One. Even men older than Savimbi would address him as such. Others spoke reverentially of him as The President or The Doctor, although he never became president and his academic credentials were exaggerated. Diplomats referred to him simply as Jonas, as though they had special access.

But who exactly is Jonas Malheiro Savimbi? And what drove him in his pursuit of absolute power?

If you believe in the great man and history theory, then Savimbi is your man for Angola. Born on 3 August 1934 in the small town of Manhango, this son of Angola's first black rail station master grew up in the heart of the Planalto plateau. He was raised on tales of his grandfather's humiliation at the hands of the Portuguese and was obsessed with avenging it.

Ovimbundu boys in those days made pilgrimages to the tombs of their ancestors. Tales were passed down of the great past, of kings who reigned in the hills before the Portuguese came at the turn of the century and turned them into virtual slaves. They were weaned on the humiliation of their fathers in the 1902 Bailundo uprising. If Savimbi had been born 25 years earlier he probably would have been sent up to the coffee plantations as forced labour.

But instead he received a Protestant missionary education and with it a sense that he was different. His father raised him to believe he was destined for better things. And from the time he was a boy, Jonas Savimbi acted by his own code of justice to get his way.

Bridgland recounts one anecdote told to him by Savimbi. It stands out like a harbinger of the man's later inability to accept defeat.

The story goes that missionaries arranged a soccer game between black students at Savimbi's school and white pupils from a nearby town. The white visitors brought along their own Portuguese referee who, according to Savimbi, rejected every score by the black team. This infuriated Savimbi, especially because they were playing with his ball.

So he stopped the game and walked off with the ball.

'My own team shouted that I could not do it because the administrator's son was playing . . . I carried on walking and the game had to be abandoned,' Savimbi said.

This was not typical behaviour of Ovimbundu boys in those days, but his schooling gave him the confidence to carry on. This special education was also Savimbi's ticket to *assimilado* status and to Lisbon, thanks to the generosity of the missionaries who paid his way. By the time he sailed to Portugal, in October 1959, to study to be a doctor as his father intended, independence fever was sweeping Africa. Savimbi was caught up in underground liberation politics. Meeting the icons of liberation – among them Kwame Nkrumah, Jomo Kenyatta, Tom Mboya, Ben Mkapa and even Che Guevara – Savimbi found a voice and a calling. His medical studies were pushed aside by his desire to be a revolutionary.

Savimbi slipped between Europe and clandestine meetings in Africa, even briefly joining the exiled government of Holden Roberto's UPA (Angolan People's Union). But eventually he decided he wanted his own movement, claiming that UPA and the MPLA did not address the aspirations of his Ovimbundu people. Savimbi formed his own group which, in his own words, was initially just a band of men with knives and a pistol donated by Sam Nujoma. His initial support came from China, which Savimbi first visited in 1964.

UNITA was officially born in March 1966 at a congress of 67 chiefs and other delegates at Muangai village, 250 kilometres from the border with Zambia in eastern Moxico province. Its first major military action took place on Christmas Day that year, against the railway town of Teixeira de Sousa on the border with Zaire. There are conflicting reports about what happened. But all concur that UNITA was repulsed, having suffered major losses and having failed to take the town. Savimbi learned his first lesson: not to attack well-defended cities.

When Savimbi returned to Angola to lead his own liberation movement, he had a message which was just what the Ovimbundu of the Planalto, long treated as second class, wanted to hear. He had been to Europe with the white men and had come back to be with his people. It was a time of black pride. Black Angolans hung posters of Malcolm X and Martin Luther King on their walls. Savimbi didn't just have a T-shirt with Che Guevara's picture – he had actually met and discussed politics with him!

Savimbi was a compelling speaker in a country where few people read and oratory is a highly appreciated art form. He was an irresistible messiah. The people of the Planalto were all his.

Peregrino Wambu was 14 years old the first time he heard Savimbi speak; his brother took him to a rally in what is today Huambo. Wambu had little interest in politics but he was from royal Ovimbundu lineage and resented the Portuguese, who used his family's crypt as a picnic site. For Wambu, Savimbi offered the promise of a life worthy of his distinguished roots.

'It was intoxicating,' said Wambu, who later became one of Savimbi's protégés. 'Agostinho Neto was not a good speaker. He had big teeth which created a sort of speech impediment. Holden Roberto spoke with a French accent. But then there was Savimbi – a good orator with a military bearing.

'You have to understand, I am descended from Wambu Kalunga, after whom Huambo province was named. He won fame fighting in the sixteenth century against the Portuguese. These were noble roots I was proud of. Savimbi touched that spirit. He didn't just speak of independence but also of dignity.'

Savimbi's spell was not just limited to the Ovimbundu. His two main lieutenants, Miguel N'Zau Puna and Tony da Costa Fernandes, were from faraway Cabinda, and closer ethnically to Roberto. But they felt Savimbi was the most capable of the three liberation leaders.

Unlike the leaders of the other two liberation movements, Savimbi won the support of the peasantry because he actually lived with them. He walked long distances between villages like a preacher of war. His little band of men infiltrated villagers to set up intelligence gathering and self-defence cells. They graduated from ambushes and training with wooden sticks in the early fight against the Portuguese, out-gunned by the MPLA, to a well-disciplined force that liberated areas. He became a legend, helped by rumour and a way of life where telephones didn't exist. It seemed that tanks and soldiers could never catch him.

By the time independence arrived in 1975, the country was split between the three liberation groups and foreign powers were intervening on behalf of their chosen proxies. Savimbi sought the help of Pretoria, which by September 1975 had more than 1 000 men in Angola versus the MPLA's foreign backing of 20 000 troops. On 9 February 1976 Cuban troops rolled into

Huambo. The next day the MPLA took UNITA's strongholds of Lobito and Benguela.

Savimbi mustered a few hundred of his supporters and began the first of several long marches down to Jamba. For the next 16 years he relied on South African and American aid and presided from his south-western bush retreat, until the 1992 elections and his fall from grace.

✣

I spent a lot of time trying to figure out Savimbi's charm. I heard many stories about how Savimbi had reduced people to hysterical laughter on aeroplanes, telling jokes in eight languages. His magnetism eluded me. I was never forced on long marches or physically maltreated by UNITA. But I found him callous. He kept people waiting and he misled them about his intentions. He insisted that his aides stir his tea.

The first time I met him the word 'petulant' came to mind. It was January 1990 and he couldn't accept that no one was terribly interested in his triumphant return to Lisbon after 30 years away, to discuss what were embryonic peace moves. Savimbi panicked when most journalists ignored the begging by his press people that they attend his daily press conferences.

'But the president has something to say,' said one of the press men, visibly anxious at hearing that we didn't want to go. 'It is necessary to hear what he says.'

Then again, Savimbi was never at his best off his territory when he couldn't control things. And by the time I met him he knew he was under pressure by his backers to end the war and sign up for peace.

But most people who met Savimbi in his prime described another man, a simpler man who was so mesmerising that they couldn't help being drawn to him.

'It was almost like being in love,' said Tony da Costa Fernandes of his initial reaction to Savimbi.

What was the secret of his aura? Savimbi articulated the aspirations of Angola's disenfranchised black peasantry whose dignity had been quashed under 500 years of Portuguese colonialism. He told them they were worth more than living in thatched huts, eating corn porridge and working on someone else's land. He stoked the yearnings for the lost glory of the Ovimbundu, who had started out as chiefs and ended up as slaves.

True to his Protestant upbringing, a rally with Savimbi in the old days was like an evangelical sermon. He shouted at the crowd like a preacher and they chorused back. They wore their Sunday best. It was like a party; there were sandwiches and beer. The Jamba night rallies could be dramatic affairs with spotlights on a wooden stadium, the drummers and dancers going wild in the mist.

Savimbi could manipulate an international audience just as well. He had the vision to exploit the gaps in the superpower rivalry, astutely realising that the South Africans and Washington needed a black ally in the Cold War battlegrounds of Africa. He crafted an image of reasonable affability with the help of a slick public relations network which spanned Washington, Paris, Lisbon, Brussels, London and the UN. But back in Jamba he heaped scorn upon his backers and took hostages. He had an uncanny ability to convince people with opposite interests that he was on their side. Scornful of colonialists, he enjoyed the patronage of Portuguese and South African white racists. A Maoist, he won the backing of American anti-communists. He persuaded them he was their man, mastering the rhetoric of freedom while running a totalitarian movement based on fear.

It is impossible to consider Savimbi's allure without putting it in an African context. In Europe it would be inconceivable that thousands of people would follow a man who killed their cousins and never said sorry. But Savimbi did what big chiefs had done in Angola for years – monopolise authority and act with impunity. The only difference was that he did it with one third of a nation instead of with only a clan.

In a culture where people believe in witches and in the vengeance of ancestors, a chief has to be anointed with supernatural powers to exert his influence. Savimbi had an extraordinary capacity for physical endurance which imbued him with a powerful mystique.

'He could walk 60 miles a day when the rest of us were exhausted,' said Fernandes. 'I don't know how he did it, but he could refrain from urinating for 12 hours. We'd all be sitting at a meeting and eventually have to ask permission to get up. But Savimbi would never need to excuse himself to go to the toilet.'

He was an Angolan James Bond who used spells instead of grenade watches, but had just as potent a penis. Like all giants of mythology, Savimbi reputedly had an insatiable lust. Everyone I met from UNITA told stories of maidens brought to him nightly as he lay waiting on his bed.

Then there were the great escapes and disappearances. During the decade I reported on Savimbi he died at least 15 times – shot, poisoned, bombed or by suicide. Each time he arose from the grave like Jesus Christ. One million Angolans died in the war, but Savimbi survived. His top lieutenants were ambushed in Luanda, but he was safe. The MPLA air bombed his villa in Huambo, but Savimbi escaped.

When Savimbi left Luanda suddenly in October 1992, people insisted they had seen him escape in a coffin. Others maintained he was dressed as a woman, hiking the 800 kilometres to Huambo. He was later allegedly spotted in the Ivory Coast, Morocco, a Pretoria hospital and Zaire.

'He's like Elvis Presley. He's everywhere,' quipped one American diplomat, only half jokingly.

The MPLA, obsessed with Savimbi's evil, regularly pumped out rumours of his death, inadvertently bolstering his prestige rather than weakening his followers' morale. The more times Savimbi was resurrected, the more his mystique grew.

Those tracking Savimbi are like Kremlin watchers –

analysing every little change to discern a shift in leadership or state of mind. His clothes were the biggest signposts. If Savimbi wore Western dress or his Nehru-collared suits he was deemed conciliatory. Fatigues meant belligerence. When Savimbi withdrew to Bailundo, he was seen at various public events in the same wide-lapelled outfit which made him look like a Las Vegas crooner. The pundits asked: Was this a sign of hard times? Didn't Savimbi have any other clothes?

Savimbi relished the role-playing, donning special outfits for each persona and each audience. Savimbi the superman goes into his bunker, instead of a phone booth, and out pops the Revolutionary Leader wearing fatigues and a pearl-handled pistol who motivates his weary troops on the front line. Meeting bankers, The Democrat puts on a sober suit to discuss free trade over a working lunch. His favourite part was The Statesman – taking his Lear jet to Washington to exchange views with the likes of George Bush.

People believed Savimbi because they needed to believe there was someone in Angola who served their purposes. Savimbi had a cunning intuition of what people wanted to hear. A servant in Cuito wants a house? Yes! UNITA will deliver. Washington wants elections in Angola? But of course! Why, that is UNITA's platform! Underneath it all, Savimbi cynically pursued his primary aim, which was to rule Angola.

I witnessed this naked cynicism one overcast October evening in Huambo, when Savimbi withdrew there in 1992 after losing the elections. In defiance of the peace accords, the UNITA flag of the black cockerel was raised in the airport tower and his troops walked brazenly in uniform through the streets. To any observer, it looked like an occupied city on the verge of war.

South African foreign minister Pik Botha had flown down to talk some sense into his 'brother'. They conferred for several hours inside Savimbi's villa, and then came out to address the press and international observers assembled outside. With Botha

241

standing by his side, Savimbi gave a speech about his commitment to democracy. This fighting could not go on, he said. His eyes looked pained as he spoke of the suffering of the Angolan people.

'We so much want peace,' said Savimbi. He looked earnestly at us.

Botha nodded contentedly; his protégé had been brought into line.

The South African boarded the plane back to Pretoria, expressing his confidence that all was well. UNITA didn't even wait for the aircraft to take off before the shooting began. That night Savimbi's men assassinated a prominent MPLA activist. More murders followed.

✝

Looking back, if I had to sum up my one overriding impression of UNITA it would be control of people. They controlled where people slept, with whom they slept, and what they ate. You couldn't walk where you wanted to if they didn't want you to.

During my brief visit to Jamba, they kept me isolated in the 'hospitality' suite, a rondavel separated from the rest of the camp by a five-minute drive. I was the only guest and felt I was being watched. And I was. At one point, having run my hand over a cactus and then accidentally touched my face, my eyelids began burning. I rubbed my eyes, hoping to soothe them. Suddenly someone was at the door with a cup of water. 'Take this, you are hurting.' What else had they seen?

They hovered over me as I ate, commanding me to take another portion of precious beans. I didn't want to take more. But my minder sat at the opposite end of a long empty banquet table and told me to eat. He watched me chew, willing me to eat a second helping.

That inimitable control was everywhere I visited in UNITA

territory. The discipline was more Germanic than African. In the demobilisation camps in 1992, and then again in 1996, the UNITA men pitched their tents in immaculate formation. Elsewhere in Angola, people discard orange peels and used tissues on the streets. Even in the MPLA's capital, Luanda, people complained loudly and drunkenly about the government. But UNITA towns were quiet and clean, with none of the spontaneous vibrancy which marks the rest of Angola. People cheered when they were told to. Each person in the 'liberated' zones had a place. For all of Savimbi's talk about democracy, he presided over a society where people couldn't express themselves freely.

The MPLA minders would follow you around, but at least they would loosen up, go to the discos and never refuse an offer of drinks. But the UNITA men were more austere and judgemental. They weren't just watching you. They were being watched themselves.

There was a passivity about the inhabitants of UNITA's 'liberated territory'. One day in November 1992, at the start of the second war, I flew to the town of Cazumbo near the border with Zambia. The town had switched sides several times, but the huge wall murals of O Mais Velho showed that it was still in rebel hands. The pilot realised that we didn't have enough fuel to reach our next destination, but he remembered that there had once been a bladder of fuel on the dirt landing strip. He asked the villagers if it was still there. The question was met with blank stares. He asked again. They didn't respond until someone went to fetch one of the men with guns.

The huts were set far apart in Jamba. Sometimes when people disappeared it would be weeks or months until others realised they were gone. They were living in the land at The End of the Earth and no one could help them.

Besides his network of spies, Savimbi used distance to maintain his command. He was rarely seen with a wife by his side. There was no nuclear family for him, no tears. Aides said that he went off into the bush if he had to cry.

We see photographs of Savimbi animating his troops. Or sitting on soft couches talking with world leaders. But where are those of him with his arms around his children? Or relaxing in a T-shirt in the shade?

Savimbi loved to keep people waiting. Even his own people. The 1996 UNITA congress at Bailundo, for instance, began about five hours late. But Savimbi was in town; it wasn't as though he was travelling from very far away. If you told your editors you were covering a UNITA event you never could say when you'd be back. I never once attended an interview where I didn't have to wait at least a few hours. For such a well-disciplined movement, it surely wasn't a matter of lack of organisation that they'd hold reporters three extra days, or more, at Jamba. No, it was a way to exercise power.

No matter how far away Savimbi was, his picture adorned the wall murals. He was like Stalin or an African president, his image staring from the walls, ever watchful.

Traditionally among the people of southern Angola, the serious illness or death of a chief is kept hidden from the people. The chief and his ministers of justice are allowed to order executions of those who do not properly respect the sovereign leader.

This was no exception within UNITA.

Colonel Fred Oelschig, who served as a South African liaison officer in Jamba, said fear was a form of social control used by UNITA. Bodies were thrown into the river, opponents were burned as witches. Oelschig shrugged, a sort of 'this is Africa' shrug.

'It was no secret that dissidents died,' he said. How many? No one knew.

Even three years after Savimbi left Luanda UNITA dissidents there feared him. One of them appeared unannounced at my hotel room for an interview. He was too scared to call first in case the telephone was tapped. He fiddled with the desk lamp, convinced there were bugs.

'Let's talk in the car,' he said.

Tony da Costa Fernandes was nervous, too. He came to my room for an interview that was more like a confession. He had a gold watch, a nice house in London, and he proudly showed me his new laptop computer with the latest Windows program. But riches do not buy one safety and he did not linger in Luanda too long. Savimbi the bogeyman could get him.

This long-distance fear was expressed by other UNITA dissidents. Savimbi kept their families hostage in Jamba as a way to manipulate them.

'I did whatever Savimbi wanted me to. I was worried about my wife and kids. They were in Jamba and he wouldn't let them leave,' said one senior official. He was too scared to make the jump that Fernandes had.

☦

Ultimately, things backfired for Savimbi. He believed too strongly in his own impunity. And when the fall came, it came from a place and a man – Luanda and Tito Chingunji.

Savimbi and his men were already on the decline when they returned to Luanda in 1992 to contest the elections. He had been pushed into peace and the foreign support which had made him feel so important was about to end. He appeared to be drinking, and for the first time his aides saw him lose control publicly.

Savimbi hated Luanda. For a man accustomed to living a tightly controlled simple life in combat or in the bush, it was another world. He couldn't control things quite the same way in the city. Certainly not in a city which was the headquarters of his enemies.

From the moment Savimbi returned to Luanda in September 1991 everything started to go wrong.

A long red carpet led out along the tarmac where dignitaries awaited the aeroplane carrying the great man. At each end of the tarmac stood pre-teen girls dressed in white, holding doves of peace. Someone played a drum and people were dancing. Savimbi came off the plane in full battle dress and strode towards the crowd.

The girls were supposed to throw the birds up into the sky in a noble gesture. But, like a bad omen, the doves plopped to the ground in front of Savimbi's approaching military boots, instead of soaring to the heavens. Their wings wouldn't open because they had been held for too long.

Any pretence at dignity evaporated, according to South African journalist Patrick Collings.

'Savimbi deftly avoided crushing the birds, which were hopping around the tarmac. Meanwhile, a couple of men ran after them and tried to catch them,' he said.

The rally itself was not that well attended. Independent estimates put the crowd at 70 000 at most – not much for a city of two million people who had little to do that day.

People were crammed into a square, standing on top of cars and climbing trees to get a look at him. Many people said they had come to see Savimbi out of curiosity – they just wanted to see what he looked like.

They were not impressed. He never again drew such a crowd in Luanda.

But it was the unclear circumstances of Tito's death that really undid him. Any hope of winning the hearts and minds of the people of Luanda evaporated.

Tito was a rising star. He was the popular young representative in Washington, the movement's acceptable face abroad. He had been a protégé of Savimbi, slated for great things. And now, suddenly, he and another senior aide, Wilson dos Santos, were dead. And two high-ranking UNITA officials, foreign affairs chief Fernandes and interior minister N'Zau Puna, defected in February 1992, accusing O Mais Velho of killing the pair the previous July.

Savimbi denied ordering the deaths. US Assistant Secretary of State for Africa Herman Cohen flew to Luanda for an explanation in April 1992. He left with Savimbi's pledge that UNITA would hold an internal investigation into the deaths and would respect human rights. But doubts remained.

The allegations were damaging not only for Savimbi's international image. Many Angolans in Luanda were appalled and he lost whatever burgeoning support he had.

The incident was a major turning point.

One of the great myths of Savimbi was that he was self-reliant militarily and a phenomenal strategist. But he was dependent on the outside world and that was part of the problem with Jamba. South Africa had sought him out not because Pretoria liked him, but because UNITA was a convenient way to contain the ANC and SWAPO. By 1979, Savimbi claimed he controlled much of the southern third of Angola. But he neglected to mention that it was South Africa which provided the tanks, protective cover and the missiles.

Allies like Pretoria cost Savimbi support in black Africa. But for him, the courtship by South Africa was intoxicating. Southern Africa's bully-boys, who jailed and hanged black men in their own country, were offering him weapons for his own fight!

His vanity swelled further when, after Ronald Reagan was sworn in as US president in January 1981, the Americans began to throw in their full support. Life was glamorous, now that he was courted by the world's most powerful country. Savimbi began to lose touch with his people and the nationalism and patriotism which brought him to the armed struggle. He listened less to dissent and became more infatuated with his own image.

The inner circle tightened to those from his own clan and the Huambo clique. His closest advisers were three of his relatives – General Bock, Ben Ben and Salupeto Pena. People from other groups – N'Zau Puna and Fernandes – were reminded frequently that they weren't Ovimbundu and didn't quite belong.

Around that time the abuses grew worse. They had begun in the 1970s. People would disappear, but in Jamba no one liked to talk about it. Some of the executions were disguised as witch-burnings, a convenient way to dispose of one's rivals. Savimbi's wife Vinona died a mysterious death, ostensibly struck by lightning. Questions were asked but never answered.

The deaths seemed to increase in the mid-1980s, when UNITA began to lose its foreign support. Savimbi's aides traced it to 1986-87, after the battle of Cuito Cuanavale when the MPLA launched a big assault on UNITA positions, confirming for the South Africans that there was a blatant military stalemate. Pretoria was ready to withdraw and had agreed to do so with the 1988 Tripartite Accords. The fall of the Berlin Wall only deepened Savimbi's gloom. UNITA was nothing without the Cold War.

And then Tito died. Tito had had a high profile inter-nationally, garnering much respect abroad for doing the groundwork for the 1988 Tripartite Agreement. He was popular in Washington. In addition, it was well known within UNITA that Tito had once been the lover of Savimbi's wife Ana, before she became his secretary and married him. The gossips said that she and Tito continued to see each other clandestinely.

Bridgland said he knew categorically that something was wrong when Tito was suddenly recalled from Washington in 1988. Earlier that year Tito had briefed Bridgland in detail about what had been done to his family. Tito said that his parents, brothers, sisters, aunts and a cousin had been killed back home while he represented UNITA abroad. Savimbi had told Tito they had died at the hands of the enemy. But relatives informed Chingunji that his parents had died by torture and beatings in a 'rehabilitation centre'.

Bridgland said he asked Tito when he could use the information. His friend replied: 'When I give the signal. Or, if certain things happen, you will have to make your own judgement.'

Bridgland made his judgement during a macabre meeting with Savimbi in December 1988. Rumours had circulated that he was being held prisoner and Bridgland went for himself to confirm whether they were true.

'I was ushered into a circular hut. Mr Savimbi was sitting in a big red chair facing the 13 members of his politburo, including General Puna and Mr Fernandes. Since Mr Chingunji's return to Jamba, UNITA had announced his removal from the politburo and dismissal as foreign secretary. But there he was, seated right in the middle of the uniformed politburo men.

'When I explained why I had come, Mr Savimbi exploded in a way I had never seen before and shouted at me for something like two hours.

'"You have come here to insult me. You think you can still come to Africa to patronise us, puffing yourself up and saying Tito Chingunji is your brother and getting him into a lot of trouble."'

Bridgland said the tirade lasted a while. Then Savimbi apparently calmed down and made a gesture of reconciliation. But as the journalist left the room he heard laughter. He never saw Tito again.

According to Fernandes, Tito's detention would be covered up when foreign visitors came to Jamba. Savimbi would take Tito out of jail and place him in a chair with the politburo in scenes like the one Bridgland described.

'His pistol holster would be empty,' Fernandes said. 'He was growing thinner and thinner. So I went to Savimbi in January 1992 and suggested we feed him properly since a US senator was coming to visit. Savimbi looked at me strangely and said: "Tito was killed a long time ago." I was shocked. He gave no explanation and then suddenly ordered me out.'

The facts were never cleared up regarding other murky deaths of men in the movement who had questioned the

UNITA leadership. Among them were the former foreign secretary Jorge Sangunba, and two of Peregrino Wambu's brothers, Anibal Piedoso and Waldemar.

'Didn't you ever think of leaving the movement?' I asked Wambu in 1995.

Even 20 years later, he was circumspect.

'I believed in UNITA. We were fighting a war we felt was just. Anyway, what could I do? Questioning was not a good idea.'

✢

There is not much in the way of tourism in the ruins of Cuito in 1995, but Pedro the primary school teacher wants to show me the remains of what was once Savimbi's villa. We walk through the rubble of Africa's Dresden as Pedro points out the houses where he had hidden during the siege. We reach Savimbi's former home and Pedro stares at the building a long time with victorious satisfaction. Very little is intact, only some walls, part of the roof and a section of the stairway still remain. Pedro guides my hand over the shattered concrete and twisted metal. He urges me to admire the destruction well after I have seen enough.

'How we hated him,' he says.

The scene is repeated in Huambo and in Luanda. Savimbi's shattered villas are like museums of defeat. People take their kids to see them. Look, and you shall learn, they say. In Huambo it is more surreptitious; I suspect some of the visitors may secretly be paying homage. UNITA is just a few hours' drive down the road. Who knows if they will come back?

But equally potent as these symbols of Savimbi's fall in the 1992-94 war is the shrine to his latest resurrection, Bailundo. By now, 1996, he has lost the war. He is far from what he wanted, total power. Peace accords have been signed and Jamba is abandoned. The US has switched loyalties to the MPLA.

250

UNITA soldiers have deserted.

But somehow this remarkable man continues to bounce back. No matter what he's suffered he manages to remain the big chief and refuses to be downtrodden.

✢

It is September 1996 and I am looking through the lens of Liebenberg's television camera. I use my good eye, the left one, and squint with the other closed so that I can better see the images. Savimbi's velvety face looks large as it fills the frame.

Liebenberg has just come back from UNITA's congress in Bailundo and is showing me what he shot. I was unable to get to the congress; after all these years I am still forced to view Savimbi at a distance. I do not have a television set on hand so I have to look at the film through the camera's viewfinder. It shows proud images of opulence and calm. I expect to see a depressed man, but instead Savimbi looks the best he has in years – fresh and healthy. His paunch is reduced, his skin is luminous. Even through the small frame of the viewfinder you can see there are no grey hairs on his head. O Mais Velho exudes vitality.

The street scenes are reminiscent of Jamba. Few people are walking around and those who are avoid looking into the camera, as though they guiltily know they shouldn't be out mixing with foreign cameramen. The buildings show signs of artillery fire from the war but otherwise are clean. There is no rubbish outside the houses. There are no street children rowdily asking for money as in Luanda. There are no children on the streets, period.

Practically the only people outside are the heavily armed UNITA guards, draped in ammunition cartridge belts and new automatic rifles, and the party officials who drive up to the congress hall in new 4x4 Toyotas and Hyundais.

Wherever the povo, *the people, are, they are missing a great party inside. This is a party unlike any that UNITA threw in Jamba. This is a party of people who are not making sacrifices for war. The troops are being well fed by the UN in assembly camps and UNITA is making*

251

good money from diamonds. So why not have a good time?

Gone are the warm beers and stringy chickens of the Jamba days. This is food worthy of a wedding in Lisbon. There is a triumphant spread of deep fried codfish, sausage, rice and tomatoes. A roasted pig's head lies on a tray surveying the crowd, surrounded by toothpicks and sliced lemons. Huge jeroboams of Laurent Perrier champagne are lined up like missiles. The UNITA generals laugh and play to the camera as they open the bottles and spray them like fountains. The champagne sprays so high that it drenches the paper confetti decorations festooned from the ceiling.

Soon it is time to cut the cake. It is an anniversary cake, the thirtieth anniversary, they say, of the start of the great fight. It is green, like the green of the UNITA flag, the green of the bush and their uniforms.

The hardline stars are in the ascendancy now. They are the loyal generals – one-armed Bock, Dachala of Lisbon days, Dembo with deep rings under his eyes like a panda, Gato, Numa. Relegated to the back rows in disgrace are the people who negotiated the Lusaka peace accords, who Savimbi feels sold out UNITA by giving away too much to his enemies. Jorge Valentim has been replaced by Dachala as information chief. I do not see Eugénio Manuvakola on the tape, but maybe that peace accord chief negotiator is there somewhere in the background quietly eating a canapé.

But that is the party.

Liebenberg has captured some angry images of the press conference Savimbi gives. There is no discussion about the one million casualties of the war or the martyrdom of Cuito. UNITA does not feel accountable. Instead, there are sinister boos from the audience as uncomfortable questions are asked. Most of the journalists present are sympathetic to UNITA and were flown in from friendly places like Zaire and the Ivory Coast. For those like Liebenberg who are not allies, questions are censured and ridiculed.

Someone asks Savimbi if he will accept the vice-presidency.

'DO I LOOK LIKE A PUPPET?' he roars. And the crowd behind him rises, jeering.

We put in another tape of the party. Liebenberg leans over my shoulder *narrating the shots.*

'O Mais Velho *looks happy and at peace, doesn't he?' Liebenberg says, as the face with the broad nose looms back into view. I look at it carefully. Savimbi looks serene, indeed.*

Liebenberg continues. 'He looks like the King of Bailundo coming home to rest, don't you think?'

7

Remission

I

I always think of Katia's parrots as oracles of war and peace. The old one, who had witnessed the street fighting outside his front door in the Battle of Luanda, used to mimic the sound of AK-47 fire. This new one, a big African Grey with sharp talons and given to plucking out his own feathers, imitated the sounds of new wealth and business. His specialities were the alarms of jeeps and the calls of vendors coming to the door.

It was January 1995 and I had come back to Luanda for the first time in more than a year. Everything was different, not just the new parrot. This time I was working for a newspaper, not an agency. For the first time I could take Angola slowly and inhale its fetid confusion with deliberation. There were no satphones to lug about, or skeds to nurse. There was just Angola to observe with a new, more measured eye. I had come for two weeks and didn't have to write a word until I got back to Johannesburg. I had time to consider Angola's illusions and contradictions.

There was another big difference on this trip. In the past, I had always kept my sentimental life in abeyance in Angola. The country and the work were so emotionally draining that there was no time for intimacy. I kept the few relationships I had during that time secretive or fleeting, awarding them so little energy that they never could flourish.

Now I decided to share the experience with someone. I wanted a witness.

It ended up being a mistake. We walked through Huambo and Cuito and a string of other ruined towns, looking at them like the completely separate people that we were. I wanted to see every mangled building, every ruined school, the way a frenetic tourist must visit every painting in Florence. My companion just wanted to take good pictures.

'Look, this is where the fighting happened on October 31,' I'd exclaim. 'And this is where I was almost shot.' He grew sullen as I dragged him to places where I had been and, more importantly, those that I had not been to but whose agony I had written about. I finally had a chance to fill in the gaps where my imagination had gone to work before. But these were my gaps and my imagination and it was too personal a thing to convey to someone else.

'I don't know why you keep going on about Angola,' he said petulantly one day, after being shepherded to yet another place which I had missed during the fighting and now had to see for myself.

'Sarajevo was pretty bad, too,' he said. And then, dusting his camera lens: 'The light was better in Somalia. It was soft and golden. It was a bigger story.'

His oblique remarks really didn't matter in the grand scheme of things. I was drifting through my war tourism on a personal map and the passenger could just look out the window for all I cared.

I realised then that it would be difficult to explain to anyone else what the war had been like, but that I had to persevere. Giving up would be disloyal to history.

✢

My first moments back were a blur anyway. When we landed in Luanda on a newly reinstated South African Airways flight,

Katia was at the airport to meet us. Normally she sent one of the staff from the press centre but something was up and she wanted to be there personally.

She thrust a travel permit with the defence ministry stamp, a water bottle and a plastic bag of musty jerseys at me and propelled us in the direction of the airport's military section. A group of Angolan journalists was sitting on the tarmac, waving excitedly at us.

'Quick, go quickly. The generals are flying to Chipipa near Huambo to meet with UNITA. The plane leaves in 15 minutes. I've got you on the flight.'

I asked her about money. I only had dollars on me and when I was there last food and ammunition were the only accepted currencies. I did, however, have a small wad of *kwanza* that I had smuggled in which was the equivalent of $50 during my last visit.

Katia scoffed. It was now worth 50 cents.

'That will buy you enough for one bread roll. Use it to blow your nose.'

✝

The Lusaka peace accords had been signed less than two months before. When Angolans spoke of the agreements they applied the subjunctive or conditional, to convey their uncertainty.

'If this peace holds,' people would say. They wouldn't just say the word 'peace' alone, like they did in 1992 before the fighting resumed. There were always the prefaces 'if', 'maybe', or 'perhaps'.

One felt that tentativeness especially in Chipipa. We arrived there on 10 January for a meeting to review the accords, held by the military command of both sides, General João de Matos of the government and UNITA's Ben Ben. I was curious to see Ben Ben; this was the first time I had had access to UNITA since they fled the capital following the Battle of Luanda.

The meetings were held in tents in an open field and in a tiny church where the windows had cracked during fighting. The two parties agreed to cease all hostilities, disengage their troops and allow the free movement of persons.

The meeting reminded me of Namibe, that ill-fated meeting in November 1992 when UNITA denied that it was waging war and had misled Margaret Anstee. But this time the air of suspicion was greater and the men looked even more wary.

✢

The Swiss woman was running her hand along the empty place on the shelf. There was a ring of dust outlining where the jar had been.

'It's gone,' she said. 'There's no doubt, it's gone.'

The journalists covering Chipipa were camped out on the floors and couches of an ICRC centre for amputees. The crowd, a fairly boisterous one, had completely overrun the centre, causing the Red Cross people to hide in their rooms and forcing them to queue up for their own meagre bath water.

That was bad enough. But now someone had stolen the malaria tablets. It was a white plastic jar which had contained just enough pills to save a few lives. The theft was a betrayal, the latest in a long line of betrayals.

The Red Cross people were already traumatised from having been looted by UNITA before it withdrew from the city in November 1994 when the peace accords were signed.

They said the UNITA men had taunted them and stolen everything. They took their clothes, their food, their mattresses. The armed men even ripped family pictures off the walls and pocketed them. These were things they didn't need, that didn't have value for anyone but the true owners. UNITA came in jeeps and cars and when they had cleaned out everything they wanted they picked up their walkie-talkie radios and called in townspeople to come take the rest. The Red Cross considered itself impartial and had helped civilians on both sides during the war. Then UNITA mocked it. The soldiers had held several dozen people hostage, holding a gun to one man's head and laughing as he begged to be saved, his head under a blanket. When everything had finally been taken, the soldiers left them to sleep on the cold bare cement floors. This was their thanks.

Now some journalist had stolen their malaria tablets.

'Are you sure that someone hasn't put the jar in a safe place?' I asked the Swiss woman. I didn't want to believe that one of my colleagues had done this.

She shook her head. There wasn't much else on the shelf, probably because of the looting by UNITA. She ran her hand over the space, thinking perhaps about all the other things which had been taken. Then she hit her hand hard on the shelf and began to cry.

✢

The military meeting was the next day. Afterwards, the generals returned to their respective bases, UNITA driving three hours to Bailundo and the government flying back to Luanda. The other journalists went with them, the malaria pill thief among them. My companion and I decided to stay in Huambo for a few days. Our first stop was the market where I traded radio batteries for bread. As Katia said, no one would take the old currency bills.

As we drove through town, I could see that Huambo was a different city from the one I had visited three years before. There were outlines of its old self, nothing more. I recognised a familiar shop sign but it was cracked from the artillery fire and some words were missing. Every building looked like it had a chunk of masonry missing. Many lacked roofs. None had intact windows.

The damage to their occupants' psyches must have been far worse. The trauma was still raw, even two months after the peace accords. A lot of people, when they heard the word journalist – *jornalista* – simply shut up. They didn't want to be probed about what had happened. Because the city had changed sides so many times, they were scared to state who they supported. They had come this far and didn't want to threaten their survival with a political indiscretion. They didn't know who the next occupiers might be.

Nearly everyone would grow quiet when asked which side they were on. 'Neither,' they would reply. Their loyalties had been pulverised and all they wanted to do was survive.

But some people were forthcoming, without any encouragement. They included a doctor at the hospital who had survived the UNITA siege. He described how the wounded had crawled into the courtyard during the 55-day battle, and died there slowly, groaning from lack of food and medicine. UNITA, we heard from a barber, had posted spies throughout the city. People disappeared in the night. Their bodies were found days later, stuffed down wells with wire wound around their necks. Neighbourhood committees watched everyone on the block. The MPLA soldiers weren't much better behaved when they retook the town in November, a nurse at the hospital said. He took us to a ward entirely filled with women who had been shot in the legs by soldiers for refusing their sexual advances.

I thought about the Ovimbundu's beliefs in spirits and ancestors. The tradition passed down through the generations is that when a person dies the soul leaves the body and becomes a ghost, or *ocimbanda*. This *ocimbanda* can be very badly behaved. Illness or death can result if it is not appeased with a feast or treated with proper respect.

There must have been a lot of *ocimbanda* restlessly flying through Huambo, searching for some relief after their violent past. The people of Huambo had little opportunity to mourn their dead properly. In many cases, people died in the streets or squares, unable to crawl back to the safety of their houses.

259

Eventually their corpses were burned in the road or gnawed beyond recognition by dogs. No one said a prayer. There was no ceremony.

✝

In Cuito, the living were as haunted as the *ocimbanda*.

It was the children who really got to me.

Before, when I thought about the war's atrocities, I usually imagined the adults who had been affected. I hadn't really thought about a report I had read by UNICEF which described 1,5 million Angolan children severely affected by the war, many of them orphaned and struggling to survive on their own.

Visiting a place like Cuito, which suffered the worst of the fighting and the hunger, I was struck by the absence of old people. No one looked over 45. But I saw kids everywhere. So many seemed to have survived by fighting. We befriended one 15-year-old, Paulinho Cunje. He stood guard at a trench on the edge of town, part of a civilian defence unit which didn't truly believe the war was over. His automatic weapon was half as tall as he was and he struggled to walk with it.

His family had all died in the war.

'*Meu novo irmão*. My new brother,' he said, tapping the gun.

The adults in Cuito were more open about talking of their experiences than the people of Huambo. It was somewhat ironic considering that the city had suffered far worse than Huambo. Cuito was so destroyed by repeated shelling that it looked like an African version of Dresden. Maybe the greater openness of Cuito's people was because the city had never been downright occupied by UNITA, but split in half between the two sides.

In any case, you'd just walk down Cuito's main street, which had served as the front line during fighting, and people would wave from inside the buildings which looked like doll houses with their facades blown off. They'd invite you in. Or an old man would fall into step as you strolled through the ruins and would offer to show you his house where his three children, wife and cousin died. He would show you the walls which they had knocked down so that they could run to the next door neighbours' house easily, and the bunker they had set up in the basement where they hid for six months. He'd tell you about a relative who crossed the street when fighting broke out and was stuck there during the entire siege.

At least the adults could articulate the horrors they had experienced. This was not the case with the kids. Children barely have a word for house or milk, let alone rape or trauma. We visited an orphanage, which was little more than a shattered building with neat lines of bunk beds and thin, worn blankets. The kids sang a traditional welcome song for us. The words were cheerful and warm but their eyes were still and they clapped their hands automatically.

We saw a little girl, maybe two years old, who had been found on her dead mother's breast, trying to nurse on the withered teat, surrounded by other corpses in a field. All she could say was her name: Teresa.

✛

Cuito had civic problems that would have upset any authority. It lacked intact buildings, walls, running water, working electricity. But the really worrying problem was the mines. A large number seemed to have been sowed in Cuito, in the city centre itself when it was the scene of the war's most ferocious battle. Mortars jutted out of cracked walls. On one wall, a cluster of grenades hung like a bunch of fake fruit. No one could explain how it had got there. Maybe it was a booby trap left by a retreating soldier.

But the happiest kids hung around the edge of the mine-fields.

For a people deafened by the sound of a thousand shells falling each day, I thought it was odd that the kids delighted in the blast and smoke when the de-miners blew up the explosives. They squealed and giggled as the dynamite worked its way down the fuse before the final BOOM! Gangs of children would follow the de-miners around, strutting behind the modern-day pied pipers who, in their protective helmets and navy blue flak jackets, looked like spacemen strutting through the ruins of the city.

I asked some boys what they wanted to be when they grew up.

'De-miners!!'

It was the Cuito equivalent of a fireman on Main Street.

The men from Halo Trust, a British NGO, set up a garden of deadly examples of explosives in their front yard. Part of it was decorative, the bent shells serving as sculptures. Part of it was a deterrent against crime.

'This is the safest house in town,' said one of the de-miners, planting a new Claymore mine by a tree. 'No one would dare rob us.'

There were Chinese mines, Russian mines, and American, South African, Cuban, East German, and Czechoslovakian mines. There were mines that broke your legs, others that shattered your torso. Some could reduce a car to tin foil. Others were designed to tear off fingers, toes and heads. Mines had been created that jumped out of the ground upon impact, heading straight for the stomach.

Experts estimated there were ten million, or one per every single Angolan. But no one knew for sure. Every time they removed a mine, someone from UNITA or a government supporter would lay more. The de-miners' work was painstaking. Some had heavy armoured vehicles and dogs. But most sifted dirt with sticks to take samples, working just a few square metres a day. When it rained the mines shifted in formerly secure ground and claimed new victims. We met peasant women balancing firewood, cassava and plastic buckets of water on their heads. They continued to walk through the fields despite the warnings of the de-miners. The spokeswoman of the group, a withered woman of about 30 wearing a torn red dress, said they didn't have a choice.

'It's this or starve,' she said.

✢

The one place my travel companion was keen to go to, and I didn't want to, was Luena. I came up with every reason why we shouldn't go, but my friend wanted to film the de-mining. There was no strong argument that I could offer to the contrary. I forced myself to return there, worrying throughout the flight that I'd suffer a strong reaction to returning to the scene of the shelling. But as we prepared for landing the expected flashback never came. There were no rapid spirals on descent this time and no wounded waiting to be evacuated when we landed. There was no panic on the ground, just my own remembered anxiety. The soldiers welcoming us looking reassuringly bored.

The last time I landed in Luena, in January 1993, I never even made it into town because of the shelling at the airport. This time we walked leisurely around the city, careful not to stray off the main roads because of the hundreds of land-mines around the town. The land-mine situation was so bad in the fields that people were growing corn in their front gardens in the city centre. The city park was completely overgrown with chest-high grass, the swings and ladders covered with ivy and weeds. But then again, they had been like that after the war of independence so you could pretend nothing traumatic had happened recently. Until you went to the railroad station.

The Benguela Railroad was paralysed by the war, so the citizens of Luena decided to put the abandoned facilities to good use. Refugees who had poured in from the countryside camped out in the derelict rusted railroad carriages and on the platform, which offered more shelter than the tents or reed huts at the UN refugee camps. The wooden sleepers had long since vanished, having been used for firewood. It had become a phantom rail station, where people arrived but never left.

+

Katia is a fighter by nature. She stayed on in Luanda when life's daily hardships became untenable for most other European *cooperantes*. In the Battle of Luanda she watched the fighting from her living room, egging on the civilians besieging Savimbi's house. Now she was fighting with her neighbour upstairs who had opened a club on the rooftop. The club, which had a panoramic view of Luanda bay as well as the main cemetery below, was officially named *O Terraço*. But everyone knew it as *MiraMortos*, or View of the Dead. (This was a pun on the neighbourhood called *Miramar*, or Sea View.) The discothèque shook the apartment building until closing time, which was usually around 6 a.m. I was staying in Katia's flat and shared her frustration. It was impossible to sleep, even with the sponge earplugs which Katia had advised me to bring with me. Every day she charged upstairs to complain to Tino, the owner. She had consulted every lawyer she knew about how to shut down *MiraMortos*. But the club remained open; Tino was related to the ex-wife of the President and had powerful connections.

Now, however, there was a truce between Katia and Tino. Tino was the cousin of Ricardo de Mello, one of Angola's leading independent journalists, who had been assassinated just a few days before by someone carrying a silenced pistol. The murderer shot him dead on the stairs leading to Ricardo's apartment. This was not a time to complain about discothèques. Besides Katia, like the entire journalistic community in Luanda, was in shock.

My friend Aguiar told me about a death list that was being circulated with the names of other journalists. He asked me to meet him in a café, where he wrote the names on a piece of paper napkin so that he did not have to speak them aloud. One of the names was his.

'This is peacetime, this is not supposed to happen,' Aguiar said.

He is normally full of bluster and defensive jokes but that evening he was almost childlike with fear. I promised him that upon returning to Johannesburg I would contact international journalists' organisations. But that didn't reassure him much.

'These people act with impunity. Someone else will be dead by the time you come back,' he said.

Ricardo had been a figure of controversy who edited a newletter sent out by fax called *Imparcialfax*. It was a mixture of scurrilous rumours, alleged government leaks and legitimate criticisms of the regime's corruption.

I had known Ricardo since my Lisbon days; he had worked for a Portuguese radio station at one point. His journalism had been at times sensationalist and poorly backed-up. There were rumours that he was on the take from a faction of the security forces. But that did not justify being shot twice in a hallway early in the morning while your family slept upstairs, with only a penknife to protect yourself.

Before he was killed, rumour had it, Ricardo was being leaked information by disgruntled security officials. They had warned him to watch out. But he pressed ahead and published a particularly controversial story which implicated people in the highest levels of government in corruption. The result was, as Aguiar said, a death foretold.

Even the suspicions about Ricardo's connections with the security forces did not quell the indignation over his death. But several journalists stayed away from the funeral, not out of dislike of Ricardo but out of fear of being spotted there.

The funeral was bizarre. Walking well behind the shocked family and reporters were a couple of government officials who apparently felt they had to show up to prove the regime was not responsible. I caught the eye of the president's spokesman and he looked away, embarrassed, like a gatecrasher at a wedding.

Someone had spray painted de Mello's name on the outer wall of the cemetery: 'Ricardo Lives! *Viva!*'

The priest led the procession through the gates across the cemetery of broken and cracked tombstones – many of the graves had been looted by thieves looking for jewellery. Several mourners tripped over stones. They were silent except for Ricardo's widow who keened 'Why? Why? Why?'

The coffin was very heavy. The priest periodically changed the pallbearers, calling out like a drill sergeant the new category of mourners as we all took turns. 'Family.' 'Diplomats.' 'Colleagues.' When he came to 'International Media' there were only two of us – myself and a French photographer. We struggled with the coffin for a few steps before passing it on to the next group.

Several days later, I joined Tino on the roof terrace overlooking the cemetery. The heavy sky was the colour of grey slate. Tino was dressed in a white caftan, whisky in hand as he looked down at the cemetery where his cousin was buried. His green-blue eyes were set against the bronzed skin that was the pride of the *mestiço* elite. Culturally, too, Tino was in a limbo between two groups and two eras.

'It's the only place where there is peace,' he reflected about the cemetery below. 'When I was a kid I believed the ghosts would attack you on the streets, come across the wall and beat you. But now I find it is the only place in Luanda where there is tranquillity. I like the idea that I can see Ricardo's grave from here and be so close to him.'

Another cousin joined us. Her name was Rosinha and she was a pop singer with dreadlocked blonde hair extensions down to her waist and Botticellian features. She had flown in from Sweden where she lived but was too late for the funeral. A self-pronounced Buddhist, she went to the stairs where Ricardo had been shot and performed a simple ceremony 'to free his spirit'. She was jetlagged, grieving and argumentative. This was her first visit back in ten years and she bemoaned the fall of the *mestiço* hegemony.

Both she and Tino felt betrayed by the MPLA and by what they claimed were uneducated black ideologues who rose through the ranks via revolution. Tino was nostalgic for the Portuguese colonial era, painting a picture of tolerance and order for people like his family.

'We were educated, decent, even aristocrats, you could say. Not like these people,' said Rosinha. She began crying again about Ricardo.

Tino carried on. 'We believed in this. We fought for independence for them. We didn't need independence ourselves because we had it so good. When I was 12 I picked up a gun and fought in the streets. Now I wonder what for. These people will do anything for power and money.'

Tino said that any lingering interest in politics vanished with Ricardo's death. 'Now all my energy will go into the night-club,' he said. 'I want to provide a beautiful place for beautiful people, a refuge from the miseries, the dirt, the poor.'

✛

During the early months of 1995 Angola hovered in a limbo between war and peace. Just a month after the much-heralded agreement in Chipipa, the UN military chief in Angola, Chris Garuba, criticised both parties for not observing the accord. There were cease-fire violations and both sides were still being armed.

The UN had done a miserable job before. It couldn't afford to do so again. On 8 February 1995, the Security Council approved the sending of approximately 7 000 blue helmets. These new men were not mere observers like the last time. This time, they would try to oversee the demobilisation of some 140 000 troops from both sides and the formation of a new army. This time the UN would try to do it properly.

That same month UNITA held its first congress since 1990. The hardliners were definitely in the ascendancy. Sitting in positions of prominence were Generals Paulo Lukamba Gato, Demostenes Chilingutila, António Sebastião Dembo, and Colonel José Pombo Vilinga. Savimbi appeared to have been unhappy with the peace accord. Definitely out of favour were Ben Ben, Jaka Jamba and Jorge Valentim. Valentim had been replaced as information secretary by Adriano Dachala. Maybe the men were being blamed for the Lusaka Protocol having been signed at a point of such military disadvantage.

In the countryside, people were growing food again. The rains and harvest were good. But reconstruction was going slowly and the economy was still a mess. By mid-year the *kwanza* was still depreciating rapidly, to 2,25 million to the US dollar. Prices were soaring. Indeed, UNAVEM III, whose first blue helmets arrived in May, seemed to be the driving force behind the economy, handing out contracts for mine clearing and construction.

Savimbi appeared to have been chastened by the humiliations of the previous year when he had lost Huambo and, effectively, the war. He claimed that any incidents attributed to UNITA were due to rogue elements. His language was conciliatory in public, heartening negotiators. Savimbi agreed to meet Dos Santos in Lusaka on 6 May, referring to him as 'my president'. Then later that month, at a press conference in South Africa, Savimbi acknowledged the futility of his second war.

But that was as far as he would go towards national reconciliation. On 17 June, Dos Santos offered the vice-presidency to Savimbi in a future government of national unity. It was an offer that Savimbi would not accept. Savimbi still refused to leave Bailundo and its surroundings when he was in Angola. Citing the massacres during the Battle of Luanda, he said his reluctance was on security grounds.

✛

Some time during 1995 I stopped having the dream about the big wave swallowing up the village by the sea. It happened gradually; the dream would occur only a couple of times a week and then only once a week. Then one morning I awoke and realised that it had receded completely.

I felt as though Angola had turned some sort of significant corner – half-way into peace, although still not quite there. But I felt uneasy. And I wondered whether a new sort of forgetfulness and apathy would come with peace. It was a concern that many Angolans felt.

In February 1995 I attended the opening of the Africus Biennale at Johannesburg's Newtown cultural complex. Artists from across Africa were exhibiting their work. The fact that the event had happened at all seemed more important than the quality of the art, which prompted little debate. But the one exhibit which seemed to elicit reaction from everyone I knew was from Angola.

'Gruesome' was the word frequently applied. The exhibit was so vivid that I could almost smell the gangrene at the Graça Machel hospital and hear the moaning patients strapped to the metal headboards so that they didn't writhe off the operating tables.

Hanging on the walls of a dark claustrophobic space were sculptures of mangled bodies, like the torsos of martyred saints displayed in medieval chapels. They had protruding bones and flesh charred like barbecued meat. There were dismembered babies with nails stuck into their torsos, like religious sacrifices who had suffered in vain.

An Angolan friend from Luanda, Teresa, had been involved in setting up the exhibit. On the night of the opening we stood in the corner and listened to one disturbed viewer after another express their disgust.

'This is awful,' said one woman. She moved away.

We heard another woman talking to someone outside. 'It is really disgusting, I assure you. Don't bother to go in.'

I looked at Teresa to see her reaction. She was smiling broadly. 'Good,' she said. 'Very good.'

✛

I returned to Angola in September 1995. The plan was to stay for a month and not write any stories, just absorb the place without the distractions of deadlines.

There was a sense of déjà vu, from the moment the businessmen took every Club Class seat of the SAA plane to when we landed in a city busily plugging up bullet holes and repainting buildings. I was reminded of 1992 before the elections, with new hotels and restaurants opening and the word 'opportunities' resounding through the city.

But the sense of time warp stopped there. Most businesses with serious money were wary of investing too much. For Angolans, the hope was more muted than after the Biçesse accords. They still had to be convinced.

Peace had made life in the provinces better. Philippe Borel of the WFP said starvation was no longer a threat. With the air of a man satisfied with a job well done, he sat in his office surrounded by boxes, preparing to leave the mission for an emergency elsewhere in the world.

Carlos Amorim, the Portuguese hotelier who had prevented a large group of UNITA people from being killed in October 1992, was also thinking of moving on. Over lunch I congratulated him on being awarded one of Portugal's highest accolades for his valour. Having remained during Angola's darkest moments, he said he had finally reached a saturation point where he didn't want to see any more problems. I sensed that he wasn't entirely convinced that Angola was in the clear.

Over some palm wine, he spoke about his dream. 'It's a little hotel in the Algarve, by the sea. No confusão there.'

✛

Peace was viewed as something very tentative by many Angolans. Most of their energy went into surviving. A chicken cost the equivalent of a civil servant's monthly wage, or $6. I needed a plastic bag the size of a potato sack after exchanging $20 for *kwanza*.

Everybody I knew was struggling to get by. The dark streets of Luanda were filled with movement at night: prostitutes, gangs of child beggars, police. All were competing for money.

João Martins, the driver of the brown Mercedes, did the unthinkable for a proud man: he came to the flat where I was staying and asked me for a 'loan'. I gave him some cash, probably worth no more than $50. He was so ashamed that he got out of the house quickly and rushed to his car. He had trouble starting it because he couldn't afford spare parts. He let some strangers give him a push but wouldn't look at me as I stood watching from the doorway.

Zeca, the cousin of my musician friend Waldemar, was struggling too. He and his wife were among the Angolan friends with whom I had lost touch during the war. I felt terrible for having waited so long. Now it was time to make amends.

When I first met Zeca in 1992, he liked to think of himself as a man of the moment. But now, surveying the wreckage of his life's work, he conceded that his finest moments had passed. Zeca had never been a rich man, and his hopes of ever becoming one lay shattered like the fine shards of glass on the floor of his factory which had been looted when the war resumed in 1992.

In three years he had lost $100 000. His business selling detergent and chlorine was in ruins. Zeca had always felt protected by his status in the MPLA. That didn't count for much these days. He was bitter.

The expensive restaurants had been forsaken for modest cafés. At dinner he and his wife declined wine and instead watered down their beer with Sprite, to make it last longer. A look of dismay accompanied the bill, which was the equivalent of $7. But Zeca's sense of pride and hospitality was such that he tried to grab the bill from my hand so that I wouldn't pay. I stupidly held on and the paper ripped.

Driving the car on the way home from dinner, he swerved to avoid some broken glass and nails that robbers had put in the road to puncture the tyres of would-be victims. An affable man in the past, he was on a charged tirade about theft by the poor and the rich alike.

'They're all the same,' he said. 'Thieves. Stealing you blind.' The car hit the edge of a pothole and bounced. 'Thieves. All of them.'

✛

A lot of the old characters had returned to Luanda. Suddenly Johann Smith, the former South African military attaché, was driving around in a 4x4. Then I ran into Isaías Samakuva, a UNITA official whom I had not seen since the Battle of Luanda. He had just opened UNITA's first office in Luanda in three years.

This time, it wasn't always clear who was on which side. The lines were more blurred. Before the war resumed in 1992 most Angolans I met were convinced about the ideological option they had chosen. Now a lot of people were confused. There had been so much loss of hope and so much destruction that idealism wasn't a factor any more. Some people had jumped sides overtly. Others linked themselves to what appeared to be the easiest option. There were people now who were happily working for those who had mutilated them several years before. It seemed bizarre to me that they could suffer wounds during the war and now work for the very same people who had inflicted them. Money was often more important than ideology or loyalty.

Johann Smith didn't say much about what his work entailed these days. During his free time he socialised with his old buddies from UNITA. One sweltering morning he, Colonel

Américo Gato, Gato's wife and a friend of the family came by my hotel and took me for an outing to the market. We went on to see the building site for Américo's new home. It was right on the beach, in an area on the outskirts of Luanda where MPLA army officials lived. The air was fresh with a salty breeze.

Everyone was cheerful, transported far from the city's claustrophobia. All the men were wearing beach shorts except for Johann; he preferred to wear long trousers to hide the scars on his legs. While visiting the site the two of us spoke about what had happened in 1992 and why it had been so traumatic for so many people.

Johann said it was one of the most painful things he had undergone in his life. I said that surely he had experienced pretty awful things before, such as being wounded several times. Why was this worse?

He looked at the sea, in the direction of the Love Boat, where he had been stuck while the men he had trained in UNITA were being slaughtered on land. He rubbed the dent on his forehead.

'It was a feeling of complete helplessness, watching everything disintegrate in front of our eyes. There we were, sitting in sheer decadence eating crayfish. Just metres away people were killing my friends. I was unable to do anything about it. I just couldn't believe it was happening.

'I felt like my whole dream was crumbling, sitting powerless on that boat. I had invested my youth and blood in Angola. I had spent so many years there that I felt like an Angolan. I had fought to end up where we were in Angola. I really thought the process would work. I saw old people standing to vote for hours and days. They believed that what they were doing was right, even though they had no grasp of it. And then they were betrayed.'

Johann had always been circumspect about UNITA's return to war, although his sympathy for the movement was never disguised. I asked him whether he believed in hindsight that

Savimbi had fought a just war.

'It shouldn't have happened,' he said. 'Even if there were fraud, UNITA made a big mistake. If they had just swallowed their defeat and left the MPLA to make mistakes, there would have been elections this year. And they would have walked an election. No, it is sad what happened instead. That's what hurts.'

Américo stood nearby, listening to our conversation. He didn't join in. He was one of the UNITA military men who had been captured during the Battle of Luanda and held in detention. The official MPLA story was that these men had switched loyalties and abandoned UNITA. But I wasn't convinced of Américo's conversion.

Like other UNITA men who had 'gone over' to the MPLA, Américo talked about starting up a business. Another who did so was General Peregrino Wambu. Once one of UNITA's rising stars and a favourite of Savimbi, Wambu was caught by the MPLA during the Battle of Luanda. After several months, he openly joined the MPLA military. Now he was living in a coveted large flat in an apartment block of the elite, and had a new 4x4 vehicle. Wambu had married into Luanda's *mestiço* elite, which was hated by Savimbi, taking as his wife a woman who was a close relative of the Cardinal. Savimbi saw him as a sell-out. But contradictory loyalties remained. Savimbi's henchman Chivukuvuku remained close to his childhood friend Wambu, even becoming the godfather of Wambu's new child.

I spent a fair amount of time with Wambu this trip. He sought me out after a mutual friend told him I wanted to speak to him, arriving unannounced at my hotel room. He was wary and did not identify himself on the telephone, saying only: 'Judite, you know who this is.' After the first meeting, we subsequently held conversations in his car or at his house.

I asked him about the woman who had been his companion during the UNITA days. He played with some cake crumbs on the table, rolling them into a ball between his fingers.

'She remained behind,' he said.

His biggest desire was to leave Angola, and earn a university degree somewhere.

'I need a change,' he said. 'Things are different now.'

The MPLA also wasn't fully convinced of the political reincarnation of Fred Oelschig, who had been a colonel under apartheid and one of the main liaison officers of the South African Defence Force stationed at UNITA's Jamba base. Now Fred and other former apartheid soldiers were working for South Africa's defence company Mechem with a contract to clear mines.

Fred and his team were sitting in the newly refurbished Hotel Continental, drinking heavily out of frustration most nights. Mechem had heavy armoured vehicles and a contract to clear more than 5 000 kilometres of armed roads. But they couldn't get to work. Their de-mining equipment was held up at the port and they were losing thousands of dollars a day because of the delays. They thought the government was holding them up because they refused to pay bribes. But people I spoke to in the MPLA said they were suspect because of their former ties.

The levels of strangeness went even deeper. The government was more tolerant of other Afrikaners, the South Africans who had fought on the side of UNITA in earlier days and were now working for Executive Outcomes. EO was first spotted helping the government in Soyo in 1993 and then in Huambo the following year.

They, too, were hanging around Luanda bars. Under the Lusaka Protocol all foreign 'mercenaries' were supposed to have withdrawn from Angola. But now about 350 of the EO men had been re-deployed in companies of the likes of Branch Energy, Shibata Security, Stuart Mills International, Ibis Air, Saracen International and Bridge Resources. I passed on some of their business cards to a friend who was an investigator in South Africa. He said some of the companies appeared to be nothing more than a fax machine, if that.

The men were pretty conspicuous, with their loud Afrikaans, large bellies and khaki shorts. They converged every Tuesday and Thursday night at two expatriate clubs called the Viking Club and French Pink Palace, where they'd drink after playing rugby. These were white male domains where any woman who entered was catalogued by hungry gazes and where the talk was of exploits in Sierra Leone, Somalia and Zaire.

The men were an embarrassment to the new black-led government in Pretoria. 'Frankly I wish they'd just go away,' said a senior South African diplomat.

Whatever its employees' past credentials, EO cleverly presented itself as a respectable firm which offered clients an unbeatable package – peace, democracy and stability. But these loud barrel-bellied men were not corporate representatives. They were men trained and skilled in one thing – war. Many of those recruited were formerly of the notorious 32 Battalion – the Buffalo Battalion – which was involved in destabilising activities west and north of South Africa during apartheid. Other recruits came from the dreaded paramilitary *Koevoet* (crowbar) unit or had served in Ian Smith's Rhodesian forces.

EO's success, first in Angola and then in Sierra Leone, was an irritant to more established security companies such as DSL (Defence Systems Limited) of Britain which prided themselves on their professionalism.

I sat in on one lunchtime meeting where a de-mining man from DSL tried to woo a new client from the World Vision aid agency. He seemed more like a financial broker than an expert in explosives. In a crisp blue Oxford shirt and red tie, he offered a variety of services in the reassuringly professional voice of a stockbroker advising clients on unit trusts.

'Perhaps you need some mine clearance on the road? Call us. How about some guards?' he said, handing the would-be client some literature to study. 'We're at your service.'

+

Naim Martins Cardoso was a big Brazilian man who did not scare easily. But when he went to work at the Catoca diamond mine he took along soldiers with automatic weapons in the back of his jeep. We drove slowly on the road from Saurimo, on the look out for land-mines and bandits. Naim's company, the Brazilian mining and construction firm Odebrecht, had just won a contract with the government to dig a giant hole to mine a kimberlite pipe which they presumed would yield some of the world's finest quality diamonds. But to do their work, they had to contract a special force of 300 crack soldiers to protect their workers. The diamond area had become a morass of confusion, carved up into fiefdoms run by warlords.

'We call it the Wild East,' Naim said, looking over his shoulder brusquely as we passed another jeep full of soldiers coming from the opposite direction.

'Supposedly the war is over. But not here.'

The roads, unlike anywhere else I had been in Angola, were immaculately tarred. But the colonel joining us in the jeep informed me that only three hours' drive down the road ten people had just been killed in an attack. Either one side got you or the other did. No one was safe.

Diamond mining had begun in Angola in 1912 when deposits were found in the rich reservoirs of the Cuango River Valley. At its peak, legal exports amounted to $243 million in 1990. Now UNITA had forced the closedown of the state diamond firm Endiama with its wildcat mining in the Lunda Norte areas which the rebels conveniently captured at the start of their second war.

By September 1995 the war was officially over. Peace had come to most of the country except in the northern diamond fields. In fact, the end of the war seemed to have made the anarchy worse in the Lundas. Syndicates now flourished on both sides. At the height of the diamond rush, the *garimpeiros*, or illegal diggers, looked like ants from the air. Thousands of them dug diamonds out of the ground with shovels and their bare hands. Diamonds were the cause of many deaths.

Angola is the world's fourth biggest diamond producer, in value, after Russia, Botswana and South Africa. It is believed to harbour more than 10 per cent of the world reserves and has some of the best quality stones anywhere, fetching between $140 and $350 a carat. But much of the money now was going to the syndicates. The *garimpeiros* would earn just a few dollars a month, barely enough to feed their families.

Both UNITA and government generals tried to strengthen their holds in the Lunda Norte and Sul provinces before some sort of workable order was restored. The *garimpeiros* had been operating in the Lundas since 1992 after the diamond prospecting rules were liberalised. Now the area had become carved up into fiefdoms divided only by a river or a stream and run by warlords or generals, who were often UNITA and MPLA military men. There was a sense of collective impotence. The UN could do little to halt the illicit activity. High-level government officials running their own syndicates were certainly not going to stop it. UNITA was mining an estimated 90 per cent of the country's diamond production, making more than $500 million a year in sales. Savimbi was not going to give up his main source of income.

Everywhere you went in Saurimo and the smaller diamond towns people came up to you and offered stones. They whispered '*diamantes*, diamonds' in the markets, on the streets, even outside the churches. I didn't know much about diamonds and the offerings looked like dirty pebbles or bits of worn glass to me. They were often wrapped in dirty newspaper or tissue paper. A lot of the accents of the sellers were French, West African or Zairian French.

✛

I wanted to visit the riverbeds where the *garimpeiros* were operating but Naim advised against driving there. The first

278

flight Odebrecht had to Dundu, the main diamond smuggling town near the border with Zaire, was in a week's time. I decided to go back to Luanda and try my luck there.

There were a variety of ways to get in because so many people were operating there. The least comfortable method was to hitch a predawn ride with the South African pilots who flew private charters for the smugglers. The private shipments that I saw were of normal cargo – beers, soft drinks, and fish. But locals whispered that they also flew in weapons.

While in Luanda I tried to hear De Beers' side of the situation. I knew they probably wouldn't see me, but decided to try anyway out of perverse stubbornness.

De Beers officials had been pretty accessible before the war resumed in 1992. But now the company was on the defensive. It had just lost a lucrative prospecting contract to some rivals. The anarchy in the Lundas was eroding its control of the world diamond market. Meanwhile, the company was coming under public criticism for helping to fund the continuation of the war by buying up UNITA's main source of income – diamonds.

De Beers officials consistently maintained that they didn't ask questions when they bought diamonds. It may have been a moral dilemma for some, but the top management insisted they were doing no wrong. Now, De Beers' main office in downtown Luanda was run as though its officials were terrified of imminent attack. A colleague and I made the mistake of dropping by without telephoning first, as one could three years before. The company was obsessed with security and even the receptionist in her bullet-proof, glass-plated refuge avoided human contact thanks to a special electronic device which accepted calling cards.

She was not reassured by what she read on them.

'Journalists?' She pointed us to a sterile white waiting-room, which seemed to be hermetically sealed and sound-proofed. We had the sensation, while sitting on the black leather couches, that we were being watched. Several minutes passed and then a man from DSL led us to the electronic door.

'No one will see you.'

Several days later I had better luck dropping in at De Beers' buying office in the city, which a diplomat had helpfully pointed out. It was an unobtrusive house in a residential area which looked like every other house on the block except for the new Discovery jeeps parked outside. Again, there was no sign on the door identifying the nature of the business being conducted inside. The guards were in plainclothes. There were four sets of heavy metal doors with metal detectors and viewing screens and four sets of guards announcing one's presence. The system was designed to protect clients' confidentiality. Visitors entered through one door and left via another, without passing each other.

Upstairs two young British men were examining stones. They seemed surprised to see me, but were frank.

'Great quality,' said one, holding up a stone which had come from the Cuango. 'It's among the best.'

✢

When we finally decided to fly to Dundu, on the commercial state airline TAAG, we almost didn't make it because of the soldier with the grenade.

The problems started when a policeman seeking a Friday night bribe to pay for his weekend drinks tried to arrest my travel companion, a Brazilian reporter. The purported offence was taking a photograph of a vending machine while we were trying to buy tickets at the airport. Just purchasing tickets was a major production. Unlike most countries, you couldn't just walk up to the desk and hand over your money. The staff would always say the flight was overbooked. So you had to appear the night before the flight as the desk was closing and, with the help of someone who knew a member of the staff, pay off an individual to issue the ticket.

Chaos is an accepted part of the Luanda airport experience. People wait for hours, sometimes for days on end, for their delayed flights to finally leave. There are no assigned seats on local flights. There is always more baggage piled on the ground than room in the cargo hold. The muggy lounge provides ripe opportunities for arguments. Shouting is the norm.

But the hollering which we heard that night was different. We were waiting for the airline official in an airless dark room to hand over the tickets when the noise erupted in the check-in section. It was nothing less than hysterical screaming and we rushed out of the room to witness the pandemonium that 150 people create when they all try to check in for the same flight at once.

I heard someone shout: 'He's got a grenade.' The crowd surged back from the check-in counter and, like a human wave, rolled towards the exit to get outside the building.

I caught a glimpse of the soldier, standing alone in front of the counter. He had pushed to the front of the queue, brandishing a hand grenade to disperse the crowd. Now he stood there alone and defiant in front of the counter, still ready to pull the pin although his competition for seats had all fled.

I reflected further on the endless anarchy of Angola as we boarded, with some trepidation, the reeking TAAG flight to Dundu the following day. The flight was only three hours late which the Angolan friend who drove us to the airport reminded us was 'not bad'. The seats smelt as though they had not been cleaned for 20 years and the stench permeated my own shirt. I held the newspaper I was reading close to my face, deeply inhaling the newsprint to block out the odours of the plane.

✛

There is a quiet submission one huddles into when facing armed authority in Angola. Your shoulders hunch over and your voice grows softer. You try to drain your face of any expression

281

and you try not to show anxiety, like a threatened dog. The aggressiveness of armed authority is always worse on Saturdays when the policemen get drunk.

It was a Saturday when we disembarked in Dundu. The police were no more than 16 years old. They were enjoying the dominance that came with their uniforms. They demanded our papers and passports, refusing to let us leave the airport on the grounds that our travel permit issued by the military command in Luanda was not valid. Cristina, the Brazilian journalist, objected, pointing to the date on the documents. But that did not deter our policemen, who were enjoying our discomfort. They appraised our breasts, debating who would take which woman.

They ordered us into a back room for questioning. We did not want to leave the tarmac and moved closer to the one man on the tarmac who was not wearing a uniform. He was a priest in a long robe, the white cloth a sharp contrast to his dark skin.

'Leave the women alone,' he murmured to the police. They were distracted – a new victim!

'*Padre*, you are wearing a dress,' they mocked. 'You are not a real man.'

They demanded to see his papers, although he had already cleared them with immigration.

'Everything is in order,' he said. He kept his eyes on the tarmac.

The thugs were enjoying this. They pushed him. He did not look up. They pushed him again like a toy, and taunted him as he fell, his white gown sullied by the filth on the ground. We were appalled but didn't dare intervene.

The police turned to me again.

'Give me your drink, whitey,' the bigger one demanded, pointing at my plastic water bottle. I lied, saying that I had a mouth infection and did not want to make him ill.

He insisted. I turned away, sick of being bullied, and pretended I did not understand his Portuguese. But I understood it well and heard him tell his companion that he believed white meat tasted sour.

We were saved by a red-haired Irish priest who loved Eric Clapton.

He suddenly appeared at the airport like a vision and walked purposefully into the immigration room where the police had taken us.

'That's them. Those are my visitors,' he said firmly to the police, as though he had been expecting us for some time. 'That will be all. Let's go, ladies.'

The police stepped back and nodded respectfully. The priest steered us outside to a jeep.

'They get a bit rowdy on the weekends,' the priest explained as we rattled towards Dundu in his jeep at 100 miles an hour. 'By the way, what are your names? And what the devil are you doing here?'

We told him what we were looking for. The Father wasn't impressed. He invited us to stay with him at his house but was reluctant to help get us to the *garimpeiro* areas. 'Diamonds. They've ruined this place.'

We realised during our two-day stay, however, that there wasn't much to do in Dundu if you weren't into diamonds. Even the museum, which had housed treasures of the Congo kingdom collected by the Portuguese, had been looted and closed down for the time being. But for the red-haired Father, life in Dundu was bliss. He had been there for ten years and even the guns and *garimpeiros* didn't spoil his idyll. He sat each afternoon and evening on the veranda of his simple wood frame house, sipping beer with the local nuns and cracking peanuts from their shells. A worn Eric Clapton tape blared from the ghetto-blaster inside. He zoomed around in his jeep, trying to give spiritual comfort to those lost in lawlessness or poverty. The Father maintained his equilibrium, somehow finding the absurd rather than the ugly in that forsaken place.

There were plenty of others who did not share his love of

Dundu. The members of the UNAVEM peace observer team who were posted there were also unsure of their mission. There were five of them – a Pakistani, a Jordanian, a Uruguayan, a Portuguese and a Zimbabwean. They ate in separate groups because of their different dietary habits. Besides meals, they seemed to do very little together, including going on patrols. I wondered what they put in their reports to headquarters, as they avoided the areas thickest with illicit action. They were very nervous about being seen with reporters, as though anyone would report back to New York that they had divulged important secrets.

'You want to see the *garimpeiros*?' one asked incredulously. 'Good luck. We wouldn't go anywhere near there. It's too dangerous.'

✜

On 25 September 1995, a few days before I returned to Johannesburg, I sat on my hotel bed and watched a live satellite television transmission from Brussels. The clattering of the air conditioner practically drowned out the sound, but the images were clear enough by themselves.

The two old foes, Savimbi and Dos Santos, appeared in a united front to convince donors that their pledges of $1 billion in reconstruction aid would not be misspent. The condition for the donation was that progress should be made towards peace.

It was a consummate public relations show. The two men had perfected the obligatory handshake that they had performed on so many previous occasions. Both wore dark suits, Savimbi with the black cockerel UNITA pin in his Nehru collar. UNITA might have lost the war, but of the two men Dos Santos looked like the loser, grey and stiff. Savimbi had risen splendidly to the occasion, as radiant and composed as a prophet. Despite all he had suffered the past year, he succeeded in upstaging his rival with his intuitive diplomacy.

Dos Santos mumbled something banal about peace. Savimbi made a speech in impeccable French. 'I am saying this in French so that there will be no misunderstanding: Jonas Savimbi will not go back to war,' he said in his rich deep voice. The moment was his.

The next month Savimbi declared in Lusaka that he regretted ever having returned to war in 1992. Then, on 2 November, UNITA troops begin to appear at UNAVEM-supervised assembly points as the first stage in demobilisation.

But would it last? Would UNITA adhere to the accords this time around? Or had Savimbi tricked everyone yet again?

II

July 1996. This is Lisbon's second moment of diplomatic revival. Biçesse didn't go according to plan. But this new venture – the formation of a Lusophone commonwealth – is being heralded as a fresh start in Portugal's relations with its former colonies. The founding ceremony is held at the Belem cultural centre, overlooking the river and the Jeronimos monastery – the site where the Discoveries had been launched. It is a sparkling sunny summer day with a fresh breeze blowing off the river. A good day for diplomatic glory.

Angola's former prime minister, Marcolino Moco, is voted secretary general of the new organisation. He looks puzzled and uncomfortable, taking his seat at the front of the hall in which the ceremony takes place. He mumbles a short speech and leaves it to the other six member countries to pronounce on the significance of the moment.

The new body will probably be just as ineffectual and haphazard as Portugal's withdrawal from the colonies was, most diplomats scoff. But there is a beguiling 'family' feel to the embraces by men in elegant suits. After all the destruction that followed independence, everyone remarks, there's a friendly atmosphere. And, like everything Portugal does with its former subjects, there is an informality. This is a vaguer sort of arrangement than the British Commonwealth or the French-African franc zone. Delegates admit that the body will probably serve best as a good opportunity to shop in Lisbon; already at its first meeting delegates discuss the fact that the grouping duplicates other existing organisations.

But Portugal doesn't have any illusions, its officials say. The CPLP, as the new Commonwealth is known by its Portuguese acronym, is more than a mere fraternity of nations who speak the same language. The new body is another way for Portugal to try to reassert its influence over Angola. Portugal is Angola's largest source of imports and is the biggest investor outside Angola's oil sector. The only foreign banks operating in Angola are Portuguese. Everywhere in Luanda one sees signs of Portuguese construction companies.

I pay a couple of visits to António Monteiro, who was Portugal's main representative on the Troika in Luanda when the war resumed in 1992. He has been rewarded for his Angolan ordeal and is now head of political affairs at the foreign ministry under the first socialist government in more than a decade. Sitting in his office at the Palacio de Necessidades, the pink foreign ministry adorned with seventeenth-century *azulejos*, António looks tanned. He seems more relaxed than at any other time in the seven years I've known him. The topic moves on to Angola, inevitably, and António reflects on what's happening there. He is fairly upbeat about Angola now, although he admits that the peace process is far from finished. But the debacle of Biçesse will not be repeated, he believes.

We reflect on how long it took for the international community to acknowledge that UNITA was resuming its war in 1992.

'No one would listen to us when we warned them that this was war,' he remembers.

António tells an anecdote about his mother. She telephoned him after seeing him on Portuguese television broadcast from Luanda the day the massacres began. His tie was askew and he had deep dark rings under his eyes.

'Son, you look terrible,' he recounts in a high voice.

'But Mama, there is a war going on.'

'That doesn't matter. You're on television.'

We laugh. Then there is a quiet moment. Monteiro looks at the *azulejos* and then out the window. 'Those were such awful days,' he says.

The next day, Portugal holds a party after the inaugural ceremony of the CPLP. There are fireworks. Musicians from each of the member countries perform – Brazil, Portugal, São Tomé and Príncipe, Angola, Mozambique, Cape Verde and Guinea-Bissau. Bonga, UNITA's muse, sings on behalf of Angola.

I spent my last evening in Lisbon at a party with Bonga's rival, my musician friend Waldemar Bastos. Waldemar was singing again, after a long, depressed break following the resumption of the war. He was ecstatic. Finally, people outside this narrow Lusophone world had discovered his music. Waldemar had made it internationally. He was going to be a star, or at least be heard across the Atlantic. The party was held in honour of Waldemar's trip to New York, where he was making a record that was to be produced by David Byrne. Waldemar's wife Lauriana cooked a *muamba* chicken stew and a spinach dish with prawns. They invited family and a small group of friends to the party, which they held at a Fado club. Waldemar sang as he had not done for years – lyrical, acoustic and gentle. He was happy.

Waldemar told me he had adopted my birthplace, New York, as his town. I mentioned that I had bought a house in Johannesburg and wanted to prolong my assignment with my newspaper in Africa.

'Judite, you're becoming Africanised and I'm becoming

New York-ised,' he said in his hoarse voice.

'Will you go back to Luanda?' I asked. I reminded him about his song which had been a hit in 1991, *Angola Minha Namorada*, 'Angola My Love'. The lyrics insisted that he would never leave Angola. I rephrased the question. 'When will you go back?'

He shrugged. 'Not now. Maybe never. For what?'

✛

The Angolan state was sick and falling apart. The reason why Moco was free to take the job as secretary general of the CPLP was because he had been sacked for criticising Dos Santos and for writing a self-promotional book which overshadowed the president.

Dos Santos and Savimbi held another summit, in Libreville in March 1996. The UN Security Council expressed concern about delays in applying the Lusaka accords. UNITA troops began slowly to report to assembly points, old men with old weapons. Meanwhile there were unconfirmed reports of weapons still coming into Negage and Uíge from Zaire.

Robbed of its favoured bogeyman, UNITA, the MPLA now had to account for the economy's decline. UNITA could not be blamed if the electricity was cut off since UNITA was no longer sabotaging the pylons or the water supply. Its fighters were sitting complacently in assembly camps, fattening up on cornmeal gruel provided by the international community. Dos Santos tried to assign blame for the government's failures. On 3 June he sacked Moco, his cabinet and Central Bank Governor António Furtado. But most of the cabinet members were rehired shortly thereafter. The new prime minister, Fernando França Van Dunem, had been prime minister for a year from 1991 and had held various ambassadorships and cabinet portfolios.

One couldn't really blame the new cabinet if it had problems improving the economy. It was an impossible task. Money was being siphoned off. Nearly half the population was under 15 and looking for work. One out of five Angolans was dependent on foreign aid for survival. Even employees at the Angolan consulate in Johannesburg had not been paid for five months.

The *kwanza* was now trading at 250 000 to the dollar versus 2 500 the previous year. As small consolation, the government pointed to the fact that it had come down from 300 000. Annual accumulated inflation had risen above 3 000 per cent. Civil servants earned $15 a month. A chicken cost $10 and a beer $1. The only thing which kept Angola from appearing on the list of the world's poorest countries was its oil exports, which amounted to nearly $4 billion in 1995. But the oil was mortgaged ahead for several years to pay for debts and weapons. Wealth from oil didn't make a difference to the lives of most Angolans.

Even party stalwarts Paulo Jorge and former MPLA secretary general Lucio Lara were critical of the mess the generals and Dos Santos had wrought. Frightened of civil unrest, the government banned several public demonstrations in 1996 fearing they would descend into complete mayhem. And more worrying for many was that Dos Santos had sidelined the one moderate, clever man who could probably save the country. Lopo do Nascimento.

According to some of the diplomats, diamonds were the key to war and peace. As long as Savimbi held on to his diamond territory he could continue to make a lot of money. Industry sources estimated that UNITA had sold about $500 million in diamonds in 1995. For the government generals, too, diamonds offered a contingency plan, an escape valve in case they lost political power. According to the industry sources, even General João de Matos had his own mine.

'It's chaos there,' said an official of the De Beers' Angola operation. Hearing that I was going to Angola, he handed me a pile of posters bearing the picture of a South African acquaintance who had disappeared on a mission to buy diamonds. He was believed to have been kidnapped or to have had his throat cut. The official asked that I circulate the posters and report back if anyone had information.

There were some 30 diamond consortia operating in Angola. It was a nightmarish scenario for a cartel struggling to maintain its monopoly. Some of the consortia were linked to generals or to maverick South Africans with mining knowledge.

The state diamond company Endiama was trying to negotiate with Savimbi about dividing up the diamond area so that some order could be restored. However, it was difficult to imagine Savimbi relinquishing control in exchange for receiving equity or concessions – for mines that he already effectively controlled.

✢

Some things never change. The same brown cardboard boxes were at Johannesburg airport, stacked near the check-in counter for the flight to Luanda. This had been a continual problem ever since direct flights were initiated in 1992. Now, in September 1996, even with four direct flights a week, we had to wait more than four hours for the flight to take off because of the *confusão* of the boxes.

There were cooler boxes filled with food, and suitcases and sacks bulging with contraband to sell in Luanda's markets. A woman complained to the airport staff, worried that her month's supply of meat would rot in the sun. Passengers filed out to identify their luggage. The white expatriates were irritated as they consulted their watches, thinking about missed meetings. The Angolans who checked in the excess baggage were expressionless.

I had only hand luggage and sat on the plane chatting to the stewardess. She said this was the flight which the cabin crew dreaded.

'What exactly is inside those boxes?' I asked her. It's funny,

I'd been taking these flights for four years and I'd never thought to enquire about the source of all this frustration.

'Diapers, onions, potatoes, clothes, lingerie,' she recited. 'Dried milk, washing power, sanitary napkins. Oh, and earrings. They're very big this season.'

So much time had elapsed that the crew's shift was over. A fresh team of pilots and stewardesses took their place. The trays of breakfast bacon and eggs which had not been served during the long delay were replaced with a lunch of beef and broccoli.

'It can also serve as dinner if the delay lasts any longer,' said the stewardess.

✛

Landing at Luanda hours later, I returned to an airport which had been spruced up with fresh paint and travel posters. The waiting-room had new seats. I noted with pleasure the new electronic flight announcement board, just like an airport anywhere in the world. But I had learned from 1992 to be cautious of the signs of peace.

Luanda was as clogged as ever with intrigue and rumour. The latest was that Dos Santos was ill with prostate cancer. Some diplomats pointed to how long he had spent in France, ostensibly to seek treatment. But then there were others who scoffed at the hearsay, pointing to his recent dancing at a public function. The question of a successor was worrying even to those who believed Dos Santos enjoyed good health. The popular wisdom was that Savimbi would not negotiate with anyone but Dos Santos. A commonly expressed fear was that João de Matos would stage a coup, but worries about military takeover have been a perennial fear in Angola at the best of times.

I immersed myself in the speculation, although I was visiting Angola for just one week. Angola was just another of my sub-Saharan beat of 47 countries which I covered for my newspaper.

Yet it was different. I felt emotionally attached to Angola, unlike the other places I reported on. Every rumour, every lie was of importance. Angola for me wasn't just a place where I needed to sketch in the outline of a story. It was a place where the nuances had some meaning for me.

✛

One night in Luanda I sat with some friends making jokes about the seemingly endless rounds of UNAVEM. Someone likened the growing numerals attached to UNAVEM to Rambo movies.

'How about this,' she said. '"UNAVEM III. They're back – bigger and better".'

We laughed. More beers were poured.

'No! I've got a better one,' someone else said. '"UNAVEM III. This time they'll get it right".'

But were they getting it right? I reflected on this the next day. The man from the State Department who sat next to us on the plane from Johannesburg said the process was working overall, despite some delays and 'a few wrinkles'. But that's what the US embassy said in 1992 before the ill-fated Angolan elections.

I went to see Beye to hear his comparisons with Biçesse.

We agreed that the UN had learned from the lesson of 1992, when it was ill-prepared and political will was lacking. The UN had learned from the positive example of Mozambique, where the formula of 7 000 peacekeepers and a gradual process had worked. Now they had duplicated the crucial elements which had made Mozambique a success. The UN deployed the same number of blue helmets under UNAVEM III and drew up a more reasonable timetable for demobilisation. No elections would be held until the troops were properly disarmed. This time 4 500 kilometres of mined road had been cleared by Mechem on the main arteries in the country's north and centre.

I found Beye's public optimism uneasily reminiscent of his predecessor's misguided faith back in 1993. Beye shrugged off what seemed to be worrying signs. So what that 10 000 UNITA troops had defected from assembly points? So what that roads were being re-mined? It was of little importance that old men and old weapons had reported to assembly points and that the crème de la crème were believed to be absent. He urged me not to focus on the 5 000-strong police force which had been set up across the country, in violation of the peace accords. Beye was not perturbed by the fact that the MPLA was rearming its military with new supplies.

Beye had just come back from meeting Savimbi, who had rejected the vice-presidency a week earlier at a UNITA congress in Bailundo. UNITA appeared to be employing delaying tactics, in the hope that the longer the country remained in suspense, the economic crisis would increasingly make the country ungovernable for the MPLA. Savimbi was also trying to take advantage of the fact that the mandate of the current parliament would run out in November 1996. Knowing that the country would not be ready for new elections, he withdrew UNITA's initial support for extending the mandate until a poll could be organised some time in the distant future. UNITA's latest demand was that the parliament should be dissolved and a constitutional assembly established in its place.

Savimbi, probably quite rightly, refused to go to Luanda, citing fears for his life. Several months before a gunman had shot at – and missed – Ben Ben when he was driving in the Angolan capital. Savimbi would be crazy to take such a chance, UNITA said.

Beye was concerned about the foot-dragging. He, like the Americans who were footing one-third of the $1 million a day peace mission, was insisting that the February 1997 deadline for the end of the UN mission had to be met.

There were some disturbing echoes of 1992 – both sides were making military contingency plans. UNITA was getting fed at the assembly camps, the government was rearming and retraining its soldiers.

✢

UNAVEM exuded a new openness towards the media now. Over the past couple of years, Beye had ordered news blackouts and could be very aggressive during interviews. 'You are very unhelpful by making us look bad,' he had accused me in 1993 when I wrote about the slowness of peace talks. Press releases were near impossible to obtain, and UNAVEM didn't want to take journalists on their flights.

Now all that had changed. Gone was the cagey suspicion of the media. Beye was feeling confident about the peace process and the fact that a cease-fire had largely held for nine months. He greeted me warmly when I called at his small house in the UNAVEM compound.

Beye had employed an efficient new press man, who was dedicated to helping rather than obstructing the flow of information. He issued helpful statistics. He offered to get me and a colleague from *The Economist* on a flight. Things seemed to have changed from the days when I had to bring my own food provisions, hitch rides on cargo flights or sleep on concrete floors.

'I booked you into Negage and Uíge where the Indian peacekeepers are. The vindaloo is smashing but I recommend you steer clear of the seafood curry,' the pressman said. 'Oh, and bring a warm nightie. It gets chilly at night.'

A warm nightie?

The media man's high praise for the Indians' cooking did not prepare us for the hospitality which lay ahead. The commander deployed the regimental band complete with bagpipes, tartans and turbans. It marched around the tarmac in our honour. He also assigned a platoon of white-gloved waiters to follow us around with silver trays of samoosas, cashews and sugary lemon juice. We were given proper beds with starched sheets in private rooms in the compound, erected behind the bombed-out hangar. And that was not all. Our hosts had thoughtfully provided us with a jar of Ponds face cream, scented talcum powder and tortoiseshell combs, all flown in from Madras.

The Indians were exemplary hosts and their presence, like peacekeepers across the country, served as a welcome buffer between the two warring sides. As the Indians drove through town in UN jeeps, civilians waved from the side of the road and held out their hands in begging gestures. The Indians tossed out packets of biscuits. ('Win their hearts and minds,' the commander said, reaching into his bag for another offering.)

The Indians acted in the best of faith but it seemed some of their efforts were a waste of time and money. They set up a training school for the locals. But what good would it do for young Angolan children to pronounce the alphabet in English, when they couldn't even read Portuguese? Some villagers showed up at the mechanics class hoping only to get more biscuits. A tailor signed on for the sewing class seeking only to take home cloth for his business. Few new skills were taught.

The peacekeepers were particularly proud of their refurbishment of the municipal swimming pool, which had been repainted a magnificent salmon and royal blue while the rest of the city remained in a state of severe disrepair.

The Indians had refilled the pool with water and were now looking at its murkiness with undisguised dismay.

'It's absolutely filthy,' said one of them, pointing to the brown slime just below the surface.

'That's probably because people have been using it,' another said.

Four cages were lined up against the wall behind the pool. During colonial times it had been a small zoo. Now all we found were a small black pig and a duck.

The pool attendant, a tiny woman in a blue dress,

approached with pride.

'We're restocking the zoo,' she said, clucking at the pig. 'Unfortunately these were the only animals we could find. However, someone has offered us a pair of rabbits. That ought to fill the cages quickly.'

✛

How effective were the men in blue helmets in checking the airplanes which were reportedly bringing in arms to UNITA? And what would happen after they left?

It turned out that no one in the Indian battalion spoke the local language. This had the unfortunate consequence that every time I tried to interview Angolans in their native Portuguese 15 Indian gentlemen, resplendent in turbans and brass, would hover protectively, hoping to glean important insights.

'What's he saying?' interrupted the commander, swooping into my conversation with a man standing at a checkpoint. 'What'd you find out?' He looked at me with anxious anticipation.

We had actually been talking about the rainy season, which was imminent. I hated to disappoint him.

'The weather.'

The Indians were proud of and homesick for things back home. They played cricket and badminton next to the shot-up hangar and attack helicopters which UNITA had destroyed in the war. For further amusement, the Indians brought a stack of videos of voluptuous singing movie stars, their own wheat flour to make chapatis and a memorial plaque to honour members of their 16 Guards Battalion who had been killed in battle back home.

✛

I had been curious to visit Uíge for a long time. The last time I had been there was in January 1993, just two months after

UNITA had captured the town. Then, the rebels had given me 45 minutes to drive around town while the UN relief plane was unloaded. The streets had been deserted except for guerrillas.

Now both Uíge and Negage were like movie sets of shot-up towns. The corrugated metal roofs of buildings had been shot off and windows and walls were missing.

But beans and rose bushes were blooming in front of homes where women had the leisure to sit on verandas chatting. Kids played soccer noisily in the streets. Other women were hoeing tapioca root by the sides of the road, and burning grass in the fields to cultivate more crops. At a checkpoint in a no man's land they bartered salt for sugar. Life was getting back to normal, slowly.

+

More trays of samoosas awaited us at the assembly camp, where a UNITA colonel with the nom de guerre *Tuyula* (Whirlwind) took us for a tour. This particular camp had closed and technically anyone outside was a bandit and could be shot by government troops. But it was UNITA which was policing the area, with police who were deployed in violation of the peace accords.

The big fear, Tuyula said, was what would happen when the rains came. The camp was just a collection of plastic and canvas tents housing several men and their families. The rains would convert the camp into knee-high sludge. Tuyula said no one wanted to contemplate the ensuing unrest.

Without the rains, however, the set-up at the camps was impressive with that inimitable UNITA order. These former guerrillas looked well nourished. 'If Savimbi is planning to go back to war he's done well by feeding his people here,' I thought. But would these be the people who would fight? A lot of the soldiers were kids, only 15 years old, if that.

Just as something did not look quite right about the soldiers, so the weapons locked up at the airfield were not impressive. The quality was downright dismal. The anti-air missiles were non-functional. Practically no ammunition had been handed over.

'Garbage,' said one of the peacekeepers, kicking at the pile of splintering wood and old metal. He walked on top of the AK-47s, which covered a big section of the tarmac when laid out. I hestitated to walk on top of them but the officer waved me on.

'They've seen worse. They're not worth very much.'

'So where are the working ones?' I asked.

The Indian colonel straightened a rusty AK-47 which had slid off the pile.

'Where do you think? With all the able-bodied soldiers who didn't report here.'

✢

A full yellow moon shone in the sky over the patio outside the Indians' compound. The Indian band was wearing red jackets, playing 'River of Babylon' slightly out of key on an electric piano. Red Christmas lights were strung on the bushes.

Thirty Indian military men in elegant houndstooth jackets and silk ties chatted pleasantly while the waiters passed around trays of chicken tikka and drinks. Kids looked in from the darkness on the other side of the razor wire on the compound's periphery.

The guests of honour, UNITA and MPLA brass, stood awkwardly on opposite sides of the patio. If this was a measure of the new trust, Angola was damned.

Colonel Jaime Nobre of the government side, whose job was to select UNITA men for the new army, was visibly nervous. He was a thin man, dressed in a frayed cotton shirt and khaki trousers that looked as though they had been washed on river rocks for several years. The UNITA brigadier was wearing a splendid dark wool suit.

'I don't like them at all,' Nobre said. He reached for another whisky from the waiter's silver tray. 'They're still the same bad men.'

He was talking a lot, and quickly.

'I wouldn't be here tonight if it weren't for the Indians. I don't go out if I don't have a UN escort. Otherwise UNITA would kill me. If I can't get an escort I stay in at night. It's boring, there's nothing to do here. But I can't risk it,' he said.

The Indian commander came over, white-gloved waiter in tow with a tray of chicken tikka.

'What were you talking about?' he asked us pleasantly.

'How well the peace process is going,' Nobre lied.

I went across the patio and sat in the free chair next to Colonel Job Sunguete. The colonel, whose nom de guerre was Longfellow, measured about 6 foot 3 inches. He was dressed in a black wool suit that would have been more appropriate for a dinner party in Lisbon, where it had been bought, than in Uíge's dilapidated ruins.

Like everyone else at the cocktail party, Longfellow expressed a deep desire for peace but stressed that he did not trust the MPLA. Like others in UNITA, he insisted that proper security arrangements had not been provided. To change the topic, I asked him whether he personally would like to join the new army if proper security could be guaranteed.

Longfellow considered the question. He asked for English tobacco while he thought. It just so happened that I was carrying a packet of Benson and Hedges.

He lit up and inhaled, his sternness relaxing. 'Ah, Britain,' he said, with a dreamy look.

I asked him if he had ever been there. He said that he hadn't, but he wanted to visit London when he finally left military life. 'Leave the military? How's that?' I asked, curious about his motives.

'No! I'm tired of all that,' he said. He looked into his glass of whisky.

'What would you like to do instead?' I asked.

'Go into business.'

'Any particular area?'

'Diamonds,' he replied. 'I've done a bit of diamond trading and I like the work.'

So that's what paid for the suit. I was probably thinking about the suit while Longfellow tried to judge my reaction. 'We've been at this a long time,' he said. 'We're not getting anywhere with this fighting. We're normal guys who want a normal life.'

✝

I felt this was like a valedictory trip to Angola. I certainly wanted it to be my last. I felt that I had to make a break somehow. I couldn't keep coming back to this place. Either I moved to Angola, or left it for good. Moving was out of the question. I had to get out, get it out of my mind, finally.

I was visiting places as though for the last time, bidding a farewell to those where I had despaired for Angola and then regained some faith.

I had to get away from Angola simply to connect with the rest of the world. I decided that when I returned home to Johannesburg I would take down the photos of Angola that I had hung on my filing cabinet. Maybe I would replace them with a map of Africa. Or pictures of somewhere else. Or leave the space empty. My new job, which wasn't so new any more, involved covering 46 countries other than Angola. For two years I had travelled constantly in Africa, averaging about a country a month. Angola was my frame of reference, although it was far from the most important country on the continent. It lacked South Africa's wealth or Nigeria's size. But articles about Angola were the first I turned to when I opened the African magazines

I subscribed to. I drew parallels to Angola wherever I was; it had become the benchmark by which I judged other situations or countries.

My job had taken me to other areas of conflict – Zaire, Sudan, Rwanda, Burundi, Mozambique, Sierra Leone. Over a period of two years I had visited 26 airports and had seen the political detritus of other failed UN peacekeeping missions. I maintained that Angola in 1992 was a case study of how not to conduct such a mission. But there had been plenty of fatal mistakes elsewhere.

I was growing exhausted, or jaded, with the seemingly endless multitude of militias and displaced people with clothes faded to that familiar beige-grey. I realised something was terribly amiss one afternoon in a refugee camp somewhere in Africa. For a moment I forgot where I was. I listened to the refugees speaking. It was French. The process of elimination began. I thought, OK, I'm not in Sierra Leone because they speak English there. No one was speaking Portuguese so I wasn't in Mozambique or Angola. Therefore, I must be somewhere in the Great Lakes. I was too embarrassed to ask where we were. Eventually it came back to me that I was on the outskirts of Bujumbura in Burundi.

On the ride back to town, I thought about how my reactions had changed since I unwittingly found myself in a war in Angola in 1992. It was not that I had lost my compassion. It was more that I had regained my distance. I had found myself accidentally in the middle of a conflict in Angola and was so open to its horror because I was unprepared for it. I was still able to feel revulsion and dread, of course. But generally I tried to protect myself. I avoided getting as connected to a place as I had been to Angola. I made my trips short. The role of a journalist is to make sense of the unexplainable as an impassive observer. I had failed terribly at this calling in Angola. Elsewhere, it was easier to be neutral because I was not as intimately linked.

After every trip to Angola, I left with a sense that something was not quite resolved. I had to get Angola out of my mind for good. I suppose I wanted to see Angola firmly back on the track to peace and the optimism of 1991 restored. I didn't want to be one of those journalists who just flew in for the story and then let it go. But I had to accept that nothing I did would make a difference. It was bad enough that I had spent one-half of the precious three weeks of my vacation time going to Angola. Other people went to Mauritius or Paris. I chose to go to a place which was falling apart and still couldn't set itself right after the war had ended.

I was beginning to comprehend the futility of continually returning to a place which other people were trying to flee. Going back wasn't going to make things all right. It wasn't going to raise the dead, or rebuild Cuito. It wasn't achieving anything except prolonging my myopic search for things which weren't getting better. Going back wasn't assuaging any guilt. My dispatches were not changing any policies. If I couldn't let go, I should move there and call it my own country. But I didn't want to do that. I decided I should cut the ties and finally move on.

+

I began to make my rounds, in an ostensible farewell.

First I went to the Lello bookshop in town, where I had bought the few reference books I had on Angola over the years. Now I crammed into my canvas satchel every book that would fit – on anthropology, on life in Luanda in the 1800s, on the colonial war, on folklore and poetry. I bought some new additions about the Biçesse peace process and why it had broken down.

Driving through town towards my next destination, the *musseques*, I passed Neto's mausoleum. The red crane was still poised half-way up the tower in the same position it had been three years ago. Nearby one could still see the vestiges of campaign posters plastered to poles.

I said goodbye to the *musseques* and to people I knew there. I couldn't find João Martins and his brown Mercedes, though. I dropped by the Hotel Tivoli to call on Honório Van Dunem, who was savouring his assumed role as the premier UNITA defector. He was finally planning to move into a house.

I visited places which had been inaccessible during the war. One of them was the Barra da Cuanza. It was a tranquil spot on the edge of the Kissama nature reserve, at the mouth of the Cuanza River. It was a favoured day trip out of Luanda in the old days. The Barra da Cuanza had been too dangerous to visit during the fighting, but now apparently those with cars and money were coming back.

On the road we passed only a couple of 4x4 vehicles. The area was sparsely inhabited and there were few signs of war destruction amid the coconut groves, baobab trees and towering cactus. The air was salty and light. The driver, Casimiro, and I were the only guests at the restaurant, which had been a favoured weekend retreat before the war. We sat on the terrace overlooking the swamp and its water lilies. The owner said that manatees had been spotted at the lagoon nearby. They hadn't been there for years, he said.

'It seems they've come back now that the war is over,' he added. 'Maybe the people will come back, too.'

Back in Luanda I was trying to bid farewell to everyone and everywhere. I invited some friends to have some final beers. The old bars had closed and so we went to a new one. It was the same crowd that I had seen in Luanda bars for five years, just a new venue. I saw several women I knew well. They were managing, just. One woman was working as a call girl. Another was taking risks as a diamond courier.

It felt like the old days, especially the uncertainty. Everyone was still struggling. The talk was still about whether war would return. No one knew exactly what Savimbi was doing in Bailundo.

Teresa is a big woman. She practically suffocated me in a hug as she spotted me coming out of the bar. 'So you're back. I thought you'd be back sooner. She always comes back,' she said, turning to another woman.

Someone at our table had moved from beers to *aguardente*, firewater, and had become philosophical.

'There's one thing which has remained the same – Angola is still entrancing and it's still a mess. Five years from now we'll still be meeting for beers with our debates about war and peace and where this country is going,' he said. 'Don't fool yourself. You'll be back here next year.'

Teresa waved to another friend in the corner and moved on to greet her. I contemplated the defence ministry, which loomed yellow and illuminated in the distance through the window. A smell of raw sewage rose from the bay beyond. I didn't like what the man at the table was saying. But he was probably right.

✝

I stopped by at Katia's to give her some detective novels. She was preparing a new salvo against Tino, who had closed and then reopened the club on the roof of her apartment building. Her shopping list, faxed before I arrived, had the shrillness of battle: 'Urgent! *MiraMortos* is back! Earplugs please!'

Katia's parrot stared at me when I walked in the door. He was not very talkative and he gazed at me scornfully as though to say: 'You're still here?' For the first time that I could remember in five years, a parrot of Katia's was silent. Maybe he was in a sour mood; the weather was sticky and he had plucked all the feathers from his chest. But I couldn't coax him to say anything. If the parrot had any clues about Angola's future, he wasn't revealing them.

Epilogue

Well before the Portuguese came to Africa 515 years ago, Angola and Zaire were joined together. The Bakongo kingdom, in what is now northern Angola and south-western Zaire, was the first African monarchy with which the white explorers and missionaries had contact. It was a formidable realm, yet a trusting one. It was not long before the Bakongo people were separated, torn apart by the adventurers and slave traders who mapped their own boundaries and endowed them with strange names.

On 18 May 1997, I drive along a road leading to Kinshasa's airport and see the severed blood ties congealing again in unity.

It is the day after the rebels of Laurent Kabila came and liberated the city. They entered Kinshasa with barely a fight after Savimbi's great protector, Mobutu Sese Seko, flew out of the city. I ride behind Red Cross workers who are collecting the bodies of people killed when the rebels arrived. It was not a big battle, maybe a few hundred dead, but for the Red Cross workers who are paid by the corpse each one means a precious warm meal. They sing lustily behind their surgical masks, songs of full stomachs.

Their white truck stops in front of a plastics factory with a high wall. The workers carry three bodies inside. As we follow them, it becomes apparent that the factory's garden enclosure serves as an impromptu barracks. Or perhaps it serves an even worse purpose, if the sound of methodical shots from outside the wall's perimeter is anything to judge by. The firing could well be the solitary bullets of execution. There are eleven pairs of army boots piled at the entrance to the enclosure on a

305

square of maroon-stained grass.

A lone soldier stands guard at the deep pit where the Red Cross stretcher bearers unload their offerings. He is uncomfortable that three whites have come to observe, pens and notebooks in hand, and responds to our French and Swahili queries with irritated incomprehension. He answers in full sentences in his own language, in the compulsive way of people who want to communicate but can't.

'Vais embora,' he says in Portuguese, moving his body between us and the grave. 'Get out of here.'

'Porqûe? Why?' I ask and he turns with surprise and relief to look at me. Here, finally, is something familiar; suddenly we are brother and sister.

The soldier babbles on about the village in Angola where he comes from, how he fought to help Kabila as a fellow African . . . One Nation, One People . . . Estamos Juntos . . . the MPLA slogans flow out as he savours his regained articulateness.

Two more shots are fired with rhythmic precision and he is reminded that we should go.

'Vais embora,' he says, more gently this time.

Back in the car, we continue on the airport road, the same one which leads towards Kenge only a day's drive away. Kenge was the last major battle for Zaire before Kabila's men reached Kinshasa. And, in fact, maybe it was one of the last major battles for Angola too.

Kenge was one of the fiercest confrontations during the seven-month rebellion, mainly due to the involvement of the MPLA and UNITA. The MPLA sent men and transport planes to back Kabila. In turn, more than 1 000 UNITA men defended Mobutu's final days. It was probably need more than loyalty which prompted UNITA's actions. Savimbi's men had to protect their diamond routes and get their arms, reportedly 2 000 tonnes of it, out of the country before Kabila arrived. But UNITA failed and, along with Mobutu, lost.

Perhaps Kabila's rebellion did more in seven months to end Savimbi's war than five years of UN peace initiatives. In April 1997, a new Angolan national unity government was finally inaugurated in Luanda. But that limbo between peace and war wasn't lifted. Savimbi refused to go to Luanda, for the ceremony or afterwards, citing his usual preoccupation with security. He remained in Bailundo, or the nearby Andulo. Did this mean there would be another war? people asked.

Maybe this will be renewed war, or at least the final battle, after what has happened in Zaire. Initially, Savimbi looked closer to defeat than ever before. With the fall of Mobutu, he lost his outlets in Kinshasa. The cargo planes no longer fly out of there with arms to northern Angola. He has been forced to sell his diamonds through Pointe-Noire, inconveniently far away in Congo, and other distant places like Togo.

On the day that I visited the plastics factory in Kinshasa, the MPLA back in Angola moved in with a vengeance to take advantage of UNITA's unaccustomed weakness. They targeted UNITA positions in the diamond areas of Lunda Norte, in what diplomats said was the heaviest fighting in Angola in two years. The MPLA's excuse was that it wanted to secure its border with what used to be Zaire. But UNITA knew otherwise and primed thousands of its men in defence. They seemed to have no shortage of men or fighters. The UN, as usual, watched impotently from afar.

Reportedly, one of Mobutu's final acts before leaving Kinshasa was to cremate the body of his Rwandan friend Juvénal Habyrimana. He regarded the former Rwandan leader as one of his children and soulmates, rather like Savimbi. These are the last of the old guard, who have been sidelined by the end of the Cold War and a new generation of African leaders. Unlike Habyrimana, Savimbi has been left alone, ensconced deeper than ever in his refuges in Bailundo and Andulo. While his men went to Luanda or the front in the Lundas, he remained behind. O Mais Velho is no longer the all-powerful, venerated Elder. He has become an old man, with irrelevant dreams of ancient kingdoms.

List of Acronyms

ANC	African National Congress
APC	Armoured personnel carrier
CCPM	Comissão Conjunta Político Militar (Joint Political Military Commission)
CIA	Central Intelligence Agency
CNE	Conselho Nacional Electoral (National Electoral Council)
CPLP	Community of Portuguese Language Countries
FAA	Forças Armadas Angolanas (Angolan Armed Forces, the joint army)
FALA	Forças Armadas de Libertação de Angola (Armed Forces for the Liberation of Angola, the UNITA army)
FAPLA	Forças Armadas Populares de Libertação de Angola (Popular Armed Forces for the Liberation of Angola, the government army)
FLEC	Frente de Libertação do Enclave de Cabinda (National Front for the Liberation of Cabinda)
FNLA	Frente Nacional de Libertação de Angola (National Front for the Liberation of Angola)
ICRC	International Committee of the Red Cross
IMF	International Monetary Fund
MPLA	Movimento Popular de Libertação de Angola (Popular Movement for the Liberation of Angola)
NATO	North Atlantic Treaty Organisation

NGO	Non-governmental organisation
RENAMO	Resistência Nacional Moçambicana (Mozambique National Resistance)
RPG	Rocket propelled grenade
SWAPO	South West African People's Organisation
UNAVEM	United Nations Angola Verification Mission
UNHCR	United Nations High Commission for Refugees
UNICEF	United Nations International Children's Emergency Fund
UNITA	União Nacional para a Independência Total de Angola (National Union for the Total Independence of Angola)
UPA	União das Populações de Angola (Union of the Angolan People)
WFP	World Food Programme

Bibliography

Bender, Gerald. *Angola Under the Portuguese: The Myth and The Reality* (Heinemann, London, 1978).

Birmingham, David. *Frontline Nationalism in Angola and Mozambique* (James Curry, London, 1992).

Bravo, Manuel (ed). *Angola: Transição para a Paz, Reconciliação e Desenvolvimento* (Hugin Editores, Lisbon, 1996).

Bredin, Miles. *Blood on the Tracks: A Rail Journey from Angola to Mozambique* (Picador, London, 1994).

Bridgland, Fred. *The War for Africa: Twelve Months that Transformed a Continent* (Ashanti Publishing, Rivonia, 1992).

———— *Jonas Savimbi: A Key to Africa* (Coronet, London, 1986).

Burchett, Wilfred. *Southern Africa Stands Up: The Revolutions in Angola, Mozambique, Zimbabwe, Namibia and South Africa* (Urizen Books, New York, 1978).

Correia, Pedro de Pezarat. *Angola: do Alvor a Lusaka* (Hugin Editores, Lisbon, 1996).

Crocker, Chester. *High Noon in Southern Africa: Making Peace in a Rough Neighborhood* (W.W. Norton and Co Inc, New York, 1992).

Ervedosa, Carlos. *Arqueologia Angolana* (Ministério da Educação,

Luanda, 1978).

Fonseca, António. *Sobre os Kikongos de Angola* (União dos Escritores Angolanos, Luanda, 1989).

Heywood, Linda M. 'UNITA and Ethnic Nationalism in Angola'. *The Journal of Modern African Studies*, 27, 1 (1989), pp. 47-66.

Jeal, Tim. *Livingstone* (Pimlico, London, 1996).

Kapuściński, Ryszard. *Another Day of Life* (Picador, London, 1987).

Knappert, Jan. *African Mythology: An Encyclopedia of Myth and Legend* (Diamond Books, London, 1995).

Lamb, David. *The Africans: Encounters from the Sudan to the Cape* (Mandarin, London, 1990).

Marcum, J.A. *The Angolan Revolution, Volume I, Anatomy of an Explosion (1950-62)* (MIT Press, Cambridge MA, 1969).

—————— *The Angolan Revolution, Volume II, Exile Politics and Guerrilla Warfare (1962-76)* (MIT Press, Cambridge MA, 1978).

Minter, William (ed). *Operation Timber, Pages from the Savimbi Dossier* (Africa World Press Inc, Trenton, 1988)

—————— *Apartheid's Contras: An Inquiry into the Roots of War in Angola and Mozambique* (Zed Books, London, 1994).

Monteiro, Renato and Farinha, Luís (eds). *Guerra Colonial: Fotobiografia* (Publicações Dom Quixote, Lisbon, 1990).

Ntyamba, Jorge. *Huambo: 56 Dias de Terror e Morte* (Editora Jango, Luanda, 1994).

Pacavira, Manuel Pedro. *Nzinga Mbandi* (União dos Escritores Angolanos, Luanda, 1985).

Pepetela. *Mayombe* (União/Endiama, Luanda, 1982).

—————— *Lueji (O Nascimento dum Império)*. (Edições ASA, Porto, 1989).

Rebocho Vaz, Camilo. *Norte de Angola 1961: A Verdade e os Mitos* (Gráfica Pampilhosense, Mealhada, 1993).

Roque, Fátima. *Angola: Em Nome da Esperança* (Bertrand Editora Lda, Lisbon, 1994).

Santos, José de Almeida (ed). *A Velha Loanda: nos festejos, nas solenidades, no ensino* (Edição da Câmara Municipal de Luanda, Luanda, 1972).

———— *Crónicas da Velha Cidade* (Edição da Câmara Municipal de Luanda, Luanda, 1972).

Savimbi, Jonas. *Por um Futuro Melhor* (Nova Nórdica, Lisbon, 1986).

Smock, David R. (ed). *Making War and Waging Peace: Foreign Intervention in Africa* (United States Institute of Peace Press, Washington DC, 1993).

Sommerville, Keith. 'The Failure of Democratic Reform in Angola and Zaire'. *Survival*, Autumn 1993.

Stockwell, John. *In Search of Enemies: A CIA Story* (W.W. Norton and Co, New York, 1978).

Stok, Danusia (ed). *Kieślowski on Kieślowski* (Faber and Faber, Boston, 1993).

Van der Waals, W.S. *Portugal's War in Angola: 1961-1974* (Ashanti Publishing, Rivonia, 1993).

Venâncio, Moisés. *Political Transition and Post-Cold War Conflict-Resolution: Lessons from Angola*. Speech delivered at Conference on Peace and Regional Cooperation in Southern Africa, Lisbon, 11 February 1994.

Vieira, José Luandino. *Luuanda* (Heinemann, London, 1980).

Wolfers, Michael and Bergerol, Jane. *Angola in the Front Line* (Zed Books, London, 1983).

Selected Index